Joseph S. [from old catalog] Brewster

Outline Evolution of Empire and Prophecy

Joseph S. [from old catalog] Brewster

Outline Evolution of Empire and Prophecy

ISBN/EAN: 9783743308657

Manufactured in Europe, USA, Canada, Australia, Japa

Cover: Foto ©ninafisch / pixelio.de

Manufactured and distributed by brebook publishing software (www.brebook.com)

Joseph S. [from old catalog] Brewster

Outline Evolution of Empire and Prophecy

OF

EMPIRE AND PROPHECY

BY

JOSEPH S. BREWSTER Esq.

"*In the study of History, a general view of the whole enables the mind to form a truer judgment on the several parts.*"—POLYBIUS, Book 2, c. 1.

"*The predictions of Scripture, if carefully examined, will be found to contain the great outlines of the History of the world.*"
—Preface to SCOTT'S COMMENTARIES, page 8.

"*Lord Bacon recommends works comparing History with the prophecies.*"
—NEWTON ON THE PROPHESIES, Dissertation 26, page 635.

NEW YORK:
J. S. OGILVIE & COMPANY,
No. 31 ROSE STREET.

PREFACE.

THE object of these pages is to present briefly a connected view of general history and to show its relation to prophecy. A proper understanding of the subject will require a sedulous perusal of those portions of the prophetical writings referred to in the foot-notes and an impartial comparison of them with the events of history, as detailed in the text. The leading authors cited will be found to throw great light on both the historians and the prophets, and should be carefully examined. Empires have been selected as the topics of reflection, since it is of them the prophets mainly write. If the labor of acquiring or recalling the knowledge of imperial events, as related to the prophetical records, is lightened and aid afforded to any one who is in search of the truth, or a desire excited in any mind to examine the historians and the prophets, the author's wishes will be accomplished.

CONTENTS.

INTRODUCTION.

THE WORKS OF THE LEADING HISTORIANS CONSIDERED IN
CONNECTION WITH EMPIRES............................ 19

Empire of the Assyrians. Portions of Diodorus applicable to it.
Empire of the Medes and Persians. Herodotus; when he flourished; substance of his work. *Empire of the Greeks.* Plutarch. Thucydides. Xenophon's Affairs of Greece. Parts of Diodorus to be consulted on this period. Arrian, the historian of Alexander. *Empire of the Romans.* Livy. Sallust. Cæsar. Pansa. Polybius. Justin. Tacitus. Suetonius. Marcellinus. Zosimus. Eutropius. Orosius. *Eastern Empire of the Romans.* Procopius. Zonaras. Choniates. Gregoras. Cantacuzene. Chalchondites. *Empire of the Turks.* Augustan History. Modern times afford general historians, as well as those of epochs. Elmakin. Ockley. Cantemir. *Western Empire of the Romans.* How and when destroyed. *Neustrian Division of the Empire of the Franks.* Crow. Paris. Froissart. DeComines. Guicciardini. De Thou. Davila. Sully. Thuanus. Racine. Brienne. DeRetz. Villars. Noailles. Dumourier. DeStaël. Thiers. Blanc. *Austrasian Division of the Empire of the Franks.* Kohlrausch. Cox. *Powers of Europe connected with the Empire of the Franks.* Sweden. Prussia. Russia. Spain. Portugal. United Provinces. Belgium. Denmark. Switzerland. Two Sicilies. Papal dominions. Austrian dominions in Italy. Sardinia. Voltaire. Geijer. Prescott. Robertson. Watson. Motley. *Empire of the Anglo-Saxons.* Hume. Smollett. Bisset. Gildas. Bede. William of Malmesbury. Hoveden. Diceto. Paris. Brompton. Fitzstephens. Froissart. Walsingham. Vergil. Hall. Holinshed. More. Stowe. Speed. Baker. Clarendon. Neall. Burnet. Rapin. Coote. Alison. Carlyle. D'Aubigné. Robertson. Macaulay. *Anglo-Saxons and Franks in America.* United States. Mexico. Yucatan. Central States. Brazil. Paraguay. Argentine Republic. Peru. Bolivia. Granada. Venezuela. Colombia. Chili. Holmes. Ramsay. Marshall. Irving. Bancroft. Hildreth. King. Kidder. The Sacred Scriptures afford the best clue to general history. Newton. Scott.

CHAPTER I.

THE EMPIRE OF THE ASSYRIANS............................ 43

Extent of the Empire of the Assyrians. Ninus. Semiramis. Ninyas. Description of Babylon. Palace. Temple of Belus. Canals. Lake.

Hanging-garden. Nameless Emperors. Sardanapalus. Chaldeans and Medes divide the empire. Nahum.

COMMENCEMENT OF REIGNS.

	A.M.		A.M.
1. Ninus	about 2054	4. The Nameless Emperors occupy a period of about eleven centuries.	
2. Semiramis	" 2061		
3. Ninyas	" 2103		
		5. Sardanapalus*	about 3257

CHAPTER II.

THE EMPIRE OF THE MEDES AND PERSIANS.................. 49

Defection of Medes. Deioces. Ecbatana. Phraortes. Cyaxares. Nineveh. The Scythians. Astyages. Mandane. Cyrus. Darius the Mede. Lydia. Capture of Babylon. Massagetæ. Cambyses. Smerdis the Magian. Darius. Hystaspes. Xerxes. Overthrow in Greece. Isaiah. Jeremiah.

COMMENCEMENT OF REIGNS.

	A.M.		A.M.
1. Deioces	about 3294	6. Cambyses	about 3474
2. Phraortes	" 3347	7. Smerdis the Magian. Usurper.	
3. Cyaxares	" 3369	8. Darius Hystaspes	about 3483
4. Astyages†	" 3409	9. Xerxes‡	" 3519
5. Cyrus and Darius the Mede	" 3444		

CHAPTER III.

THE EMPIRE OF THE GREEKS............................ 63

States of Greece. Cecrops. Danaus. Cadmus. Pelops. Amphictyonic Council. Athens. Sparta. Messenia. Themistocles. The Piræus. War with Persia. Treason of Pausanias. Flight of Themistocles. Cimon. Aristides. Pericles. Peloponnesian war. Pestilence. Spartan war with Persia. Agesilaus. Lysander. Disturbances in Greece. Thebes. Corinth. Argos. Conon. Place of Antalcidas. Sparta and Thebes. Epaminondas. Pelopidas. Leuctra. Mantinea. Divisions of Greece. Philip of Macedon. Alexander the Great. Thebes. Persia. India. Arideus. Perdiccas. Antipater. Craterus. Polysperchon. Cassander. Antigonus. Battle of Ipsus. Lysimachus. Ptolemy. Seleucus. Isaiah. Jeremiah.

COMMENCEMENT OF REIGNS.

	A.M.		A.M.
1. Philip of Macedon§	about 3644	4. Cassander, Lysimachus, Ptolemy, Seleucus	about 3706
2. Alexander the Great	" 3668		
3. Arideus	" 3681		

---

* Dio. Sic., Bk. II. ch. ii. Justin, Bk. II. ch. iii.; note pp. 18, 19.
† Her., Clio, pp. 50-52. Justin, p. 5.
‡ Lardner's Chron. Tables.
§ Lard. Ch. Tab.

CHAPTER IV.

THE EMPIRE OF THE ROMANS TO THE TIME OF AUGUSTUS
CÆSAR.. 77

Flight of Æneas from Troy to Italy. Romulus founds Rome. Sabines. Tarquin the Proud. Violation of Lucretia. Junius Brutus. Consuls. Dictator. Tribunes of the people. Coriolanus. Cincinnatus. Laws of the Twelve Tables. Decemviri. Appius. Virginia. Camillus. Gallic invasion. Samnite war. Valerius. Pyrrhus. Carthaginian wars. Conquests of Macedon, Asia, Greece. Accession to Pergamus. Gracchi. Jugurthine war. Marius. Sylla. Mithridatic war. Pompey. Cataline. Cicero. Cæsar. Crassus. Civil war. Pharsalia. Assassination of Cæsar. Octavius. Antony. Philippi. Actium. Noah. Daniel.

COMMENCEMENT OF REIGNS.

	A.M.		A.M.
1. Julius Cæsar*........	.about 3962	2. Augustus Cæsar........	about 3980

CHAPTER V.

THE STATE OF SOCIETY IN ALL EMPIRES TO THE COMMENCEMENT OF THE CHRISTIAN ERA.—THE INCARNATION.—THE APOCALYPSE.................................. 99

Preliminary suggestion. *Egypt.* Government. Judiciary. Laws. Polygamy. Idolatry. Animals worshipped. Trial of the dead. Artificers. Husbandmen. Shepherds. Irrigation of the soil. Army. Buildings. *Carthage.* Religion. Moloch. Constitution. Commerce. The Jews. Military power. Learning. Hannibal. Mago. Hasdrubal. Terence. *Persia.* Judiciary. Mode of trial. Division of the empire by Cyrus. Posts. Military science. Arts. Music. Medicine. Astronomy. *Greece.* Athens. Sparta. Government. Lycurgus. Solon. Socrates. Plato. Aristotle. Arts. Sciences. Differences between the Athenians and Spartans. Revenues. *Romans.* Civil divisions. Army. Revenue. Senate. Tribunes of the people. Plebeians. Patricians. Master and slave. Consuls. Prætors. Censors. Ædiles. Quæstors. Dictator. Twelve Tables. Suits. Religion. Time. Festivals. Downfall of religious systems. The Incarnation. The Apocalypse.

CHAPTER VI.

THE EMPIRE OF THE ROMANS TO THE TRIUMPH OF AURELIAN
OVER THE GOTHS..................................... 134

Death of Augustus Cæsar. Tiberius. Caligula. Claudius. Nero. Galba. Otho. Vitellius. Vespasian. Titus. Domitian. Nerva. Trajan. Hadrian. Antonines. Commodus; his character; acts; assassination. Pertinax; his melancholy death. Sale of the purple. Julianus. Niger. Albinus. Severus; marches to Rome; seizes the sceptre; defeats

---

* Eutropius, Bk. VI. ch. xix., xx.

Niger and Albinus. Prætorian guards abolished. Another corp created. Humiliation of the senate. Corruption of the people. Vicious character of the empress. Contentions of Geta and Caracalla. Emperor's expedition to Caledonia. Accession of Geta and Caracalla. Geta slain by his brother's guards. Murder of Papinian. Caracalla killed. Macrinus. Bassianus. Alexander Severus. Maximin. Balbinus. Maximus. Gordian III. Rise and fall of Philip the Arab. Defeat of Decius by the Goths. Æmilianus. Franks. Goths. Alemanni. Persians. Overthrow and imprisonment of Valerian in Persia. Gallienus. Claudius. Aurelian; his victory over the Goths.

COMMENCEMENT OF REIGNS.

	A.D.		A.D.
1. Tiberius	14	18. Did. Julianus	193
2. Caligula	37	19. Septimius Severus	194
3. Claudius	41	20. Caracalla and Geta	211
4. Nero	54	21. Macrinus	217
5. Galba	68	22. Elagabalus	218
6. Otho	69	23. Alexander Severus	222
7. Vitellius	70	24. Maximin	235
8. Vespasian	70	25. Balbinus	237
9. Titus	79	26. Gordian III	238
10. Domitian	81	27. Philip	244
11. Nerva	96	28. Decius	248
12. Trajan	98	29. Æmilianus	253
13. Hadrian	117	30. Valerian	253
14. Anton. Pius	138	31. Gallienus	259
15. M. Antonius	161	32. Claudius	263
16. Commodus	180	33. Aurelian*	270
17. Pertinax	192		

CHAPTER VII.

THE EMPIRE OF THE ROMANS TO ITS EXTINGUISHMENT IN THE WEST.. 143

Murder of Aurelian. Tacitus. Probus. Carus; his wars. Diocletian. Division of power. Constantius. Maximian. Galerius. Abdication of emperors. Death of Constantius. Accession of Constantine; sole power; troubles. Constans. Constantine. Constantius. Division of empire. Destruction of the Flavian family. Escape of Gallus and Julian. Constantius succeeds to the entire empire. Julian. Persian war. Jovian. Sallust. Valentinian. Valens. Division of empire. Barbarian inroads. Gratian. Valentinian II. Theodosius; his course with the Goths. Defeat of Maximus. Arcadius and Honorius. Stilicho. Alaric. Sack of Rome. Adolphus. Placida. Attila. Maximus. Sack of Vandals. Odoacer. Extinguishment of Western Empire by Theodoric, king of the Ostrogoths.

---

* Mosheim's Chron. Tables.

COMMENCEMENT OF REIGNS.

	A.D.		A.D.
1. Tacitus	276	13. Gratian and Valentinian II	375
2. Probus	276	14. Theodosius the Great	379
3. Carus	282	15. Arcadius and Honorius	395
4. Carinus	283	16. Valentinian III	425
5. Numerianus	284	17. Maximus	455
6. Diocletian and colleagues	284	18. Avitus	455
7. Galerius and colleagues	305	19. Majorian	457
8. Constantine the Great	324	20. Libius Severus	461
9. Constans, Constantine, and Constantius	340	21. Anthemius	467
		22. Olybius	472
10. Julian	361	23. Julius Nepos	474
11. Jovian	363	24. Romulus Augustulus	476
12. Valentinian and Valens	364		

CHAPTER VIII.

THE EMPIRE OF THE ROMANS TO ITS EXTINCTION IN THE EAST BY THE OTTOMANS 151

Death of Arcadius. Pulcheria. Death of Theodosius. Marcian. Leo. Basiliscus. Zeno. Anastasius. Justin. Justinian. Invasion and conquest of Africa by Belisarius. Italy subdued by Belisarius. Narses. Justin. Tiberius. Maurice. Phocas. Heraclius; his triumph over the Persians. Constantine. Constans. Theodosius. Constantine. Justinian. Philippicus. Anastasius. Theodosius. Leo. Constantine. Leo. Constantine. Irene. Nicephorus. Saturacius. Michael. Leo. Michael. Theophilus. Michael. Basil. Leo. Alexander. Constantine. Zoe. Romanus. Theophano. Phocas. John Zimisces. Basil. Constantine. Zoe. Romanus. Michael. Michael. Theophano. Isaac Comnenus. Ducas. Romanus. Nicephorus. Alexius. John. Manuel. Alexius. Andronicus. Isaac Angelus. Alexius. Alexius. Ducas. Latin conquest. Baldwin. Henry. Peter. Robert. John. Restoration of the Greeks. Michael. Andronicus. Cantacazune. Manuel. Constantine. Conquest of Ottomans. Prophecy.

COMMENCEMENT OF REIGNS.

	A.D.		A.D.
1. Pulcheria and 2. Theodosius	408	15. Constans II	641
		16. Theodosius, Constantine IV	668
3. Marcian	450	17. Justinian II	685
4. Leo	457	18. Philippicus	711
5. Leo, Basiliscus, Zeno	474	19. Anastasius II	713
6. Anastasius	491	20. Theodosius III	716
7. Justin	518	21. Leo III	718
8. Justinian	527	22. Constantine V	741
9. Justin II	565	23. Leo IV	775
10. Tiberius	578	24. Constantine VI	780
11. Maurice	582	25. Irene	792
12. Phocas	602	26. Nicephorus	802
13. Heraclius	610	27. Saturacius, Michael I	811
14. Constantine III	641	28. Leo V	813

	A.D.		A.D.
29. Michael II	820	52. John	1118
30. Theophilus	829	53. Manuel	1143
31. Michael III	842	54. Alexius II	1180
32. Basil I	867	55. Andronicus I	1183
33. Leo VI	886	56. Isaac II	1185
34. Alexander, Constantine VII	911	57. Alexius III	1195
35. Romanus I., Constantine VIII	919	58. Alexius IV	1203
36. Romanus II	959	59. Ducas	1204
37. Nicephorus, Phocas	963	60. Baldwin I	1204
38. John Zimisces, Basil II	969	61. Henry	1206
39. Constantine IX	1025	62. Peter	1217
40. Romanus III	1028	63. Robert	1221
41. Michael IV	1034	64. John, Baldwin	1228
42. Michael V	1041	65. Michael Palæologus	1259
43. Zoe and Theodora	1042	66. Andronicus II	1273
44. Constantine X	1042	67. Andronicus III	1338
45. Michael VI	1056	68. John Cantacazune	1347
46. Isaac Comnenus	1057	69. John Palæologus	1353
47. Constantine Ducas	1059	70. Andronicus IV	1390
48. Romanus III	1067	71. Manuel	1392
49. Michael VII., Constantine XII.	1071	72. John VI	1425
50. Nicephorus III	1078	73. Constantine Palæologus	1448
51. Alexius I	1081		

CHAPTER IX.

THE CONDITION OF THE EMPIRE OF THE ROMANS FROM THE AGE OF AUGUSTUS CÆSAR TO ITS OVERTHROW BY THE OTTOMANS.. 159

Extent of empire. Army. A legion. A camp. Discipline. Navy. Government. Slaves. Arts. Posts. Highways. Commerce. Diocletian. Constantine. Magistracy. Roads. Taxes. Constantine's conversion to Christianity. The principal persecutions of the Christians. Constantius espouses Arianism. Julian changes religion. Civil changes. Toleration of Jovian and Valentinian. Valens a persecutor. Theodosius destroys Arianism and paganism. Arcadius and Honorius. Monastic life. Justinian. Origin of popery. Silk introduced. Taxes. Monopolies. Court preferments. Temples. Laws. Succeeding ages. Heraclius. Bounds of empire. Income. Silk. Royal family. Processions. Navy. Greek language. Effect of the Latin conquest.

CHAPTER X.

THE EMPIRE OF THE SARACENS, TURKS, AND OTTOMANS FROM ITS RISE TO THE PRESENT TIMES....................... 178

Mohammed. Flight from Mecca to Medina. Creation of a Feud between these places. Conquest of Mecca and Arabia. Abubeker. Omar. Othman. Ali. Ommiyades. Abbasides. Almanzor. Mohadi. Haroon. Rasheed. Al-Maroon. Decline of Saracens. Motassem. Turks.

Toghrul. Beg. Alp-Arslan. Malek Shah. Monguls. Ottomans. Osman. Orchan. Amurath. Bajazet. Mohammed I. Moorad II. Mohammed II. Bayezeed. Selim. Decline of Ottomans.

COMMENCEMENT OF REIGNS.

	A.D.		A.D.
1. Mohammed	622	17. Mocktader	908
2. Abubeker	632	18. Toghrul Beg	1038
3. Omar	634	19. Alp-Arslan	1065
4. Othman	643	20. Malek Shah	1072
5. Ali	655	21. Sanjar	1092
6. Moawiyah	661	**EMPIRE OF OTTOMANS.**	
7. Merwan I	683	22. Osman	1299
8. Almanzor	750	23. Orchan	1326
9. Mohadi	775	24. Amurath	1359
10. Rasheed	785	25. Bajazet	1389
11. Al-Maroon	813	26. Mohammed I	1413
12. Motassem	833	27. Moorad II	1422
13. Motawakkel	847	28. Mohammed II	1451
14. Mostanger	861	29. Bayezeed	1481
15. Moteyov	866	30. Selim	1512
16. Mohtadi Billah	869	31. Suleiman	1520

CHAPTER XI.

THE NEUSTRIAN DIVISION OF THE EMPIRE OF THE FRANKS TO THE DEATH OF LOUIS XII. 185

Clovis destroys the power of the Romans and Visigoths; founds the Empire of the Franks. Division of kingdom. Clotaire II. Dagobert; successors. Pepin Heristal. Charles Martel. Pepin. Charlemagne conquers Italy. Germany, Spain; is declared Emperor of the West. Louis. Lothario. Civil wars. Division of empire. Constitutions of Mersen. Fall of Carlovingians. Hugh Capet. Robert. Henry. Philip. Council of Clermont. Crusade. Peter. Louis VI. English war. Vassals reduced. Louis VII. Philip Augustus. Louis VIII. Albigenses. Louis IX. Philip III. Sicily. Philip IV. The pope. The Templars. Louis X. Philip V. Charles IV. Philip VI. War with England. John. Treaty of Bretigni. Charles V. Charles VI. Treaty of Troye. Charles VII. Joan d'Arc. English conquered. Louis XI. Charles VIII. Louis XII.

COMMENCEMENT OF REIGNS.

	A.D.		A.D.
1. Clovis	486	10. Charles the Bald	875
2. Clotaire	511	11. Louis the Stammerer	877
3. Clotaire II	613	12. Louis III	879
4. Dagobert	632	13. Charles the Fat	884
5. Pepin	751	14. Charles III	898
6. Charlemagne	771	15. Robert	922
7. Louis	814	16. Rodolph	923
8. Lothario	840	17. Louis the Stranger	936
9. Louis II	855	18. Lothario	954

		A.D.			A.D.
19.	Louis V	966	30.	Philip IV	1285
20.	Hugh Capet	987	31.	Louis X	1314
21.	Robert	996	32.	Philip of Valois	1328
22.	Henry I	1031	33.	John	1350
23.	Philip	1060	34.	Charles V	1364
24.	Louis VI	1108	35.	Charles VI	1380
25.	Louis VII	1137	36.	Charles VII	1422
26.	Philip Augustus	1183	37.	Louis XI	1461
27.	Louis VIII	1223	38.	Charles VIII	1483
28.	Louis IX	1226	39.	Louis XII	1498
29.	Philip III	1270			

CHAPTER XII.

The Neustrian Division of the Empire of the Franks to the Accession of Louis XIV 194

Francis I. Milan. Quarrel with the Emperor Charles V. Wars. Treaty of Crespy. Henry II. War. Treaty of Chateau Cambresis. Francis II. Duke of Guise. Catharine of Medicis. League of Bayonne. Civil war. Massacre of St. Bartholomew. Death of Charles IX. Henry III. Henry IV; means by which he attained the crown. War with Spain. Edict of Nantes. Murder of Henry IV. Louis XIII. Civil commotions. Cardinal Richelieu. Accession of Louis XIV.

Commencement of Reigns.

		A.D.			A.D.
1.	Francis I	1515	5.	Henry III	1574
2.	Henry II	1547	6.	Henry IV	1589
3.	Francis II	1559	7.	Louis XIII	1610
4.	Charles IX	1560	8.	Louis XIV	1643

CHAPTER XIII.

The Neustrian Division of the Empire of the Franks to the Execution of Louis XVI 203

War about Brabant. Treaty of Nimeguen. Offensive measures of Louis XIV. League against France. War. Treaty of Ryswick. War about the Spanish succession. Treaty of Utrecht. Louis XV. Regency. John Law. War about Poland. War with Austria. Treaties of Dresden, Breslau, Aix-la-Chapelle. French ambition in America and India. War. Treaty of Paris. Internal troubles of France. Louis XVI. Notables. States-general. War with Austria. Execution of Louis XVI.

Commencement of Reigns.

		A.D.			A.D.
1.	Louis XV	1714	2.	Louis XVI	1775

CHAPTER XIV.

THE NEUSTRIAN DIVISION OF THE EMPIRE OF THE FRANKS TO THE DOWNFALL OF LOUIS NAPOLEON BONAPARTE AS EMPEROR.. 116

Foreign war. State of parties. Napoleon Bonaparte. Treaty of Campo Formio. Fall of the directory. Consulate. Treaty of Amiens. War. Treaty of Presburg. Decree of Berlin. Treaty of Tilsit. Acts of Napoleon. Spain. Portugal. Holland. Attack on Russia. Retreat of French. Failure in Spain. Leipzig. Elba. Louis XVIII. Irruption of Napoleon. Waterloo. St. Helena. Charles X.; causes of his abdication. Louis Philippe I. Louis Napoleon Bonaparte as emperor. Republic.

COMMENCEMENT OF REIGNS.

		A.D.			A.D.
1.	Napoleon Bonaparte	1799	5.	Louis Napoleon Bonaparte	1848
2.	Louis XVIII	1814	5.	Napoleon III	1852
3.	Charles X	1824	6.	Republic	1871
4.	Louis Philippe I	1830			

CHAPTER XV.

THE AUSTRASIAN DIVISION OF THE EMPIRE OF THE FRANKS FROM THE ELECTION OF CONRAD OF FRANCONIA TO THE DEATH OF MAXIMILIAN I.............................. 230

Election of Conrad by the Germanic states. Enumeration of states. Henry the Fowler. Otho I. Otho II. Otho III. Henry of Bavaria. Conrad. Henry III. Henry IV. Rudolph of Suabia. Henry V. Lothario. Conrad. Henry of Bavaria. Guelphs. Ghibellines. Frederick Barbarossa. Henry VI. Contest for the sceptre by Philip. Otho. Frederick; his success. Interregnum. Rudolph of Hapsburg. Adolphus of Nassau. Albert. Henry VII. Intrigues of Louis of Bavaria and Frederick of Austria. Battle of Muhldorf. Charles IV. Wenceslaus. Rupert, Sigismund. John Huss. Jerome of Prague. Albert II. Frederick. Maximilian I.

COMMENCEMENT OF REIGNS.

		A.D.			A.D.
1.	Conrad I	911	16.	Otho IV	1197
2.	Henry I	919	17.	Frederick II	1215
3.	Otho I	936	18.	Rudolph	1273
4.	Otho II	973	19.	Adolphus	1292
5.	Otho III	983	20.	Albert I	1298
6.	Henry II	1003	21.	Henry VII	1308
7.	Conrad II	1024	22.	Louis	1314
8.	Henry III	1039	23.	Charles IV	1347
9.	Henry IV	1056	24.	Wenceslaus	1378
10.	Henry V	1106	25.	Robert	1400
11.	Lothario	1125	26.	Sigismund	1410
12.	Conrad III	1138	27.	Albert II	1438
13.	Frederick I	1152	28.	Frederick III	1440
14.	Henry VI	1190	29.	Maximilian I	1493
15.	Philip	1197			

CHAPTER XVI.

THE AUSTRASIAN DIVISION OF THE EMPIRE OF THE FRANKS TO THE PRESENT TIMES.................................... ... 239

Charles V. Proceedings against Martin Luther. Confession of Augsburg. Emperor's acts against the Protestants. Turkish war. Maurice. Peace of Passau. Settlement of diet. Council of Trent. Evangelical Union. Catholic League. Controversy as to the duchies. Ferdinand I. Edict of Restitution. War. Gustavus Adolphus. Peace of Prague. War continued. Peace of Westphalia. Ferdinand III. Leopold. Joseph. Charles. Maria Theresa and Francis I. Joseph. Leopold. Settlement of Vienna. Francis II. Ferdinand. Francis Joseph I.

COMMENCEMENT OF REIGNS.

	A.D.		A.D.
1. Charles V	1520	9. Joseph I	1705
2. Ferdinand I	1556	10. Charles VI	1711
3. Maximilian II	1564	11. Francis I	1745
4. Rudolph II	1576	12. Joseph II	1765
5. Mathias	1612	13. Leopold II	1790
6. Ferdinand II	1619	14. Francis II	1792
7. Ferdinand III	1637	15. Ferdinand	1835
8. Leopold I	1658	16. Francis Joseph I	1848

CHAPTER XVII.

POWERS OF EUROPE CONNECTED WITH THE EMPIRE OF THE FRANKS.. 251

Denmark. Norway. Sweden. Union of Calmar. Margaret Waldemar. Eric. Stene Sture. Christian II. Gustavus Vasa. Eric. John. Sigismund. Charles IX. Gustavus Adolphus. Christiana. Charles Gustavus. Charles XI. Charles XII. Ulrica Elenora. Frederick Gustavus III. and IV. Charles XIII. Bernadotte. Oscar. Charles XIV. Prussia. Frederick III.; successors. Russia. Peter the Great. Catharine; successors. Spain. Ferdinand and Isabella; successors. Philip II. United Provinces. Treaty of Breda. Princes of Orange. Louis Bonaparte. Settlement of Vienna. Belgium. Philip IV.; successors. Portugal. Denmark. Switzerland. The Two Sicilies. Papal dominions. Austrian dominions in Italy. Sardinia.

COMMENCEMENT OF REIGNS.

	A.D.		A.D.
UNION OF CALMAR.		4. Sigismund	1592
1. Margaret Waldemar	1397	5. Charles IX	1599
2. Eric	1412	6. Gustavus Adolphus	1611
3. Christian II	1513	7. Christiana	1632
		8. Charles Gustavus	1654
SWEDEN.		9. Charles XI	1660
1. Gustavus Vasa	1520	10. Charles XII	1697
2. Eric	1560	11. Ulrica Elenora	1719
3. John	1569	12. Frederick Adolphus	1751

	A.D.
13. Gustavus III	1771
14. Gustavus IV	1792
15. Charles XIII	1809
16. Bernadotte	1818
17. Oscar	1844
18. Charles XIV	1859
19. Oscar II	1872

PRUSSIA.

	A.D.
1. Frederick William I	1713
2. Frederick the Great	1740
3. Frederick William II	1786
4. Frederick William III	1797
5. Frederick William IV	1840
6. Wilhelm I	1861

RUSSIA.

	A.D.
1. Peter the Great	1682
2. Catharine I	1724
3. Peter II	1727
4. Anne	1730
5. Ivan III	1740
6. Elizabeth	1741
7. Peter III	1762
8. Catharine II	1763
9. Paul	1796
10. Alexander	1801
11. Nicholas	1825
12. Alexander II	1858

SPAIN.

	A.D.
1. Ferdinand and Isabella	1479
2. Charles I	1516
3. Philip II. (*United Provinces*)	1555
4. Philip III	1598
5. Philip IV	1621
6. Charles II	1665
7. Philip V	1701
8. Ferdinand VI	1746
9. Charles III	1759
10. Charles IV	1788
11. Ferdinand VII	1808
12. Isabella	1833
13. Amadeus	1871

PORTUGAL.

	A.D.
1. John I	1383
2. Edward	1433
3. Alfonso V	1438
4. John II	1481
5. Emanuel	1495
6. John III	1521
7. Sebastian	1557
8. Henry	1578
9. Spanish Conquest.	
10. John Duke of Braganza	1640
11. Alfonso VI	1656
12. Pedro II	1667
13. John V	1706
14. Joseph	1750
15. Mary	1779
16. John VI	1792
Removal of court to Brazil	1807
17. Don Maria (Dom Pedro regent)	1826
18. Louis II	1856
19. Dom Pedro	1863

CHAPTER XVIII.

The Empire of the Anglo-Saxons to the Fall of Richard II 269

Picts and Scots. Saxons. Angles. Heptarchy. Egbert. Ethelwolf; successors. Alfred the Great, the founder of the empire. Danish invasions. Edward; successors to the division of England with Canute the Dane; successors till the time of the Norman invasion. William the Conqueror; his successors to Richard II.

Commencement of Reigns.

	A.D.
1. Egbert	827
2. Ethelwolf	838
3. Ethelbald	857
4. Ethelbert	860
5. Ethelred	866
6. Alfred the Great	872
7. Edward	901
8. Athelstan	925

		A.D.			A.D.
9.	Edmund	941	21.	William the Conqueror	1066
10.	Edred	948	22.	William II	1087
11.	Edwy	955	23.	Henry	1100
12.	Edgar	959	24.	Stephen	1135
13.	Edward	975	25.	Henry II	1154
14.	Ethelred	978	26.	Richard	1189
15.	Edmund	1016	27.	John	1199
16.	Canute	1017	28.	Henry III	1216
17.	Harold	1035	29.	Edward I	1272
18.	Hardicanute	1039	30.	Edward II	1307
19.	Edward the Confessor	1041	31.	Edward III	1327
20.	Harold	1066	32.	Richard II	1377

CHAPTER XIX.

THE EMPIRE OF THE ANGLO-SAXONS TO THE DEATH OF JAMES I. 280

Henry IV. Wickliffe. Henry V. Warwick. Gloucester. Suffolk. York. Henry VI. Civil war between the houses of York and Lancaster. Edward IV.; succeeding kings. Mary. Elizabeth. Affairs of Scotland. James I. The controversy about prerogative and privilege.

COMMENCEMENT OF REIGNS.

		A.D.			A.D.
1.	Henry IV	1399	7.	Henry VIII	1509
2.	Henry V	1413	8.	Edward VI	1547
3.	Henry VI	1422	9.	Mary	1553
4.	Edward IV	1461	10.	Elizabeth	1558
5.	Richard III	1483	11.	James	1602
6.	Henry VII	1485			

CHAPTER XX.

THE EMPIRE OF THE ANGLO-SAXONS TO THE ESTABLISHMENT OF WILLIAM PRINCE OF ORANGE IN POWER 290

Charles I. King's debts. Parliament refuses supplies. National grievances. Arbitrary taxation. John Hampden. Scotland. Strafford. Ireland. The Thirteen Bishops. The Five Members. Civil war. Fairfax. Cromwell. Disagreement between the army and parliament. Execution of Charles I. Navigation Act. Dutch war. Instrument of government. The Protector. War with Spain. Richard Cromwell. Charles II. Algernon Sidney. Lord Russell. James II. William Prince of Orange. Act of Settlement.

COMMENCEMENT OF REIGNS.

		A.D.			A.D.
1.	Charles I	1625	4.	James II	1685
2.	Cromwell	1653	5.	William and Mary	1689
3.	Charles II	1660			

CONTENTS. 17

CHAPTER XXI.

The Empire of the Anglo-Saxons to the Present Times. 298

Toleration. Battle of the Boyne. Conspiracy to restore James II. Anne of Denmark. Union with Scotland. House of Brunswick. George I. The efforts of the Pretender. Sir John Blount. George II. George III. East India Company. Canada. Union with Ireland. George IV. William IV. Alexandrina Victoria.

Commencement of Reigns.

	A.D.		A.D.
1. Anne	1701	5. George IV	1820
2. George I	1714	6. William IV	1830
3. George II	1727	7. Alexandrina Victoria	1838
4. George III	1760		

CHAPTER XXII.

The United States of America to the Administration of the Year 1872 306

Causes that led to the rupture between the thirteen colonies and England. Revolutionary war. Treaty of Paris. Shays' rebellion. Constitution. Administrations of Washington. Administration of the elder Adams. Administrations of Thomas Jefferson and James Madison. Treaty of Ghent. Administrations of James Monroe and the younger Adams. Administrations of Andrew Jackson and Martin Van Buren. Administrations of William H. Harrison and John Tyler. Administration of James K. Polk. Treaty of Guadalupe Hidalgo. Administrations of Zachary Taylor and Millard Fillmore. Administrations of Franklin Pierce, James Buchanan, Abraham Lincoln, Andrew Johnson, and Ulysses S. Grant.

Presidential Terms.

	A.D.		A.D.
1. Washington, two terms	1789-1797	10. Polk, one term	1844-1848
2. Adams, sr., one term	1797-1801	11. Taylor, deceased. Fillmore, Vice-President, one term	1848-1852
3. Jefferson, two terms	1801-1809		
4. Madison, " "	1809-1817		
5. Monroe, " "	1817-1824	12. Pierce, one term	1852-1856
6. Adams, jr., one term	1824-1828	13. Buchanan, one term	1856-1860
7. Jackson, two terms	1828-1836	14. Lincoln, two terms { Johnson, V. P., last term {	1860-1864 1864-1868
8. Van Buren, one term	1836-1840		
9. Harrison, deceased. Tyler, Vice-President, one term	1840-1844	15. Grant, two terms	1868-1872

CHAPTER XXIII.

American Nations Connected with Branches of the Empire of the Franks 327

Mexico. Independence. Empire. Iturbide. Federal constitution. Pedraza. Guerrero. Bustamente. Central government. Santa Anna.

Herrera. Paredes. Farias. Santa Anna; successors. Yucatan. Central States. Brazil. John VI. Dom Pedro I. and II. Paraguay. Argentine States. Rosas. Urquiza. Peru. Simon Bolivar. Santa Cruz. New Granada. Venezuela. Congress of Panama. Colombia. Chili. The world's future history.

CHAPTER XXIV.

NATIONAL PROGRESS IN EUROPE AND AMERICA FROM THE FALL OF THE EMPIRE OF THE ROMANS IN THE WEST TO THE PRESENT TIMES 337

The feudal system. Chivalry. Crusades. Reformations in social system. Discovery of the pandects. Commerce. Literature. The compass. Navigation. The Portuguese. Columbus. Cortes. Pizarro. Magellan. The Dutch. The English. Cabot. Raleigh. Virginia. Jamestown. Maryland. Plymouth. New England. The Carolinas. New York. New Jersey. Pennsylvania. Georgia. Russia. France. The Reformation. Jesuits. Learning in England. Commerce. English and Dutch in India. Colbert. Effect of the revocation of the Edict of Nantes. Buccaneers. The social system. Jansenists. Jesuits. Learning in France and England. Juan. Ulloa. Navigators of all nations. Northern passage. Fur-trade. Commerce of Europe. Learning in Europe and the United States. American commerce. Inland navigation. Effect of revolutions. The quadrant. Electricity. Steam.

INTRODUCTION.

THE WORKS OF THE LEADING HISTORIANS CONSIDERED IN CONNECTION WITH EMPIRES.

TIME has made sad havoc among many of the ancient historians. Mere fragments remain of some of their best works. From these, however, the world derives most of its knowledge as to the empires which began their existence before the Christian Era.

Diodorus the Sicilian wrote his "Historical Library" in the reign of Augustus. When originally complete it contained forty books; of which only fifteen are extant. In the first five there is a minute detail of the manners, customs, and laws of the Egyptians and a full account of the founding of the First or Assyrian Empire, by Ninus, as well as its extent, continuance, division, and final overthrow by the Median power. Here there is an hiatus, caused by a loss of books; which compels us to look to another source for the particulars connected with the Second or Medo-Persian Empire. This is fully supplied by Herodotus. The author then, in the eleventh book, commences with the expedition of Xerxes into Greece and continues on for five books, to the beginning of the reign of Philip of Macedon; and in the five succeeding books traces the destruction of the Second and the formation of the Third or Grecian Empire, and its divisions for years after the death of its projector, Alexander, commonly styled the Great.

The distinct manner in which Diodorus narrates the

history of the Assyrian or First Empire required, for the sake of order, that he should be first noticed; although in so doing apparent violence is committed upon the rights of the great Halicarnassean who has been for ages most properly denominated "the father of history," and to whom reference is made at all times with the greatest satisfaction. Herodotus was born at Halicarnassus in Caria, B.C. 484. On his arrival at manhood, he left his native place and travelled throughout Greece, Scythia, Egypt, and the other portions of the world then famous. In this manner he collected such information as was calculated to enable him to form correct ideas of the origin and condition of the nations which he visited. After this journey he retired to the isle of Samos, where he compiled his History. When thirty-nine years of age, he recited his composition at the Olympic games. It delighted the multitudes so much that they bestowed upon it the highest evidence of their approbation, by affixing to each of the nine books into which it is divided the name of one of the muses. Of his merits a more perfect idea can be formed by a careful consideration of the general design which directed his efforts. This author gives a view of the first empire which existed, the Assyrian; of its utter demolition; of the second empire, the Medeo-Persian, which arose; its youth; its maturity; and of the third empire, the Grecian, which was about attaining greatness as he closes his narration. His mode of commencing is a little circuitous, but upon mature reflection it will be found to be perfectly natural. After a cursory review of the causes of quarrel which brought Persia and Greece into war, he very naturally casts his eye over Asia Minor, his own country, from its earliest periods. All this portion of the world, he says, was once under the power of Crœsus, the Lydian king. After a full review and description of the people and government, he proceeds to show how domestic feuds brought Crœsus into contest with his Eastern neighbor, Cyrus of Persia. Upon the success of the latter, his dominions being extended to the Mediterranean, he becomes, both in the size and the opulence of his kingdom, the greatest prince in the world. Now, says the historian, as the reader is prepared to say, "Who is this Cyrus, and by what means did the Persians obtain the empire of Asia?" The solution of this question involves the historian in a description of the Assyrian Empire, which is the first one mentioned by any historian or prophet, and forms a coincidence which finds a parallel in all the cardinal points of history and prophecy during every age of the world; none of which can be accounted for by supposing a common design between the historians and prophets to deceive, or explained away by asserting that the prophecies were written after the histories; inasmuch as the former supposition is refuted by the position of the prophets and the historians, as well as the chronology of their writings, and the latter assertion is disproved by the concurrent testimony of the conflicting sects among the Jews and the admission of pagan authority.

The true explanation of the coincidences between history and prophecy is to be found in the fact that prophecy is the text of God's providence in the events of the world, and history is the commentary upon it (Dio. Sic., B. II. c. ii.; Josephus, Antiqs., B. IX. c. xi. § 3; Gen. c. ix. vs. 26, 27; Dan. c. ii. vs. 27, 43; Rev. c. iv. to xxi., inclusive; Newton on the Prophecies, Introd); but in all cases it must be borne in mind that prophecy refers more to dynasties than to single individuals, and is to be understood more in regard to the world's advancement in scientific, moral, political, and religious truths than to the agents that Providence uses in promoting them. (New. Dis. i. p. 15.)

Broken of its power by the independent position of the Medes, the history of that distinguished people is traced from the founding of their dynasty by Deioces down to the reign of Astyages. The delusions which disordered the brain of this monarch are sketched in a touching manner. The dreams which excited his jealousy of his daughter Mandane; his consultation of the Magi; the marriage of his child to the Persian prince, as if to defeat the decrees of heaven; for the same purpose, his removal of her to his own court; the birth of her child Cyrus; his preservation by the herdsman; his final conquest of Media, and the overthrow of his grandfather, are graphically described. In reference to all these topics Herodotus, however, candidly admits that there are other accounts; but he thinks that after the most careful investigation he has obtained and given the one most to be relied upon. Xenophon in his "Institution of Cyrus" very considerably differs from Herodotus. This book, however, was evidently written more with a view to inculcate good statesmanship than good history. In this respect it accomplishes all its author designed, and the reader being put in possession of this great prize, pardons the fiction by which it is communicated. But let the particulars of the birth, education, and establishment of Cyrus be what they may, this is asserted by Herodotus, that Cyrus was the founder of the Second or Medeo-Persian Empire; and in this he is undisputed by Xenophon. Having traced Cyrus to the possession of empire, he follows him through all his progress of conquest and government until Babylon, the last fragment of Assyrian power, is made his dependant. With a far greater empire in his possession than was the one which first existed in the world, Cyrus, according to this author, sought to overwhelm the Massagetæ or Turks, a Scythian tribe, and in the attempt lost his life.

In the reign of Cambyses, the son and successor of Cyrus, the bounds of the empire were extended to Egypt; and thus the entire civilized world, as known to the ancients, was embraced within its limits, except Europe—then considered but in the inception of refinement. The detail of this transaction is preceded by a full and minute description of Egypt and its inhabitants from the earliest time. As is invariably the case with this author, much gossip occurs in his narration; but it is told with an ease amounting in most instances to elegance; and in all cases he apprises the reader, before proceeding to his narrative, whether he is to expect this description of matter or such as he avers upon his own knowledge. Herodotus never deceives by a false gloss, never deludes by an arrogant assertion; if he knows a fact worth telling, he gives it truly and at large; if he has merely received it upon the information of others, he communicates it in that form.

This expedition, though fortunate in its primary object, was attended by the threefold calamity of the murder of Smerdis, the brother of Cambyses, his own death, and the usurpation of the Magi. Though the race of Cyrus was thus extinguished, his great empire was not doomed to fall a prey to the turbulence of faction or the imbecility of his unprincipled successors. The cheat of the Magi was soon discovered, and the resolution of seven men rid the people of their oppressors. Whatever may be thought of the arguments which agitated the convention for the settlement of the state, no one can withhold his approbation of the masterly manner in which the historian sketches the various forms of government which were proposed. It seems, however, at that period of time, the intelligence of the people was not sufficient to demand, or the power of the aristocracy was great enough to refuse, a republican constitution. The result was that Œbanes, the hostler of one of the conspirators, by causing his horse to neigh before those of his conspirators, conferred upon his master the sceptre of Cyrus. Thus was brought to power Darius, the son of Hystaspes, who first penetrated Europe. To his son Xerxes he left the work of laying at once the foundation of Grecian greatness and Persian overthrow. The immense preparations of this emperor for the invasion of Greece are described with an accuracy which is not surpassed in any work. Greece and Grecians are delineated from the first mention of them in history. The manners, customs, political condition of the rulers, in fine, all the peculiarities of the country and people, are set forth with the accuracy of one who had seen what he described. With the calamitous result of this mighty struggle to Persia and its glorious consequences to Greece, the history of Herodotus is brought to a close.

Plutarch in his lives of Aristides, Themistocles, Pericles, and Cimon fills up about forty-eight or fifty years after the Persian invasion. Greece now became the scene of what is denominated the Peloponnesian war, which lasted for twenty-seven years. Twenty years of this melancholy contest form the subject of the history of Thucydides, which the author divides into eight books. In the first book the historian traces the Greek states from their commencement, showing the means by which each attained its strength and importance. Corinth, which was the first to embark in maritime adventures, is sketched with precision. Her colony at the island of Corcyra, it seems, according to this author, became in the course of time her rival. The bitterest jealousies arose, which eventually ended in lasting enmity between the two powers. Their contests disturbed the harmony of two centuries and terminated in a furious war. Corcyra appealed to Athens for assistance, and Corinth threw herself upon the magnanimity of Sparta, the great capital of the peninsular states, formerly called the Peloponnesus, in recent times the Morea. Both succeeded in bringing into the war these great states of Greece; and the remaining seven books contain the incidents of it, given with a vigor of description which has elicited universal admiration. The work breaks off unfinished in the twenty-first year of this war.

Xenophon takes up the subject in "The Affairs of Greece" where Thucydides drops it. The course of the war is traced by this writer in his first two books to the victory of the Spartans in the sea-fight at Ægos Potamos and the subjection of Athens. The overthrow of the thirty tyrants in that once powerful capital by Thrasybulus is then described. Sparta now proceeds to carry war into the Persian dominions under Agesilaus, and in the midst of its successes the Persian king excites trouble at home and raises a third capital in Thebes, which disputes the palm of power. Athens in the general confusion regains much of her importance by means of the exertions of Conon. Matters are somewhat arranged by the peace of Antalcidas; but under pretext of a clause in this treaty, Sparta interferes for some of the cities. Thebes is revolutionized, and eventually she and the Lacedæmonians are thrown into bloody conflict. Two dreadful battles are fought, one at Leuctra, the other at Mantinea; and though the Theban general, Epaminondas, was slain at the latter, that republic was triumphant. The portrait of these times cannot be considered perfect unless Plutarch's lives of Agis, Agesilaus, Conon, Pelopidas, and Epaminondas be consulted. Although not a historian, this author abounds in incidents and reflections, which serve admirably to enforce and illustrate all history. He died in the one hundred and fortieth year of the Christian era.

Xenophon's "Expedition of Cyrus" is indispensable to a

proper understanding of this period of the world. It contains a full account of the contest between Cyrus and his elder brother for the sceptre of Persia; the connection of the Greeks with it; and forms a perfect preface to the designs of the Macedonian Philip and his son Alexander.

The conflicts which for years rent asunder the states of Greece were watched with unceasing anxiety by the Macedonian monarch. The ultimate object of his ambition was Persia. To accomplish this, he well knew that he must be general of the Grecian forces. Every art, every scheme, therefore, was brought to bear to enable Philip to sway the destinies of Greece. His success finally aroused the ire of Demosthenes, who delivered philippic after philippic against the cunning tyrant, and was able to form a powerful league to repel his aggressions. The army which this brought into the field Philip overpowered at Chæronea, and eventually triumphed over all opposition. But the dagger of Perdiccas scattered the plans of ambition which he had formed. Plutarch's life of Demosthenes and the contemporary characters will give a full view of the incidents of this period: but Diodorus must not be neglected here or afterwards.

Philip's death placed his son Alexander on the throne. By him was the Persian Empire finally destroyed, and his almost boundless domains were divided among his principal generals, after his early death; all of whose dominions were eventually subjected to the Roman or Fourth Empire. Arrian is properly the historian of Alexander. He flourished about A.D. 140, and was honored with the government of Cappadocia by M. Antoninus. His "Expedition of Alexander" consists of seven books, written in the clear, succinct style of the old historians. Arrian commences at the accession of this hero to the throne of his deceased father; traces him to the states of the

Peloponnesus, whose decree in favor of him, as the head of the army against Persia, he records; notes the dissent of Sparta to this action, the sympathy of Athens for the policy of that city, but its speedy accession to the Peloponnesian league, under awe of the power of the young Macedonian; carries him back to his own territories, to subdue the rebellious Triballi and Illyrians; narrates the conspiracy of the Thebans and the overthrow of Thebes; the passage of Alexander into Asia ; the battle at the Granicus; the conquest or submission of the states of Asia Minor, until Alexander arrives at the Straits of Issus, where his victory over the army of Darius is described, as well as his progress from that place to the ultimate limits of his expedition into Egypt and Arabia. The final triumph at Gaugamela, or, as it is commonly called, Arbela, is delineated, as also Alexander's invasion of Scythia on the north and India on the east. Thus possessed of power to the Hyphasis on the east, through Egypt in the south, to the Tanais on the north, and master of Macedon and Greece in the west, courted by both Carthage and Rome,—in a word, enjoying all worth the thought or notice of ambition,—Alexander is brought back to Babylon, where he dies like the humblest peasant, of a dreadful fever. After a minute description of the Indian expedition, the division of this vast empire among Alexander's generals is given.

The world was distracted for years with the contentions of these men, until the battle of Ipsus divided the possessions of Alexander between Cassander in Macedonia, Lysimachus in Thrace, Ptolemy in Egypt, and Seleucus in Chaldea. Diodorus draws the picture of these distractions, along with Plutarch in his lives of Eumenes and Demetrius. Lysimachus was killed in a war against Seleucus. About two years before he entrusted his treasures to Philæterus the eunuch, who, seizing them at Pergamus, in Mysia, established a kingdom, over which he presided for twenty years. His successors were five. The last, Attalus Philomator, left his kingdom to the Romans, who expelled by arms the usurper and made it a Roman province. The successors of Seleucus, numbering some eighteen or twenty persons, commonly called the Seleucidæ, held possession of his dominions, or portions of them, until the last was conquered and dethroned by Pompey and a Roman province established. Cassander reigned near twenty years in Macedonia. Upon his death, his three sons contested the succession, but all fell by the hand of violence. Demetrius, the son of Antigonus, obtained the throne, from which he was expelled by a league between Ptolemy, Seleucus, and Lysimachus; but it finally came to his family, the last of whom, Perseus, was conquered by the Romans, their vengeance having been roused by the Macedonians siding with Carthage. Ptolemy's race held Egypt till it was subdued by Julius Cæsar.

Livy is the principal Roman historian. His compilation originally consisted of 142 books, of which but 35 are preserved, though the contents of the whole work, except the 37th and 38th books, are extant. He wrote his history in the reign of Cæsar Augustus. He traces the Romans from the time when their progenitor, Æneas, with his six hundred companions, landed in Italy, after the destruction of Troy; through the sway of kings and consuls, tribunes and decemvirs, until they became masters of all the Italian states, and gained so much fame from having expelled Pyrrhus, king of Epirus, from their borders that they stood unrivalled by any power in the West but that of Carthage. The offence taken at this African capital for its effort to subdue the Mamertines, in Sicily, in opposition to the interests of Rome, being presented; the bloody contests with it are minutely traced, and the results are set out as giving the Romans the decided preponderance of power in the West, and a cause of quarrel with Macedonia, which brought it Pergamus and Egypt as allies, and made Antiochus and Philip enemies, and eventually, in the time of Augustus, extended its sceptre from Britain to the Caspian Sea. The internal commotions of the state are vigorously described, and in so close and connected a manner as to render Livy a most bewitching author.

Sallust supplies much matter, of which but an imperfect idea can be formed from what remains of Livy. In his History of the Jugurthine War a view is afforded of the corrupt condition of the Roman nobility after the conquest of the East, and the efforts of the Gracchi to repress it. The geography, population, actual condition of Africa, incidents of the war, and the means by which Marius and Sylla rose to power are given in a succinct but enchanting manner. Having afforded a key to the characters of these men who successively scourged Rome by their ambition and cruelty, Sallust, in his Conspiracy of Cataline, unfolds one of the darkest plots that ever endangered the state or disturbed the peace of society. These two small portions of history form an introduction to the operations of Julius Cæsar of which the world would otherwise be ignorant, and thus supply what is wanting from the loss of Livy. Sallust died B.C. 33.

Cæsar's Commentaries of his wars in Gaul give the account of his overthrow of the Helvetii or Swiss, who then aspired to the sovereignty of all the nations of Gaul; the expulsion of the Germans, who had laid it under contribution; the flight of the Belgian army; the success of Galba in opening a way to Roman merchants over the Alps; Cæsar's triumph in Venice and Gaul; the triumph of Crassus in Aquitaine; the invasion of Britain by the Romans; Cæsar's success over the Pirustæ in Italy and Illyricum; over the Treveri in Gaul; over the Britons upon a second entrance into their isle; over the nations of Gaul that conspired to throw off the Roman yoke; over the Nervians and the Senones, the Carnutes and Menapians; and of the victory of Labienus, in charge of one of the legions, over the Treveri. A description of the manners and customs of the Gauls and Germans; of Cæsar's second passage over the Rhine; of his marches against Ambiorix; and of his overthrow of the great confederacy under Vercingetorix for the liberation of Gaul, is also afforded. Pansa's continuation of the Commentaries shows how Cæsar effected the final conquest of Gaul, and concludes by opening up the causes which led to the Civil War. Cæsar's Commentaries of the Civil War unfold the causes of the quarrel between him and Pompey, as well as all the incidents of the contest down to the battle of Pharsalia, in which the champion of the aristocracy was crushed and the favorite of the people was elevated to the possession of unbounded power. Pansa now appears again, and in his Commentaries describes Cæsar's reduction of Alexandria and establishment of Cleopatra in the sovereignty of Egypt; his subjugation of Illyricum and all the states of Asia; his overthrow of the Pompeian interest in Africa and Spain.

Polybius, who died before Christ 124, wrote a general history in forty books, only five of which remain, with fragments from the sixth to the seventeenth of those lost. The first book contains an account of the first Punic war and the war of Carthage, after its termination, with its mercenaries. Carthaginian progress in Spain, the advancement of the Romans in Illyria, the Gallic powers and their irruptions, together with the contests of the Grecian states, are treated at large in the second book. The causes and particulars of the second Punic war are portrayed in the third, when the affairs of Greece are resumed and reviewed in the fourth book. Greece and Asia form the subjects of the fifth book.

Justin is indispensable to a connected view of all the historians to the time of Augustus. He compiled his work in the reign of the Antonines from a larger one written by Trogus Pompeius, which is lost. It consists of forty-four books. From a total ignorance of Jewish antiquity, this author, in common with many who followed him, gives the most absurd account of that nation.

The empire attained its summit under Augustus Cæsar. It gradually declined through the influence of luxury, vice, sedition, and the inroads of the Northern and Eastern nations. In the year A.D. 364 it was finally divided between Valentinian and his brother Valens; the latter taking the East, the former the West. The West was destroyed A.D. 476, though partially restored in A.D. 537 by the army of Justinian. The Empire of the East fell before the Latins A.D. 1203, and was finally destroyed by the Turks A.D. 1453.

The first six books of the Annals of Tacitus describe the reign of Tiberius, the successor of Augustus. There is a loss of the four succeeding books and also of the fore part of the eleventh book, when the author opens after Claudius had reigned six years, and concludes in the twelfth book with a description of the means by which the emperor was poisoned by his wife, whose son Nero was placed in power. The guilty reign of this wretch is described in the thirteenth, fourteenth, fifteenth, and sixteenth books, but left unfinished by the loss of the latter part of the last book. The History of Tacitus narrates the elevation and fall of Galba; the rise of Otho, and the bloody civil war between him and Vitellius, the issue of which terminated the power of the former and brought the latter to the possession of a sceptre, which was soon snatched from his hands by Vespasian: the events of whose reign are sketched in the fourth book, which is entire, and in the fifth book, a greater part of which is lost. A very complete idea of affairs in Gaul, Germany, Rome, and Judea at this period can be gathered from these sources. "The Manners of the Germans" and the "Life of Agricola" by the same author form to this day the only proper introduction to the study of German or English history.

The compilers of the Augustan History present the leading authors on imperial affairs from the time of Augustus to the latter part of the sixteenth century. A prominent feature in this invaluable collection consists of all that remains of the writings of Ammianus Marcellinus. The work of this remarkable man originally comprised thirty-one books; at the present time only eighteen are extant. Eutropius wrote a history of the Roman Empire, which concludes at the death of Jovian, A.D. 364. Zosimus lived in the fore part of the fifth century. His narrative embraces events from the time of Augustus to that of Alaric, A.D. 410. The latter part of his first, the fore part of his second, and the conclusion of his fifth book are lost: the reign of Dioclesian and the events of the Gothic inroad are therefore wanting in this author. The remarks of Zosimus upon Constantine the Great certainly possess a severity which the accounts of contemporaneous writers, both Christian and, like himself, pagan, do not justify; still in his general narrative of facts he is so concise and clear that he becomes an agreeable companion, though not invariably a safe guide. Orosius wrote about the same time as Zosimus. Notwithstanding his work is rather argumentative than historical, it may be consulted with great profit by the student.

INTRODUCTION.

The final condition of the eastern portion of the Roman Empire is found in the pages of Procopius, an historian who wrote in the reign of Justinian. His principal work consists of eight books; two give an account of the Persian war, two of the Vandal, and four of the Gothic; and it is brought down to A.D. 567 by Agathias. The Annals of Zonaras bring the history of the eastern portion of the Roman Empire to the fore part of the twelfth century, A.D. 1119; Nicetas Acominates or Choniatus to the commencement of the thirteenth century, A.D. 1203; Nicephorus Gregoras to the middle of the fourteenth century, A.D. 1341; John Cantacuzene nineteen years later, A.D. 1360; Laonicus Chalchondites to the conquest by the Turks in A.D. 1453. The substance of these authors is arranged by the compilers of the Augustan History; in treating of each emperor, and in tracing the affairs of the Franks and Ottomans, they are equally careful to form their narratives from original sources.

The Turkish Empire, which triumphed over the eastern portion of the Roman power in 1453, dates its origin in A.D. 622. At that period Mohammed, after having in vain attempted to change the religion of Mecca, in Arabia, was compelled to fly with a handful of followers to Medina, a town some two hundred miles distant. Here he had better success, and soon set up for a temporal prince. In the short space of ten years he subdued nearly all Arabia, and during the period of thirty years, which covers the reigns of his four successors, the empire extended to the Oxus and India, the Caspian and Euxine, Africa, Cyprus, and Rhodes. Upon the assassination of Ali, the last of these khalifs and the son-in-law of Mohammed, the Ommyades succeeded and held the sceptre nearly one hundred years, when the relations of the Prophet again came to power in the descendants of Abbas, his uncle, and destroyed all the Ommyades except Abd-er-rahman, who was established in Spain. By the middle of the eighth century these bigots would have overwhelmed Europe by the way of the Pyrenees, had it not been for the power of the Franks, directed by Charles Martel. The Turkish guards which one of the Saracen khalifs created to protect his throne eventually seized the sceptre in A.D. 1055; and though the Mogul invasion in the thirteenth century destroyed the khalifate entirely, Othman, of the Turkish tribe of Oghuz, restored the splendor of the empire, after whom it is called to this day.

The narratives of ancient empires cannot be formed without resorting to the distorted writers of epochs; but the numerous standard works of modern times, in addition to furnishing a connected detail of all events of the empires which sprang from the Roman powers, afford a reference to the authors of each period and kingdom, and thus lead the student by gradual but certain steps to the fountain-head of genuine history. Elmakin gives in his History the account of the origin, progress, and dissensions of the Saracenic Empire. Ockley's History of the Saracens is more accessible, but does not come down so far as Elmakin, though the index will serve to the conclusion of the empire. Cantemir's History of the growth and decay of the Othman Empire, which concludes in 1683, completes the greatness of this remarkable portion of the human family. Since that period it has gradually dwindled to its present insignificance, and its history is to be more properly traced in that of western empires than from any other source.

Much uncertainty prevails among the Roman authors as to the origin and organization of the Northern nations which destroyed the western division of the Roman Empire. A few general statements, however, may be assumed.

Germany under its two confederacies,* the Franks and Alemanni—or the inhabitants of the lower Rhine and Weser and those beyond the Elbe, and their allies to the south as far as the western borders of the Rhine—resisted the Roman arms and harassed the dominions of the empire. The Goths, whose origin is variously traced, penetrated Dacia and Mysia; poured their myriad hosts through Greece; and, though impeded at times by other barbarians, finally uniting with them, swept the Roman Empire in the West from existence and established themselves, under various names, in Italy, Gaul, and Spain. The Vandal hordes finally seized upon Africa. Eventually the Vandals were cut off in Africa by the arms of Justinian; and the Goths and Alemanni received a fatal blow from Clovis, the head of the Franks, who left to his successors, the Merovingians, at his death in A.D. 511, a kingdom embracing the country between the Garonne and Loire. What Clovis commenced was completed by Charlemagne, who in the first year of the ninth century was crowned "Emperor of the West" at Rome by Pope Leo III. Thus at once was confirmed the power of the papacy and healed for a time the breach in the branch of the Roman Empire which embraced the Western nations of the continent of Europe.† The eastern portion of this dominion, German in its population, was called Austrasia; the western part, Romanized Gallic in its extraction, was denominated Neustria. The private quarrels of the nobles engrossed public attention among the Neustrian Franks, till the Crusades, in A.D. 1066, gave another turn to affairs. After more than a century of warfare, France yielded her sceptre to England in A.D. 1420, by the treaty of Troye; but recovering from her dis-

---

* Kol., 64, 65. Man. Ger., p. 558, note 3. 1 Gil., 145, 146.
† Kol., 86. Scott's Com., Rev. xiii. 2-4.

grace, maintained her power, under Charles VII., fifteen years afterwards. An equally favorable result followed her wars with Charles V., from A.D. 1515 to 1554. The strifes between the Huguenots and Catholics, though allayed by the accession of Henry IV. in 1589, really existed till the overthrow of the former, in A.D. 1685, by the revocation of the Edict of Nantes. The bloody wars for the conquest of Holland; to maintain the pride and tyranny of Louis XIV.; to secure the Spanish succession in the Bourbon house; to defeat the title of Maria Theresa to the imperial sceptre; and to destroy the English colonies in North America,—all of which were more or less general throughout Christendom,—which mark French history, fill up a period of one hundred and thirty-one years, from the reign of Louis XIV. in A.D. 1643 to the end of that of Louis XV. in A.D. 1774. The fearful scenes of the Revolution are then presented, which brought upon the stage Napoleon Bonaparte, after which, during a period of thirty-six years, the old dynasty was restored and eventuated in the creation of the Republic of 1848, the first head of which was Louis the nephew of Napoleon, who established an empire, and on whose downfall the present republic was formed. Lardner's Cabinet Cyclopædia (History: France) is as succinct as any that can be consulted and makes constant reference to the authors of each epoch,—which may be thus classed: Paris and Froissart to the end of the fourteenth century; De Comines and Guicciardini to the year 1530; De Thou, Davila, Sully, and Thuanus to the time of Henry IV.; and Racine, Brienne, De Retz, Villars, Noailles, Dumourier, De Staël, Thiers, and Blanc to the present time. Henault's abridgment will be of incomparable service.

In 911, the Austrasian Franks or German states, for their own protection, formed a confederacy and elected Conrad of Franconia emperor. The restraint of the Danes and Huns; the regulation of the affairs of the popedom; and the consequent operations in Italy, form the leading features of the history of this empire to A.D. 1072, when the emperor Henry IV. became involved in a thirty years' war about the supremacy of the papal power. The Crusades and civil commotions fill up the period to the elevation of Rudolph of Hapsburg in A.D. 1273. The importance of the Austrian house dates from this reign, and from A.D. 1438 it has been almost without intermission in the enjoyment of imperial authority. The accession of Charles V. in 1520 and the commencement of the Reformation about the same time were eras from which sprang the great contests that occupy European history for the succeeding century. A struggle with the Turks then ensued; towards the conclusion of which the empire was brought into a deadly feud with France, the history of which is to a greater or less extent connected with that power till the treaty of Vienna, in A.D. 1815. Kohlrausch brings his history of this empire down to that time, and his ample references to original authors and his agreeable style render him a safe and entertaining guide. Cox's History of the House of Austria will serve to facilitate the labors of the student in acquiring a correct account of this branch of empire.

The power of the Germans extended to all the Northern countries, though the authority of the emperor was not directly exercised over them. Hence it is evident in the contest with Albert, who was expelled from Sweden in A.D. 1389; and when by the treaty of Calmar, seven years afterwards, the sceptres of Denmark, Norway, and Sweden devolved upon Margaret Waldemar, and finally upon her grand-nephew, Eric of Pomerania, it was no less marked. In the reign of Christian I., which commenced A.D. 1457, it is asserted that the municipal offices were so filled with

Germans that a Swede could obtain nothing unless he chose to be a beadle or a gravedigger. The settlement of the crown in the house of Vasa, in A.D. 1544, put an end to this state of things, and the reign of Gustavus Adolphus, which began A.D. 1611 and ended A.D. 1632, made the power of Sweden more important in the empire of the Germans than theirs had ever been in Sweden. Nor was it less distinctly marked in the reign of Charles XII. in developing, in A.D. 1700, the genius and resources of Peter the Great of Russia, whose fifth successor acted such an important part in bringing about the treaty of Vienna. Geijer's Sweden, together with the French, German, and English authors cited, afford ample information on all these kingdoms, so far as they are connected with the general course of events.

Spain, the southern portion of the empire of Charlemagne, never assumed more importance than any other kingdom of a similar stamp until the latter part of the fifteenth century, when the discoveries of both it and Portugal in the East and West gave them a commanding influence in the affairs of the world. The wars to reduce the United Provinces, the wars of Louis XIV., and the revolutions of the present century in South America and Mexico have quite reduced the condition of this peninsula to what it was when but a member of the empire of Charles the Great. Prescott's Ferdinand and Isabella, Robertson's Charles V. and America, Watson's Philip II., and the authors to be cited on English history, afford the prominent events of this section of empire. As each American power is reviewed, the authorities will be noted.

In less than a century (A.D. 872) after Charlemagne re-established the Empire of the West, Alfred, having driven the Danes from the island of Great Britain, laid the foundation of the Anglo-Saxon Empire. In A.D. 1066, William Duke of Normandy became its sovereign. Henry, the second son of this line, acquired Normandy and involved himself in a war with France. His only child, Matilda, he married to Geoffrey Plantagenet, son of the Duke of Anjou, by whom she had a son named Henry. On her father's death, Stephen Count of Boulogne, grandson of the Conqueror, contested her right of succession, and a bloody civil war followed. Her son coming of age, entered England, and a decisive battle would have taken place had not a treaty settled the matter by permitting Stephen to hold the sceptre during life, when the young Henry was to succeed. His reign was embittered by a controversy with the Church, incited by Thomas à Becket, but it is famous for the improvements in the arts and sciences, literature and laws. His two successors involved everything in confusion, which brought on a contest that was settled at Runnymede, A.D. 1215, by King John signing Magna Charta, the bulwark of English liberty. He and his sons disregarded this solemn instrument, which created a civil war, in which the third Henry was successful; but peace was restored by the triumph of Magna Charta under the first Edward. In this reign the contest raged with the Scots, and the House of Commons originated (A.D. 1295). The third Edward's reign brought on the wars with France which were so glorious to the arms of England. The attention is now arrested by the causes and the course of the civil wars between the houses of York and Lancaster, which terminated in A.D. 1484 in the fall of the Plantagenets and the rise of the Tudors under Henry VII. Five reigns, including this king, brought the house of Stuart into power in A.D. 1601, the first member of which was James First of England, the Sixth of Scotland. The high notions of James on kingly power and ecclesiastical authority involved him with the popular or Puritan party, in opposing which his son Charles I. lost his life. The Commonwealth succeeded, with Oliver Cromwell at its head. Upon the failure of the movement by the death of its chief, the son of the decapitated monarch, Charles II., was reinstated in power (A.D. 1660). The tyranny of this king and his brother James II. produced the fall of the house of Stuart, in 1688, and the Act of Settlement, by which the son-in-law of James II., William of Orange, and his wife, came to the sceptre, and after Anne of Denmark the house of Brunswick, which is now in possession of power. There is no branch of the history of empires upon which as many good historians can be produced as on this. The succeeding reference, therefore, is made with great deference and is not to be considered as exclusive. Hume, Smollett, and Bisset read in connection with Neall's History of the Puritans, D'Aubigné's Protector, Carlyle's Letters of Cromwell, Robertson's History of Scotland, and Macaulay's History of England will give the student as correct a view of this empire as books can confer. Upon recent Europe, Alison should be studied. The original authors can be consulted in this order: to the end of Stephen's reign, Gildas, Bede, William of Malmesbury; to the conclusion of the reign of Henry III., Hoveden, Diceto, Mathew Paris, Brompton, and Fitz Stephens; to the death of Henry V., Froissart and Walsingham; and to the present age, Polydour Vergil, Hall, Hollinshed, More, Stowe, Speed, Baker, Clarendon, Neall, Burnet, Rapin, Coote, and Alison.

The genius of Europe discovered and the convulsions of Europe peopled America. The courage and wisdom of the first settlers and their descendants laid the foundations of mighty states. The first to strike the blow effectually were the thirteen Anglo-Saxon colonies, which from a population of three have increased to over forty millions. The settlement and colonial condition of North and South America may be collected from Holmes' Annals, Bancroft's and Hildreth's History of the United States, and Marshall's Introduction to the Life of Washington. The Revolutionary struggle of the United States is traced in Ramsay's History of that war; and Marshall's and Irving's Life of Washington not only contain the matter of that author, but bring down the history of the Republic to the conclusion of Washington's administration. Hildreth and Abbott will keep up the connection to the present period. The Rebellion is taken from the author's notes. The commonly received chronological tables have been followed throughout the work, except that the calculation is made from the creation to the birth of Christ, on the supposition that four thousand and four years transpired between these eras. In all researches into the origin of our race, its gradual enlargement through the various stages of patriarchal and national existence, the rise of four and the downfall of three empires, it will be found that no one book furnishes so constant a clue to the diffuse narratives of the ancient historians as the Sacred Scriptures. Passing from the historical portions of the divine record to those of a prophetical character, with some temperate and learned works like those of Newton and Scott as a guide, a force will be perceived in ancient and modern history of which it is destitute when studied in any other method. The investigation of history on a different principle is to tax the memory to its utmost tension, merely to obtain a dry detail of curious annals; but studied in the manner suggested, it steadily presents as the objects of contemplation the attributes and providence of God, the evolution of empires, and the accomplishment of the scheme of redemption, the rewards of virtue and the punishment of vice,—sublime truths which are calculated to enlighten the understanding, to purify the affections, and consequently to advance the best interests of mankind.

OUTLINE EVOLUTION
OF
EMPIRE AND PROPHECY.

CHAPTER I.

THE EMPIRE OF THE ASSYRIANS.

THE first empire was founded by Ninus, king of Assyria.* Determined to subdue Asia from the Tanais to the Nile, Ninus associated with himself the prince of Arabia, and, raising a large army, in the space of seventeen years made himself master of the Babylonian district, Media, Armenia, Egypt, Phœnicia, Celo-Syria, Cilicia, Pamphylia, Lycia, Caria, Phrygia, Mysia, Lydia; the provinces of Troas and Phrygia on the Hellespont, together with the Propontis; Bithynia, Cappadocia, and all the nations on the Pontus, as far as the Tanais; the Cadducians, Tarpyrians, Hyrcanians, Dacians, Derbians, Carmanians, Choroneans, Borchanians, and Parthians. He also penetrated into Persia and the nations in the Caspian straits; founded Nineveh; and subdued Bactria. Semiramis, his queen, bore him a son, whom he named Ninyas. At the death of Ninus, the son being young, his mother became regent.

---

* Jus., p. 19, note; Bk. I. ch. i., ii., iii. Dio. Sic., Bk. II. ch. i., ii. pp. 54, 65. Orosius, Bk. II. ch. i., iv.

The famous city of Babylon was built during the reign of Semiramis.* Its foundations were laid upon a spacious plain, in the form of a square, surrounded by a wall three hunded feet in height and wide enough to allow from two to six chariots to be driven abreast upon it. The wall was made of bricks cemented together by bitumen, a tenacious substance peculiar to the country. A trench was sunk around the wall; an idea of the depth and width of which may be inferred from the fact that the earth taken out of it composed the bricks of the wall. Towers adorned the wall, and twenty-five brass gates, open by day, presented as many streets, which ran the length and breadth of the city, intersecting each other at right angles. Around the squares were ranged the buildings, rising to the height of three and four stories, but extending to such a depth as left an interior space open for ventilation. The river Euphrates passed from the north to the south through the centre of the city. On each side of it walls were erected, of the same materials as those which encompassed the capital. At each street archways were constructed, in which brazen gates were placed, whence steps projected to the edge of the river, to enable the citizens to enter barges as convenience or pleasure suggested.

The Euphrates was drained of its waters and a tunnel cut beneath its bed. At the opening of the tunnel stood the old palace, a building of immense proportions. At its outlet, on the opposite side, a new structure was erected, designed for imperial purposes. It occupied nearly eight miles. The palace was surrounded by walls ornamented with every species of device expressive of daring exploits.

The Temple of Belus was erected near the old palace. A tower stood within it, half a mile in compass and a

---

* Herodotus, Clio, 178, 183.

furlong in height, from which as a base rose seven other towers. The ascent to the top was by a winding staircase on the outside of the edifice, which circled it several times. In each story spacious rooms were finished in the most elegant style and ornamented with the richest gems which Eastern splendor could command. Over the whole establishment was formed an observatory, which afforded to the Babylonians an opportunity of perfecting themselves in the science of astronomy.

Excellent as were the uses to which this portion of the temple was devoted, its other apartments were prostituted to the worship of various heathen deities, the principal of which was the god Baal. Age after age these chapels were the repositories of precious gifts, which the superstition of thousands prompted them to offer, until the accumulation of wealth was immense. This prize remained untouched, amidst all fluctuations, down to the time of Xerxes.*

The canals and lake were projected at a later period, to protect the capital against the rapacity of the Medes.† During the winter months the adjacent mountains of Armenia were covered with snow. When the spring arrived this immense mass dissolved and poured down its streams into the Euphrates. The torrent broke in the summer through all bounds, forced the banks of the river, and flooded the low country. Canals were made, which turned the waters of the river so often as to destroy its force and to render its navigation difficult. A lake four hundred and twenty furlongs in circumference was constructed, where the waters were pent up, and by means of locks and outlets distributed, as occasion demanded, for the purpose of fertilizing the country. Thus did these

---

* Herodotus, Clio, 183.   Judges vi. 28.   2 Kings x. 28; xvi. 10, 16.
† Herodotus, Clio, 185.

works answer the double purpose of protecting the inhabitants of the city and enriching those of the plain.

The luxuriousness of still later times suggested and caused to be executed a work which elicited much admiration. It was denominated the hanging garden. This was formed by large projecting terraces, one above another, at a distance of about ten feet, ascending round the walls of the palace; each terrace forming a square of four hundred feet and connected with the one above it by steps. The fabric was made permanent by arches durably formed and surrounded by a wall twenty-two feet in thickness. So firmly constructed was the work that in the garden were reared not only all kinds of shrubbery, but trees of the largest size.

Semiramis did not rest her fame solely on stupendous monuments of art. Her celebrity in arms rivals, if it does not surpass, that of her husband. Sprung from an obscure origin, she resolved to obliterate the recollection of it, in the minds of her subjects, by the splendor of her actions. Immense and opulent as were the domains left her by Ninus, she added to them on all sides. In the south she penetrated as far as Ethiopia, and established there the imperial authority. Emboldened by her success in this quarter, she determined on an invasion of the rich countries of the East. An immense army was raised and departed on the expedition. When the empress approached India, its monarch sent an embassy to demand her reason for invading his territories without provocation. The brief reply which she gave was that in a little time he should have a trial of her valor by her actions. Battle was joined at the Indus, and Semiramis was victorious: but following up this advantage by too-rapid marches, the Indians rallied, and she was defeated. Making good her way to the place on the river where she had crossed, Semiramis effected a retreat to her own empire, having lost about two thirds of her army. This calamity was followed by one of a still more serious description. Ninyas, her son, aspired to the sceptre, and plotted to wrest it from her hand. The empress declined a contest with her offspring; and after a reign of forty-two years, withdrew from public affairs.

With the accession of Ninyas, the policy of government was altered. Dreading that he might fall by the same means through which he acquired power, the emperor adopted a system of military proceedings the tendency of which was to counteract the schemes of ambition. The various divisions of the army were filled by levies from the provinces, which, under the new arrangement, were made so constantly that the entire body was composed of a new set of men every succeeding year. The commander-in-chief was the only person who was not affected by this scheme; but his influence was rendered nugatory by reason of the limited time the soldiers were subject to his order. A system whose avowed object was fluctuation, though well calculated to prevent conspiracies, was equally as fatal to military enterprise. The period of its establishment is that from which to date the decline of the empire. Thirty successive generations, extending through a space of over eleven hundred years,* produced none but debased princes. The last of them was Sardanapalus. Abstracting himself from the society of men, he spent all his time among the women of the seraglio, applying his attention to the distaff, dressing and painting himself to please his companions. Rebellion ensued. Two powerful leaders assumed the command. Sardanapalus at first shunned the contest, but when forced into it he met the insurgents and triumphed over

---

* Oros., Bk. XI. ch. i., xii.

them in three successive engagements. The leaders of the rebellion, made desperate by these defeats, prepared to hazard all in one effort, and falling upon the emperor, defeated his forces after a bloody conflict. Mortified at the success of his enemies, Sardanapalus fled to Nineveh. In that city he was besieged for two years.

In the third year of the siege the river was so swelled by continual rains that it overflowed part of the city and broke down the walls for twenty furlongs, when the king, thinking the prophecy fulfilled which had been written, according to Josephus, one hundred and fifteen years before, built a funeral-pile in the palace, and collecting his companions and treasures, burnt them, and perishing himself in the conflagration, the besiegers took the city.*

Thus fell the Assyrian Empire, which had for thirteen centuries oppressed the nations and at the time of its overthrow held captive the ten tribes of Israel. He who next succeeded to empire was pre-eminently the subject of prophecy.

How impressive are the words of Nahum in predicting the fate of Nineveh and the Assyriam Empire!

"Woe to the bloody city! it is all full of lies and robbery. . . . And it shall come to pass, that all they that look upon thee shall flee from thee, and say, Nineveh is laid waste: who will bemoan her? . . . The fire shall devour thee; the sword shall cut thee off, it shall eat thee up as the canker-worm. . . . Thy shepherds slumber, O king of Assyria: thy nobles shall dwell in the dust: thy people is scattered upon the mountains, and no man gathereth them. There is no healing of thy bruise; thy

---

*Dio. Sic., Bk. II. ch. ii. Nahum i., ii., iii. Josephus' Antiqs., Bk. IX. c. xi. § 3. Newton on Prophecies, Dis. 9. 2 Kings xviii. 9-12.

wound is grievous: all that hear the bruit of thee shall clap the hands over thee: for upon whom hath not thy wickedness passed continually?"

CHAPTER II.

THE EMPIRE OF THE MEDES AND PERSIANS.

AFTER the independence of the Medes, their affairs fell into confusion. The tribunals of justice became corrupt; men in all departments practised oppression; and that spirit which effected the national liberation ceased to animate the people. This state of things fired the ambition of Deioces. An obscure judicial circuit was occupied by him at the commencement of his career. Great propriety in the discharge of his duties secured public confidence. His spotless character gradually attracted the people in the surrounding districts. Suitors voluntarily submitted their causes to his arbitrament. Such was his fame that his judgments, though local in form, possessed the force of national law. In the midst of this prosperity, the judge suddenly withdrew from the bench, alleging that his attention to public pursuits compelled him to neglect his own interests. The abdication of the patron of order produced that scene of misrule which Deioces had anticipated. A national assembly was soon convoked to provide for the exigencies of the times. In this body Deioces had his minions. Concealing their personal predilections, they procured a declaration in favor of monarchical government, as well as a vote that he was the most proper person for its administration who had rendered the greatest amount of public services. The name of Deioces was then put forward, and he was chosen king by unanimous consent.

The first act of this reign was the building of the capital, Ecbatana. This city was surrounded by seven circular walls, "each rising above each, by the height of their respective battlements." Within the last of these stood the palace and treasury. Each wall was of a different color—the first white, the next black, the third purple, the fourth blue, the fifth orange; whilst the battlements of the two innermost were plated, one with silver, the other with gold. The people were compelled to live beyond the walls surrounding the palace. This was but a prelude to that despotism which was to be established. An edict was proclaimed which interdicted all communication between the sovereign and his subjects except through duly constituted ministers and in cases hereafter noted. All the actions of these officials were directed with precision by the terms of the law: they were not allowed so much as to spit in each other's presence or in the presence of the king; any violation of the rule being punished with the severest penalties. Causes involving the rights of private property or persons were submitted to the sovereign in a written statement, upon which he endorsed his judgment. Infractions of public law were treated differently. The criminal was arrested by spies, whom the king always kept in his service, and brought immediately to his presence, where such punishment was inflicted as his sense of justice or impulse of vengeance at the time happened to dictate.

On the death of Deioces, his son Phraortes succeeded to the throne. The son determined to use the power which the father had acquired for the enlargement of his dominions. Accordingly, the Persians were not only made tributary, but degraded. Many nations of Asia were subdued.

Victorious in every invasion, Phraortes resolved upon the conquest of Nineveh. After great preparations, hostilities were commenced; but while in progress, the king, with the greater part of his army, was destroyed. His son Cyaxares inherited the throne and possessed all the valor and ambition of his father. A more thorough system of discipline was adopted, and the army accordingly divided into companies of spearmen, cavalry, and archers. The Lydians, a powerful nation of Asia Minor, were attacked. An eclipse of the sun, in the heat of battle, suggesting to the superstitious minds of the combatants the impropriety of the contest, it was abandoned as one offensive to Heaven.

Cyaxares resolved to accomplish the work in which his father and so many of his subjects had fallen. Its vastness, however, required much caution. Alliances were accordingly formed with all the tribes beyond the Halys. Thus provided, the king undertook the expedition. The Assyrian forces met him some distance from the capital and a bloody battle was fought, in which the Mede was victorious. Nineveh was now besieged with great vigor. But the bright prospects of Cyaxares were suddenly blasted by the unexpected appearance of a large army of Scythians under the command of the intrepid Madyas. Compelled by the poverty of their own soil to seek a subsistence in foreign climes and allured by the luxuriance of Asia, these pillagers seized all the lands held by the Medes. During thirty years they plundered at will. Exaction so full of outrage finally roused the vengeance of the oppressed. An opportunity for revenge was afforded at a feast. Here the Scythians became intoxicated and the Medes put them to an indiscriminate slaughter. Having by this means regained his power, Cyaxares directed his efforts towards the subjugation of Nineveh, and not only captured it, but conquered all the Assyrians, except those within the

Babylonian precincts. Crowned with glory, the reign of Cyaxares terminated.* Astyages, his son, was invested with the sceptre. Unlike his predecessor, he was wholly occupied by domestic ills. A vision which portrayed the happy destiny of Mandane, his daughter, filled the mind of the king with the most fearful apprehensions. As if to defeat the decree of Heaven, he married his child to the Persian king. Another dream disturbed his mind. The Magi were consulted, and their interpretation betokened evil. The condition of Mandane suggested to her heartless parent an expedient by which he might avert his anticipations. The daughter was ordered to repair to her father's palace, and she complied with the mandate uninjured. Mandane was soon afterwards delivered of a child, whom she named Cyrus. Determined to destroy the infant, the king committed the execution of the deed to Harpagus, his minister. Harpagus communicated the design of Astyages to his wife. Whether from horror at the atrocity of the act or the dread of discovery by the populace, she dissuaded her husband from executing the king's order, suggesting to him to commit the child to the custody of one of the monarch's servants. A herdsman was selected whose habitation was on the mountains near the Euxine. To him was the child given, under an injunction from the minister that he was to be destroyed by wild beasts or exposure to the weather. Female tenderness saved the future sovereign of the East. The herdsman's wife had been delivered in his absence of a dead child. When the fearful mission of her husband was communicated to her, she induced him to take the dead child, arrayed in the costly robes of the living one, and cause it

---

*Herodotus, Clio. Justin, Bk. I. chs. iv. to viii. Xen., Cyropædia.

to be exposed upon the mountain-heights. In a few days the shepherd reported to the minister the execution of his sovereign's command. Snatched from an untimely death, Cyrus found a mother in the herdsman's wife. Humble as was his lot, it was nevertheless calculated to develop those powers with which God had endowed him in a pre-eminent degree. At the early age of ten his play-fellows chose him their king. One of his subjects resisted his authority. Cyrus forced him into obedience. The rebel was the son of a Mede of distinction, who was offended at this indignity to his child and immediately complained to Astyages. The monarch directed the herdsman to produce the young offender. When Cyrus appeared before the king, he avowed his right to act as he had done, affirming that he was prepared to endure all consequences.

Struck with this declaration, as well as the manner in which it was uttered, and revolving in his mind the age and the general appearance of the boy, the sovereign was convinced he had been deceived by Harpagus or the herdsman. The palace was accordingly cleared and the latter compelled to confess the truth. Astyages pretended to be satisfied, but determined to revenge himself upon the minister, and accomplished his purpose shortly after by the murder of his only son. Having thus sated his vengeance, the king sought to secure himself against the infant object of his jealousy. The Magi being consulted, they came to the conclusion that no danger was to be feared from Cyrus. The king no longer dreading his daughter's son, he was committed to the training of his parents in Persia. Here this remarkable youth rapidly increased in those mental and bodily qualifications calculated to fit him for the discharge of the trusts which God was about to devolve upon him. His grandfather was declining in years and disgusting his subjects. Stung by the king's cruelty in the murder of his son, Harpagus did his utmost to increase the general discontent and privately counselled Cyrus to provoke a revolt in Persia, assuring him that he would surrender the army to him. Such a prospect impelled the young Persian to exert all his arts upon his countrymen. A rebellion was eventually produced. Cyrus conducted the Persians against his bloodthirsty kinsman, and Harpagus, true to his promise, surrendered the forces of his sovereign. With Astyages terminated the sole race of Median kings; and with Cyrus and his uncle, generally called Darius the Mede, commenced a new dynasty.

A rising fame always begets enmity. The greatness of Cyrus excited the envy of Crœsus, king of Lydia, the wealthiest prince of Asia. Resolving to curb the ambition of his rival, the Lydian formed alliances with the Grecian states and prepared for war. Having collected a large army, he crossed the Halys, and a battle was fought on the plains of Pteria. Neither party had any cause for exultation. Crœsus shortly afterwards removed his forces to Lydia. He was now guilty of an indiscretion which admits of no apology. Under the impression that Cyrus would not pursue the war until the following spring, the mercenaries were dismissed. Arrangements were made with Assyria, Egypt, and Greece for the supply of soldiers at that time. Taking advantage of this oversight, Cyrus marched immediately into the territories of the Lydian, routed his army, subdued his capital, captured his person, and made his dominions a portion of the Persian Empire.

Nothing prevented Cyrus from grasping the sceptre of Asia but Babylon. The conquest of this city was no easy task. Determined upon its reduction, the Persian monarch was not to be driven from his purpose. The northern territories of his enemies were first subjugated; then the proud capital was encompassed by the Persian armies.

Every scheme which military experience could devise was applied in vain. As a last resort, the Persian directed the Euphrates to be drained; the gates in its bed being left open by the presumptuous Assyrians, Cyrus and his army entered at the hour of midnight, and the ancient capital fell into the hands of the Persian, who restored the Jews held captives in it to their native land: these events having been predicted by Isaiah over a century prior to the birth of the conqueror, and by Jeremiah more than seventy years before their occurrence.

No writers could be more explicit than are Isaiah and Jeremiah in regard to the advancement of Cyrus and the overthrow of Babylon:

"Remember these, O Jacob and Israel; for thou art my servant: I have formed thee; thou art my servant: O Israel, thou shalt not be forgotten of me.

"I have blotted out, as a thick cloud, thy transgressions, and, as a cloud, thy sins: return unto me; for I have redeemed thee. Sing, O ye heavens; for the Lord hath done it: shout, ye lower parts of the earth: break forth into singing, ye mountains, O forest, and every tree therein: for the Lord hath redeemed Jacob, and glorified himself in Israel.

"Thus saith the Lord, thy Redeemer, and he that formed thee from the womb, I am the Lord that maketh all things; that stretcheth forth the heavens alone; that spreadeth abroad the earth by myself; that frustrateth the tokens of the liars, and maketh diviners mad; that turneth wise men backward, and maketh their knowledge foolish; that confirmeth the word of his servant, and performeth the counsel of his messengers; that saith to Jerusalem, Thou shalt be inhabited; and to the cities of Judah, Ye shall be built, and I will raise up the decayed places thereof: that saith to the deep, Be dry, and I will dry up thy rivers: that saith to Cyrus, He is my shepherd, and shall perform all my pleasure: even saying to Jerusalem, Thou shalt be built; and to the temple, Thy foundation shall be laid." (Isaiah xliv. 21-28.)

"Thus saith the Lord to his anointed, to Cyrus, whose right hand I have holden, to subdue nations before him; and I will loose the loins of kings, to open before him the two-leaved gates; and the gates shall not be shut; I will go before thee, and make the crooked places straight: I will break in pieces the gates of brass, and cut in sunder the bars of iron: and I will give thee the treasures of darkness, and hidden riches of secret places, that thou mayest know that I, the Lord, which call thee by thy name, am the God of Israel. For Jacob my servant's sake, and Israel mine elect, I have even called thee by thy name: I have surnamed thee, though thou hast not known me." (Isaiah xlv. 1-4.)

"The word that the Lord spake against Babylon and against the land of the Chaldeans by Jeremiah the prophet: Declare ye among the nations, and publish, and set up a standard; publish, and conceal not: say, Babylon is taken, Bel is confounded, Merodach is broken in pieces; her idols are confounded, her images are broken in pieces. For out of the north there cometh up a nation against her, which shall make her land desolate, and none shall dwell therein: they shall remove, they shall depart, both man and beast." (Jer. l. 1-3.) This is a beautiful prelude to the sublime utterances that follow to v. 40.

"Now in the first year of Cyrus king of Persia, that the word of the Lord spoken by the mouth of Jeremiah might be accomplished, the Lord stirred up the spirit of Cyrus king of Persia, that he made a proclamation throughout all his kingdom, and put it also in writing, saying, Thus saith Cyrus king of Persia, All the kingdoms of the earth hath the Lord God of heaven given me; and he hath charged me to build him a house in Jerusalem, which is in

Judah. Who is there among you of all his people? The Lord his God be with him, and let him go up." (2 Chron. xxxvi. 22-23; Ezra i. 1-3.)

"Behold, I will stir up the Medes against them" (the Babylonians), "which shall not regard silver; and as for gold, they shall not delight in it. Their bows also shall dash the young men to pieces; and they shall have no pity on the fruit of the womb; their eye shall not spare children. And Babylon, the glory of kingdoms, the beauty of the Chaldees' excellency, shall be as when God overthrew Sodom and Gomorrah. It shall never be inhabited, neither shall it be dwelt in from generation to generation: neither shall the Arabian pitch tent there; neither shall the shepherds make their fold there. But wild beasts of the desert shall lie there; and their houses shall be full of doleful creatures; and owls shall dwell there, and satyrs shall dance there. And the wild beasts of the islands shall cry in their desolate houses, and dragons in their pleasant palaces." (Isaiah xiii. 17-22.)

Cyrus, though surrounded by the wealth and refinement of the world; though possessed of territory exceeding that of any predecessor; though commanding an army sufficient to secure his dominions in peace, sighed for conquests. Indeed, so ardent was his ambition that it was not restrained by the reflection that the nation whose ruin he plotted was the heritage of a woman. With all the fire of youth, he prepared to invade the Massagetæ or Turks, a people beyond the Araxes, near the wilds of Scythia. Tomyris, their queen, fearlessly told the Persian that if he persisted in his designs she would give him his fill of blood. Nothing daunted by her threat, nor compassionating her condition, Cyrus invaded the distant land, and joining battle with its enraged inhabitants, his army was defeated and his life destroyed.

The sceptre of Cyrus passed to the hands of his son Cambyses. Early domestic occurrences gave direction to the reign of this prince. His father had introduced into his household a distinguished beauty named Nitetis, the daughter of a deceased king of Egypt. It is easy to imagine the effect of this act upon the mind of Cassandane, the wife of Cyrus, who afforded the best evidence of affection in a thriving family of children. A lady of distinction on a visit to the household of the monarch, charmed with the appearance of the children, gave expression to eulogy. The dejected princess exclaimed, "Me, who am the mother of these children, Cyrus neglects and despises: all his kindness is bestowed on this Egyptian female." Stung by the severity and truth of the remark, young Cambyses vowed, when he should arrive at man's estate, to avenge his mother's wrongs by the destruction of Egypt.* This project, however, was long delayed by a dread of the consequences of conducting the army over the deserts between Egypt and the empire. Of this the monarch was at last relieved by the advice of Phanes, a Halicarnassean whose talents had given him elevation in the court of Egypt, but who had fled from it in disgust to the Persian palace. Pursuant to this, the consent of the Arabians was obtained for the passage of the Persians, the expedition completed, and Egypt subdued.

Although Cambyses increased the power of the empire by this exploit, its success elated him to such a degree that he gave loose to the worst passions. Not content with humbling a nation by conquest, he degraded its people by casting indignity upon their usages. In the midst of his exultation, the king fell a prey to a consuming disease. A

---

* Herodotus, Euterpe, Thalia. Justin, Bk. I. ch. ix., x. Orosius, Bk. II. ch. iv. New. Dis., xii. p. 167.

vision increased his torments by deluding him into the belief that Smerdis, his brother, had seized the sceptre and was acknowledged in the capital. An executioner was commissioned, with an injunction not to return until Smerdis was despatched. A real usurpation followed this horrid fratricide. The bold impostor, taking advantage of the secrecy which attended the murder of the son of Cyrus, asserted that he was Smerdis and, having been rescued from the atrocious designs of Cambyses, had taken the throne to save the sinking empire. Deceived by these pretexts, the nation acknowledged his authority. The danger which now threatened the distant monarch roused him from his lethargy to protect his power. But in this the most justifiable act of his life, the desert of his crime followed him. When mounting his horse to return to his dominions, he fell upon the edge of his naked sword. The wound soon assumed a dangerous form, and it became apparent to all that death must follow.

The usurper sought to establish himself firmly upon the throne of the departed monarch. Edicts were issued relieving the subjects for three years from the weight of taxes and tribute. This popular step would have answered the purpose of the impostor but for the act of one man. Independent of the confession of Cambyses that he had murdered his brother, Otanes, the father of a lady attached to the royal household, had reason to believe the reigning monarch was not Smerdis, the son of Cyrus. In order to satisfy himself and the public, he required his daughter to inform him if the reigning sovereign had ears. Strange as was the test proposed, it was of all others the best calculated to settle the dispute, inasmuch as it enabled Otanes to decide whether the monarch was not the villain who, for his mean vices, had been deprived of those organs by the order of Cyrus. After some time had elapsed, the female reported to her father that the king had no ears. This information was communicated to six trusty friends, who, having determined to rid the nation of the impostor, repaired to the palace, and luckily obtaining admission, he was despatched by the sword of Darius, the son of Hystaspes.

The form of government was now the object of concern among the conspirators. In their meetings the respective forms of democracy, oligarchy, and monarchy were discussed. Monarchy was finally adopted. A matter of greater difficulty arose in the selection of a person to fill the throne. After much altercation it was unanimously agreed that the conspirators should ride up next morning by sunrise to a certain street in the capital : the sceptre was to be his whose horse first neighed. The conspirators parted. What means were taken by the rest to bring about a favorable result is not known; Darius, however, left nothing untried that the art of his hostler, Œbanes, could suggest. The morning arrived; the conspirators met: Darius, the son of Hystaspes, won the prize and was acknowledged emperor of Asia.

An opportunity soon occurred of testing the emperor's feelings towards his early companions. During hours of danger the conspirators entered into an agreement that whoever might hold the sceptre, his six associates should have the privilege of approaching his presence without the formalities usual in Asiatic courts. Intaphernes, one of the conspirators, entered the palace in great haste and, being resisted by the guards, forced his way to the royal presence. Darius, roused by the temerity of the act, caused him and many of his unoffending relatives to be executed. Shortly afterwards, however, an event transpired which relieved the fame of the monarch from the odium of this wicked act. A stranger appeared at the palace and, alleging he had once conferred a favor on Darius, sought to be introduced to his presence. The king hesitated at first, but at last permitted him to enter. He proved to be Syloson, the exiled prince of Samos, who when Darius was in Egypt, an undistinguished subordinate in the army of Cambyses, made him a present of a costly cloak, though he had been unable to obtain it at an exorbitant price. The recollection of this act of kindness induced the monarch to offer wealth to the stranger, which he declined, but implored that his native isle might be rescued from servitude. Darius promised to perform the request, and a force was equipped under the command of Otanes which accomplished the object.

During the time spent in the reduction of Samos, Babylon rebelled. A year was employed in fruitless efforts for its reduction. At last Zopyrus, one of the seven who had dethroned the false Smerdis, agreed with Darius to effect the surrender of the city by treachery. His scheme was finally successful.

Thus relieved from internal feuds, the emperor determined to enlarge his dominions by an incursion into the territories of the Scythians.* At the head of an immense army he crossed the Thracian Bosphorus by a bridge of boats. Thrace was subdued, the Ister was passed, but the Persian was compelled to return to Asia without finding the wily Scythian. The invasion of Libya was still more unfortunate. Such extensive operations excited hatred against the empire. Aristagoras reared the standard of rebellion in the regions of Ionia. With Grecian assistance Sardis was besieged; but the Persians abandoned the siege and defeated the assailants near Ephesus. Notwithstanding the division thus created between the

---

* Herodotus, Melpomene to Calliope. Justin, Bk. II.

allies, the loss of Grecian aid was repaired by the auxiliaries which the Ionians received from Cyprus and Caria. Against this powerful combination Darius rose in all his strength, and victory crowned his exertions on the Asiatic and European side of the Hellespont, as well as throughout Macedonia and Thrace. The submission of Greece was demanded in haughty terms. The generals of the emperor were instructed to enforce the demand. They made fearful havoc among the Grecian isles, and passed into Attica to erect their standard. Repulsed at Marathon, they were compelled to retire into Asia, leaving the Greek commander, Miltiades, in possession of his native soil. Still determined on conquest, Darius renewed his preparations; which were but little delayed by his death. To Xerxes, his son by a second wife, Darius committed his sceptre and the execution of his towering schemes. In command of the largest army ever marshalled, this prince set out for the invasion of Greece. Crossing the Hellespont on a bridge of boats, Xerxes landed in Greece, pressed on to Thermopylæ, whose narrow pass he forced after a glorious resistance by the small band of Leonidas; gained no advantage at Artemisium; was unsuccessful at Delphi; and was defeated at Salamis by Themistocles, in command of the Greeks. Dejected by these calamities, the Persian king returned to his capital, leaving behind three hundred thousand men, under Mardonius, to subjugate Greece. This force, however, was shortly afterwards ruined and their general slain by Pausanias, in command of the Greeks, at Platæa. The Persians who survived this defeat met a dreadful slaughter in Phocis.

Thus was the palm of empire lost by the Persians. By what power it was next won will be seen in tracing the affairs of the Grecian states.

CHAPTER III.

THE EMPIRE OF THE GREEKS.

Greece, now become one of the most important powers of the world, was composed of many separate and independent states. All that portion of it which lay south of the Corinthian gulf was called Peloponnesus, in modern times known as the Morea, and consisted of the republics of Achaia, Elis, Messenia, Laconia, Corinth, Arcadia, and Argolis; that, north and east of this peninsula, more properly styled Greece numbered the republics of Acarnania, Attica, Bœotia, Phocis, Locris, Doris, Megara, Ætolia, and Thessaly.*

The arts and refinements of civilized life were early introduced among them by Cecraups and Danaus from Egypt;† Cadmus from Phœnicia;‡ and Pelops from Phrygia.§

The council composed of representatives from all the states, created by Amphictyon, one of the earliest kings of Athens, in the course of time became the senate of the country, extending its authority to religious and secular affairs.‖ Kingly power having given place in most of the states to popular authority, their progress was rapid to

---

*Butler's Ancient Geography.
† Dio. Sic., Bk. I. ch. xi. p. 13.
‡ Her., Ter. lviii. 4.
§ Plut. Theseus. Thuc., Bk. I. p. 4. Diod. Sic., Bk. IV. ch. 4; Bk. V. ch. 3. Comstock's Greek Revolution, ch. i.
‖ Tac. An., notes 4 to 14, p. 108.

national importance.* However much political weight was possessed by each of the states of Greece for centuries, two at last became pre-eminent. Athens and Sparta, the capitals of these republics, were consequently rivals; which arrested the attention and divided the affections of the entire confederacy. This condition of things may have kindled an emulation which perfected both in the arts and sciences; but it gradually engendered a feeling which broke asunder the warmest attachments, social and national.† The contests with Messenia kept alive the bitterest strife: its final subjugation to Spartan authority did not diminish them.

After the Persian invasion the Athenians resolved to surround their city with walls. The work was commenced with alacrity. No sooner had they commenced it than a delegation arrived from Sparta which protested in the name of their state against its prosecution. Themistocles, comprehending the motive of this interference, suggested to his countrymen a scheme by which it might be circumvented. Governed by his views, they appointed him at the head of a delegation to treat with the Spartans. Having arranged their plan of operations, Themistocles set out for Sparta first. On his arrival there all action was suspended until his companions should join him. One after another came in, but the last did not arrive until the walls were completed. The general now chided the envious people for their intermeddling, telling them in plain terms that Athens had determined to protect herself from any attacks which might be made against her, whether they approved or censured. The erection of the fortifications at the

---

*Her., Ter. xv., lxvi.
†Justin, Bk. III. ch. ii. Thuc., p. 7.

Piræus was a measure of equal importance. These works were constructed on such an extensive scale as to afford accommodation for over four hundred vessels.*

Sparta and Athens dropped their contentions for a time to assist their Ionian allies, now oppressed by Persia. Pausanias was put in command by the Lacedæmonians, and the Athenians committed their forces to Aristides and Cimon, the son of Miltiades. Pausanias agreed to betray his country to the Persian king in consideration of receiving his daughter in matrimony. The consummation of the perfidy was prevented by the detection and death of the traitor. Themistocles, suspected of having been privy to the design of Pausanias, abandoned Greece and found a refuge among the Molossians.† The evil effect of these pernicious examples in such illustrious subjects was counteracted by the sterling integrity of Aristides.‡ Unexpected as was the change in the life of Cimon from the excess of dissipation to a precise morality, it tended, together with the virtues of Aristides, to place the honor of Greece upon that eminence from which it had been cast by the defection of their predecessors.§ During the military command of Cimon the power of Persia was destroyed in Thrace; Scyros was reduced; the imperial forces expelled from Ionia to Pamphylia; the Asiatic fleet overthrown near the mouth of the Eurymedon; distrust spread throughout the empire; and Egypt induced to rear the standard of rebellion. The achievements of Cimon procured him so distinguished a reputation as to excite the jealousies of rivals. The veteran was banished from his country; but its exigencies produced his recall in the space of five years. Again in-

---

* Plut. Themistocles. Jus., Bk. II. ch. xv. Thuc., Bk. I.
† Justin, Bk. II. ch. xv.
‡ Plut. Aristides. Jus., Bk. II. ch. xv.
§ Plut. Cimon.

vested with the chief command, he set out to humble the powers of the East. Never was he more successful than in this expedition. The Persian was completely reduced, and was glad to obtain peace on terms the most flattering to his Grecian adversary. Cimon, however, did not survive to behold the injury he had inflicted on his enemies or the advantage he had obtained for his country.

Greece, above all nations of these times, was fortunate in the continued succession of great men. Scarcely was Cimon departed before the talents of Pericles added lustre to her arms and strength to her councils.* Powerful as was his intellect, he was nevertheless wedded to the conceit that Athens ought to govern Greece. Sparta was accordingly treated as if she was a subordinate member of the confederacy. Through the influence of Pericles, Athens was selected as the place for the assembling of the national convention to provide for rebuilding the temples destroyed in the Persian war. The indignation of Sparta was aroused by this act; the convocation prevented; and the rancor of political strife spread with redoubled fury. Athens received advantage from this disgraceful struggle, but Greece at large was injured by it.† A truce at last restored peace for thirty years. In half that time the influence of Pericles broke it by taking part in the conflict between Corinth and its Corcyran colonists. Greece now became involved in what is called the Peloponnesian war, which lasted for twenty-seven years.‡ The first act of hostility was committed by the Thebans in besieging Platæa. Athens sent forth her armies to its relief, and succeeded in expelling the Spartans. These acts ranged the powers of Greece

---

* Plut. Pericles. Justin, Bk. III. ch. vi.

† Jus., Bk. III. ch. vii.

‡ Thucydides and Justin, Bks. IV., V. Xenophon's Affairs of Greece, Bks. I., II.

under the banners of the rival cities: although some remained neutral for a time, all were compelled to fall in with one side or the other before the war had made much progress.

Presuming she could terminate the contest by a single blow, Sparta invaded Attica with an army of sixty thousand men, commanded by Archidamus. The foresight of Pericles thwarted the plan by inducing the citizens to destroy their effects, ravage the country, and betake themselves to Athens. Secure within the walls of that city, the enemy, though he continued to menace, was eventually compelled to retire. In return for this invasion, Spartan territory became the scene of Athenian inroad.

A pestilence which had made dreadful havoc in the east and south appeared in Athens during the second year of this war. Notwithstanding the exertions of the senate to stay its course, guided, as some suppose, by the abilities of Hippocrates of Cos, its desolating fury was so great that the dead and dying were hourly found in every habitation, throughout the streets, and in the temples. Afflicted as they were at home, the Athenians still conducted their warlike operations abroad. Potidæa, which had been now nearly three years besieged, yielded to their arms. A few months placed an equal advantage in the hands of the Lacedæmonians by the conquest of Platæa. A second year turned the scale in favor of Athens by the destruction of Mitylene: but the ravages of the plague deprived it of the capacity for rejoicing. The possession of Pylus by the Athenians gave them a temporary advantage. Its proximity to Spartan soil excited the Lacedæmonians to extraordinary exertions; but they were unsuccessful at this fortress, and an equally melancholy catastrophe befell them at Sphacteria, which was followed by the reduction of Cythera and the ravages of the Peloponnesian coasts. Such a train of disasters roused the greatest energies of the Spartans, and they devolved the chief command upon Brasidas, one of the ablest generals Greece ever produced. Thrace, whence Athens derived her most important supplies, was now invaded by the Spartans, and Amphipolis, its chief town, subjected to every indignity that a relentless foe could inflict.

Many years were spent in this destructive war. All Greece at length became inclined to peace. A cessation of hostilities was agreed upon for one year. During this period of time peace would have been concluded but for the influence of two men. Cleon, a citizen of Athens, without education, was possessed of that order of talent which proved to be potent with his vain and inconstant countrymen. Brasidas, the Spartan general, exactly opposite in his genius, charmed the Lacedæmonians by a career of judicious actions. After the death of these men the republics settled on a truce for fifty years. Even this would not have been accomplished but for the influence of Nicias, whose patriotism was illy rewarded by his countrymen. Just as were the views entertained by this statesman, they were assailed by the censure of the popular leaders.

Alcibiades was now becoming important. Possessed of a flowing eloquence and a large fortune, he exerted a commanding influence in the councils of Athens. This he wielded on all occasions against Nicias. In the space of a few years he rekindled the flames of civil discord. A vast force was raised for the invasion of Sicily, which was committed to the joint command of Alcibiades and Nicias. The entire weight of this arduous work was soon left upon the shoulders of Nicias, in consequence of the disgrace of his associate commander. Although the expedition was in opposition to the judgment of Nicias, he sacrificed his own views to the decrees of his country, and conducted the operations with so much ability that Syracuse, the capital of Sicily, was about to surrender as the Lacedæmonian fleet arrived. Victory turning to the oppressed, the allies charged the Athenians with such desperation as to annihilate their fleet and army. An event so important produced radical changes in both parties. Athens underwent a revolution, which brought to power a council of four hundred, whose misrule was soon succeeded by the recall of Alcibiades and his investment with the supreme control of the army. Sparta, more calculating in its movements, invested Lysander with the chief command. The Lacedæmonian general, strengthened by an alliance with the Persian court, set out at the head of the fleet, worsted the rival navy at Ephesus, and utterly defeated it at Ægos Potamos. Losing no time, the conquerors besieged Athens, brought that ancient capital to terms, and put an end to the Peloponnesian war. The government was changed to suit the victors, the authority of thirty commanders set up, and the spoils of silver and gold sent in triumph to Sparta.*

The supremacy of Sparta, however, was not of long continuance.† Scarcely was it established before the republic was involved in occurrences which led eventually to its ruin. A severe struggle at this time agitated the Persian dominions. Cyrus the younger, a son of the last king, undertook to dethrone his brother Artaxerxes. Raising a considerable army, he attached to it thirteen thousand Grecian troops under the command of Clearchus. The contest was terminated on the plains of Cunaxa, where the prince was slain, his mercenaries routed, and his allies,

---

* Xenophon's Af. of Gr.
† Jus., Bk. V. ch. ix. Xen., Ex. of Cy.

though triumphant, were left alone to fight their way home, sword in hand. After much hardship, this band arrived in Europe and entered into the service of the Thracian prince. Elated with success, the Persian monarch imposed new burdens upon the Ionian cities, which appealed to the Lacedæmonians for succor. Agesilaus,* the Spartan king, proceeded in person to Asia, accompanied by Lysander, who shared with him the command. Brave as was the prince, the fame of his general insured the regard of the citizens. Such a slight was more than the Spartan noble could bear. His indignation showed itself in acts which created implacable discord between the general and the king. Asia was soon afterwards deprived of the presence of Agesilaus by a call of the Spartan senate, which required his immediate return in consequence of the league between Thebes, Corinth, and Argos, got up by Persian gold.† Conon, the disgraced Athenian admiral, who since his defeat by Lysander had remained in retirement, took advantage of this war in the republic, and procuring the command of the Persian fleet, defeated the Spartans in a sea-fight near Cnidus. So sudden and severe a blow spread consternation throughout the Peleponnesus and severed their allies from their interest. The peace of Antalcidas put an end to these contentions. The Persian king by this treaty retained the cities in Asia and the isles of Cyprus and Clazomenæ; the rest of the Grecian cities were left free; and Lemnos, Imbros, and Sciros subjected to the Athenians.‡

Sparta, though humbled, was not less aspiring than she had always been. Determined still to effect her ambitious schemes, under pretext of the late treaty she insisted

---

* Plut. Agesilaus. † Jus., Bk. VI.
‡ Xen. Af. of Gr., Bks. IV., V.

upon the freedom of the Grecian cities. Thebes was her object: her citizens were degraded; her laws and institutions were overthrown. This triumph of brute force was not of long duration. It roused the spirit of patriotism, and brought into the field Epaminondas and Pelopidas. The counsels of these leaders drew together an army which, though small, was composed of men whose courage was irresistible. They met the Spartans at Leuctra, and, notwithstanding they were outnumbered three to one, the Thebans were victorious. This success induced the Theban generals to undertake an invasion of Laconia, in which they penetrated to the walls of Sparta, and finally triumphed at Mantinea.*

Greece was alarmed by the rise of this third capital, which seemed destined to pluck the palm of sovereignty from both Athens and Sparta. Misgivings and jealousies disturbed the public mind and distracted the national councils.

Philip of Macedon had long contemplated the conquest of Greece, but feared to attempt it even divided as it was.† The period at which he chose to accomplish his purpose was about seventy-five years after the commencement of the Peloponnesian war, when the entire confederacy was torn asunder by a religious war created in consequence of the Phocians applying to private uses certain property alleged to have been devoted to Apollo. The conduct of these people was submitted to the states-general, whose determination made it their duty to return the property they despoiled to the purposes for which it was originally devoted. The execution of this decree was resisted by the

---

* Plut. Pelopidas. Xen., Af. of Gr.
† Dio. Sic., Bk. XVI. Justin, Bks. VII.–IX. Plutarch's Demosthenes.

Phocians. A war ensued, in which Philip enforced the decree and tried all the plans which ingenuity could suggest to obtain possession of the pass of Thermopylæ. These bold movements excited the indignation of Demosthenes, who raised a warning voice against the Macedonian. Eloquent as were his efforts, they passed by the Athenians almost unheeded; though at last they were induced to send a small auxiliary force to Olynthus, from which place succor had been sought against the common enemy. The town, however, was forced to surrender. Philip lulled the Athenians into a fatal repose by inducing them to believe that his only design was to heal the divisions of Greece. By this crafty policy the Macedonian obtained Thermopylæ, subdued the Phocians, terminated the sacred war, and procured himself to be elected a member of the amphictyonic council. Domestic concerns required the return of the monarch to Macedonia, and during his stay there he enlarged his kingdom by movements in Illyria and Thrace. The good fortune of Philip forsook him for a while. He failed in his attempts upon Byzantium. But his favorite object, the sovereignty of Greece, infused ardor in the midst of misfortune. Elatea was seized by the Macedonian. The voice of Demosthenes was loud in denunciation. Inflamed by the appeals of the orator, a league was effected between Thebes and Athens to check the conqueror; but he crushed this last effort for independence at Chæronea.

The subjugation of Greece, however, was but a means with Philip by which to effect the conquest of Persia. To this account alone he turned it; procuring himself to be immediately proclaimed by the amphictyons the commander of the Greeks against their enemies, the Persians. No time was lost in making preparation for this undertaking. Promising as were the prospects of the king, his domestic broils had arrived at a crisis, and, prompting the revenge of Pausanias, the brilliant anticipations of Philip of Macedon were terminated by the dagger of that assassin. Alexander, the issue of Philip's marriage with Olympias, now twenty years of age, succeeded to the throne of Macedon.* Procuring from the Greeks of the Peloponnesus, Sparta excepted, the generalship of the projected expedition against Persia, and from Athens more honors than she had ever given to his father, Alexander proceeded first to reduce the nations contiguous to Macedon, which had thrown off his authority. In effecting this object he evinced that genius which always made his arms invincible. Thebes resolved to maintain its independence; but Alexander, with his veteran troops, appearing at her gates, compelled her to surrender, and inflicted upon her innocent citizens such a doom as struck Greece with terror. The invasion of the Persian Empire was now commenced. No sooner had Alexander reached the Granicus than a battle ensued in which he was victorious. This success was followed in a few months by the submission or subjugation of the greater part of Asia Minor. Danger brought thus near to the Persian monarch impelled him to extraordinary exertion in preparing for a final struggle. Alexander was more anxious for battle than his enemy. The sickness of the Macedonian deferred it for a time. It was at last fought near the city of Issus. The victory was so decisive that not only was the army of Darius, the Persian king, destroyed, but his wife and children fell into the hands of Alexander. Parmenio seized the imperial treasures at Damascus for the conqueror; Sidon threw open her gates

---

* Arrian's Expedition of Alexander. Dio. Sic., Bk. XVII. Jus., Bks. XI., XII. Orosius, Bk. III. ch. ix. Justin, Bk. IX. ch. viii. New. Dis., ii. Ezekiel xxvi.–xxviii.

before him; and although Tyre ventured to resist him for a while, her walls were eventually carried by storm. Palestine and Egypt were visited by Alexander at this period: to the former he granted great favors; in the latter he established his authority and founded a city distinguished by his name. Great as was this success, the object of the invasion was yet unaccomplished. Darius still existed; his sceptre was not seized; and the Persians had rallied with ardor in support of both. Marching rapidly from Egypt and crossing the Tigris and Euphrates, Alexander met his adversary on the plains of Gaugamela, near Arbela. A battle was fought. The sceptre of empire was won by the Macedonian: the kingdom of Cyrus, which had existed over two hundred years, now in the time of his twelfth successor was annihilated. Darius was shortly afterwards slain. Bessus, attempting to maintain the power of Persia, was delivered to the conqueror, who reigned without a rival. The union of the various portions of an empire is the basis of common strength. If Alexander had regarded this principle, his mission would have been a mercy to mankind and a blessing to himself; but holding his conquests in their dissevered condition, he deprived them of the benefits of good government and stimulated in his own bosom a hurtful ambition. Hence new visions of glory excited his passions as he read or heard of distant realms; and he successively subdued Media, reduced Bactria, humbled Scythia, laid much of India under contribution, and would have conquered the whole country but for the rebellion of his army. Death terminated the career of this restless conqueror at Babylon, in the thirteenth year of his reign.

Arideus, an illegitimate son of Philip, was proclaimed chief of the empire, and Perdiccas, to whom Alexander, at the point of death, gave his ring, was entrusted with executive power; while the provinces were portioned among various favorites. The Greeks both of Asia and Europe made an effort to regain their independence, but were subdued by Antipater and Craterus. Perdiccas, judging this a fit opportunity to carry out his ambitious schemes in Macedonia, attempted to destroy the power of Antipater. A league among many of the governors followed. Antipater and Craterus prepared to enter Asia at the head of a large army.* Eumenes was directed to repel them; while Perdiccas invaded Egypt, the domain of Ptolemy.† Perdiccas had not the popularity necessary for the consummation of such vast schemes, and, falling a victim to the fury of the soldiers, his power passed into the hands of Antipater. Death in the space of a year carried off that veteran soldier, and Polysperchon took his place. The ambition of two men now distracted the empire—Cassander in Greece, and Antigonus in Asia. Divisions in the royal household favored their designs. The king and his wife had become divided from the widow of Philip, Olympias, and Alexander's widow Roxana and her son Alexander. Cassander united with the first, and Polysperchon with the latter. A fortunate turn enabled Olympias to get possession of the persons of the king and his wife, who were despatched by her orders. In Asia the cause of Antigonus triumphed. Eumenes was not only defeated but taken prisoner. In her turn Olympias fell a victim to the fate to which she had consigned Arideus and Eurydice. Cassander, emboldened by his success, made Roxana and her son prisoners, married Thessalonices, the sister of Alexander, and thus confirmed his power in Macedonia. Seleucus, governor of Babylon, in dread of the power and ambition of

---

* Dio. Sic., Bks. XVIII.-XX. Jus., Bks. XIII.-XVII.
† Plut. Eumenes. New. Dis., xv.

Antigonus, fled to the court of Ptolemy, where he succeeded in forming a league between that prince, Cassander, and Lysimachus against Antigonus, who proclaimed himself the avenger of Roxana and her son and the friend of the Greek cities. A furious war raged for four years, when it was terminated by a treaty which made Cassander sovereign lord of Europe till Alexander's son arrived at age; placed Lysimachus in command of Thrace; left Ptolemy in the enjoyment of sovereign power in Egypt and the bordering cities in Africa and Arabia; declared Antigonus lord of Asia, and established among the Greeks the supremacy of their ancient laws.

Cassander soon rid himself of all fear from the succession of Alexander's son by causing him and his mother to be put to death. About one year after the peace, upon complaint that Antigonus had violated the treaty by putting garrisons into the Greek cities, Ptolemy invaded his dominions in Cilicia, but being repulsed, turned his warlike preparations against Lycia and Greece. Demetrius, the son of the Asiatic lord, passed into Greece at the head of a large force, freed all the cities, and overcame the Egyptian in a sea-fight.* From this period all the chiefs assumed the title of king. Demetrius pushed his conquests in Europe until Cassander sought his father to stay his operations. A haughty demand was contained in his reply, that Cassander should surrender to him all his dominions. This brought on another war which terminated at the battle of Ipsus, where Antigonus lost his life and his crown. By the terms settled among the victors, Cassander took Macedon and Greece; Lysimachus, Thrace and the countries upon the Hellespont and Bosphorus; Ptolemy, Egypt, Libya, Arabia, Syria, and Palestine; Seleucus,

---

*Plut. Demetrius. Dio. Sic., Fragments of Bk. XXI. p. 748.

Chaldea, Persia, and the East. All these powers were gradually subdued by the Empire of the Romans, which now claims attention.

CHAPTER IV.

THE EMPIRE OF THE ROMANS TO THE TIME OF AUGUSTUS CÆSAR.

ÆNEAS after the destruction of Troy, with a band of about six hundred exiles, sought a refuge in distant climes. Arriving in Italy, they were eventually received into the favor of Latinus, king of the Latins, and their leader married to his daughter.* Fourteen kings succeeded Æneas, when Romulus arose, who laid the foundation of a city on the banks of the Tiber (A.M. 3252), which was called, from his name, Rome. Under the influence of laws encouraging immigration, vast multitudes from all the surrounding nations flocked to the standard of the new prince. This prosperity, however, came well-nigh being destroyed by an unfortunate contest with the Sabines. With a view of procuring wives, the Romans seized some of the females of that people when attending the public amusements at Rome. A war ensued. The women who had been taken, now Roman wives, rushing amidst the infuriated combatants, implored them to cease the work of blood. This appeal putting an end to the battle, induced the parties to form a lasting league, by the terms of which the Sabine Tatius became a partner in royalty with Romulus; such

---

* Livy, Bk. I. Jus., Bk. XLIII. Eutropius' Epitome of Rom. History to Jovian. Orosius, Bk. II. ch. i to iv.; Bks. IV. to VI.

of his nation as wished had liberty to settle in Rome; and their numbers were represented by adding one hundred members to the senate.

The kingdom thus constituted increased its numbers and extended its limits for two hundred and forty-four years. At this period, Tarquin, surnamed the Proud, lost the sceptre. Sextus, his son, had gratified by force his passion upon Lucretia, the chaste wife of Collatinus, one of his companions in arms. Overwhelmed with grief, the outraged matron, plunging a knife into her bosom, fell dead in the presence of her family, having first communicated to them the whole affair. Brutus, stung to the quick by the detail of her wrongs, roused the spirit of rebellion among the citizens and soldiers. The oppressions endured by the nation since the accession of the Tarquins produced disgust of monarchy. Kingly power was consequently succeeded by consular authority. Brutus and Collatinus were first chosen consuls (A.M. 3497).

The exiled king, however, was not thus easily set aside.* The ambassadors who were sent to Rome to procure a restitution of his property formed a party among the young nobles to effect his restoration. The conspiracy was discovered by the vigilance of the consuls before it was ripe for execution. The sons of Brutus were prominent among the conspirators. Unshrinking in the discharge of his duty, this fearless patriot promptly examined the case of his children. Their guilt having been established, the consul consigned them to the same doom as was inflicted upon their companions in crime. Foiled in this attempt to regain his throne, Tarquin procured the assistance of the Veientians. Before battle was fairly joined fell both Brutus and Aruns, the son of the exiled king: the issue,

---

* Livy, Bk. II.

however, was in favor of the Roman people. The only hope left Tarquin was in the aid of Porsenna, king of Clusium. Uniting their forces, these kings assailed Rome. The downfall of that city would have been inevitable had not Horatius Cocles, by interposing his person between the retreating Romans and their enemies, intercepted the course of the pursuers until his countrymen cut down the bridge over the Tiber, when he saved himself by swimming to the opposite shore. Porsenna, still persisting in his purpose, laid siege to Rome, but at last, wearied out by the valor of his enemies, he withdrew his forces and left hopeless the cause of Tarquin. The proud exile made but one more effort to regain his power; which was unsuccessful.

Intestine troubles, as well as the dread of a war with the Sabines, led to the appointment of a new officer, called a dictator. Serious discontents prevailing among the people on account of being subjected to imprisonment for debt, they refused to enter the army. A decree was consequently passed abolishing imprisonment for debt and relieving the soldiers from all process while in service. Upon the return of peace, these wise regulations having been repealed, new troubles ensued, which brought Valerius, a man of mild disposition, into authority as dictator. After the conclusion of these commotions, the dictator pressed the senate to dispose of the persons confined for debts; but on its refusal, he resigned. The senate then directed the consuls to remove the army from the city. The soldiers withdrew without the consuls to the distance of about three miles, where they surrounded themselves by a rampart and a trench. After anxious deliberation, the senate sent a deputation to reason the case with the army. Menenius Agrippa, a senator of great reputation, managed the address. Such an effect was produced upon the minds of the legionaries by the argument of the senator that the whole army agreed to return to the city, upon condition that the people should in future elect officers from their body, who should have the power to redress their grievances. Thus were created the Tribunes of the People.

The consequences of this alarming defection were felt during the following year in a distressing famine. Supplies of corn were procured from Sicily by the senate. In distributing the article, disputes arose. Coriolanus insisted that the grievances of the patricians should be removed before any distribution was made. Popular fury was raised to its highest pitch; the senator cited to answer before the tribunes, and sentence for banishment pronounced against him. Severity so unwarranted aroused the resentment of Coriolanus. A large force was procured by him from the Volscians. Having now the advantage of his countrymen, Rome would have been subjected to a ferocious sack but for the importunities of his mother.

The calamitous turn of the war with the Æquans caused the appointment of Lucius Quintius Cincinnatus as dictator. The excitement upon the subjects of the agrarian law and consular power were consequently allayed. After having successfully terminated the war, the dictator, contented with having served his country, retired to his farm.*

The third century of the existence of Rome is distinguished by change in its laws and in their administration. Commissioners were appointed to visit Athens, the capital of science, in order to form a system of jurisprudence adapted to the age. The results of their investigations are denominated the "Laws of the Twelve Tables." A body of men were instituted, known as the decemviri, to administer the new code (A.M. 3554). Firmly established in office,

---

* Livy, Bk. III. Dio., Bk. XII. ch. iv.

these men abandoned themselves to the worst passions. They exercised military as well as civil authority. Their official position was constantly used as the means of personal revenge. Siccius was exposed to a cruel death by the treacherous decemvirs. Little justice as might be expected in the career of such wretches, humanity is nevertheless shocked at the calculating hypocrisy of Appius Claudius in the case involving the honor of the daughter of Virginius. Struck with the beauty of that female while she was yet at school, he resolved upon the gratification of his passion. Neither the maturity of his own years nor the youthful simplicity of hers restrained his desires. Having plotted the ruin of his innocent victim, he determined to execute it in such a manner as not to expose himself to punishment. A pliant tool was selected, who was to seize the child, now fifteen years of age, as his property, on the allegation of being the daughter of a deceased female slave. The pretended master appeared before the judge to prosecute his claim. Appius, after hearing the demand, deferred the case until Virginius could be apprised of the proceeding; but he immediately wrote to the decemvirs at camp not to allow him leave of absence. The letter, however, not arriving until after he had left the army, the horror-stricken parent was present at the court when the case of his daughter was adjudged, and, unable to save her honor, he plunged a knife into her heart. Hence he fled through the city and to the army. The story was given to Rome; consternation seized the projectors of the horrid deed: a revolution succeeded.

The principal changes produced by these commotions were the abolition of the decemvirs and the revival of the tribunitian power, with the right of appeal to the people. Laws authorizing intermarriages between the patricians and plebeians; enactments directing that military tribunes, with consular power, should be elected from both orders; and the creation of the censorship soon followed.*

The repose of Cincinnatus, now over fourscore years of age, was again disturbed by the call of his country, to suppress the conspiracy of Mælius, a bold demagogue whose wealth enabled him to make alarming impressions upon the populace. The veteran patriot, prompt to duty, snatched the republic from impending ruin and, regardless of personal promotion, returned to his rural retreat. Recovered from internal danger, the Romans resolved to reduce the pride of their haughty rivals, the Veii.† Camillus was entrusted with the execution of this work. Ten years were spent in war before this people were reduced. After the completion of this great national conquest, the conqueror, Camillus, was doomed upon a slight pretence to a fine by the tribunes of the people. Such is the fate of merit when envy is dominant in the bosoms of judges. In a short space of time the course of events made them sensible of their weakness and of his strength. A Gallic invasion brought Camillus to the command. The powers of his genius were unimpaired by misfortune. Rome was saved from a foe so ruthless as to treat with violent indignity its senators engaged in the councils of state.‡ Two laws of the greatest importance to the public succeeded this desperate struggle. By the one, plebeians were admitted to the consulship; by the other, all citizens were prevented from holding more than five hundred acres of land.

The arms of the Romans had subjugated only the nations immediately adjacent; now they were turned against a more distant nation, the Samnites, which inhabited the south of Italy.§ The contest was tedious and severe; but

---

* Livy, Bk. IV. † Livy, Bk. V.
‡ Livy, Bk. VI. § Livy, Bks. VII. to X.

the command of the Roman forces being committed to Marcus Valerius, his talents infused an ardor which rendered them invincible. Such signal glory as was won by the army in the war with the Samnites inflamed a portion of the soldiers with a feeling of self-importance. Seizing upon Quintius, a man of valor, they compelled him to assume their command. Rome was assailed, but the appearance of Valerius dissuaded the rebels from their rash purposes. After this timely reconciliation a successful war was waged with the Latins. The Samnites were again (A.M. 3727) arrayed against the Romans; but unable to cope with their enemies they united with the Tarentines and implored the aid of Pyrrhus, king of Epirus, the force of whose genius ranked him as the greatest general of the age.* The Romans were brought into battle the first time with their new foe on the banks of the Siris. It was a desperate struggle on both sides. The Greek fought for the preservation of his fame: the Roman for his native soil and glory. Pyrrhus, perceiving that his troops were unable to withstand the heroism of their foes, introduced into the conflict his elephants, upon which were mounted armed men who, having the advantage from their position, overwhelmed the Romans in all directions. The Greek did not feel inclined to try chances with the Romans again. The milder measures of negotiation were adopted. Cineas the orator was deputed to procure a peace. Notwithstanding the charm of eloquence which adorned the efforts of the ambassador, he was not successful. War was renewed, and in the battle which was fought at Asculum victory inclined to the Greek. " One more triumph," said Pyrrhus,

---

* Justin, Bk. XVIII. ch. i. ii.; Bk. XXIII. ch. iii. Dio. Frag., Bk. XXII. ch. xi. Frags. in Livy, Bks. XI. to XX. Dio., Bk. XIX. ch. vi. Plut. Pyrrhus.

"of this kind will undo me." Two years passed before there was another trial of skill and force between the Greeks and Romans. Roman valor proving triumphant, Pyrrhus abandoned the possession of Italy.

Carthage,* a city of Africa, which from a small Phœnician colony, planted about one hundred and thirty-seven† years before the founding of Rome, was now possessed of many portions of Africa, Spain, and all the islands in the Sardinian and Tyrrhenian seas. Through a quarrel with the Mamertines at Messana, this republic endeavored to get a foothold in Sicily. In dread of the progress of the Carthaginians, the Romans took these people under their protection. An army was sent over to Sicily, commanded by Appius Claudius, which proved to be too much for the combined power of the Carthaginians and Hiero, king of Syracuse. The latter made peace with the Romans by paying them one hundred talents of silver and restoring the prisoners without ransom. Emboldened by success, Rome equipped a fleet under the command of Regulus and Manlius, by which Carthage was invested. Attacked by sea and land, the Africans were reduced to a dreary condition. They procured the services of Xantippus, a Grecian general of great abilities, who afforded a partial relief to them by the defeat of Regulus. Eventually, however, in the consulate of Caius Lutatius, the affairs of Carthage became desperate. Peace was restored by a treaty in which the Carthaginians were bound to abandon Sicily, to abstain from making war on the allies of Rome, to deliver prisoners and deserters without ransom, and to pay a tribute of twenty-two hundred talents of silver. Thus terminated

---

* Polybius, Bk. I.
† Justin says "seventy-two;" see Bk. XVIII. ch. vi. Dio. Frag., Bk. XXII. ch. v., vi.

the first war with Carthage after a continuance of twenty-four years (A.M. 3764). A peace of fourteen years afforded the Romans an opportunity to acquire a knowledge of the arts and sciences, by which the nations of Greece had been refined. Ambitious of intellectual as well as military fame, it was improved; and Rome soon presented enduring monuments of the perfection of her citizens in those departments of knowledge which for ages had distinguished her Eastern neighbors.

The great foe of the commonwealth was humbled but not subdued.* After the conclusion of the first war with Rome, Carthage had been shaken to her centre by a contest with her mercenaries. Sardinia threw off her yoke. Upon bringing their mercenaries to terms, the Carthaginians attempted to regain this island. The Romans opposed them, liberated the island, and compelled Carthage to pay twelve hundred talents. The submission of the Carthaginians was coupled with a determination to break the peace as soon as they could acquire the pecuniary ability. When this point was attained, Hannibal, the son of Hamilcar, reared in a deadly hatred of Rome, was ordered to lay siege to Saguntum, a town in alliance with her. Hannibal, under the orders of the Carthaginian senate, marched from the Spanish town assailed for Italy, and having crossed the Alps in fifteen days, thrice defeated the Roman army. The Carthaginian then advanced unchecked to the south of Italy. Fabius Maximus was created pro-dictator, and Minucius Rufus master of horse. The coolness of the former and the impetuosity of the latter so divided the Roman populace that both were finally succeeded by Lucius Æmilius and Caius Terentius Varro, who were chosen consuls.† Battle was at last joined at Cannæ. During the

---

* Polybius, Bk. II. Livy, Bk. XXI.　　† Livy, Bk. XXII.

first day Æmilius was in command, and the cunning and experience of Hannibal were equally unavailing. On the second day Caius took charge, and, departing from the prudent course of Fabius and Æmilius, the Romans were conquered and cut to pieces. Had Hannibal marched immediately to Rome he might have terminated the existence of the republic; but either because he did not know how to improve a victory, or in consequence of not being able to rally his forces, he took up quarters at Capua. The luxuries of Italy enervated the Carthaginians, and the fortunes of their general eventually underwent a total change.* The Roman arms, triumphant at Nola, Arpi, and Capua, captured Syracuse, cut off the recruiting forces under Hasdrubal, and were victorious in Spain. Penetrating to the confines of Numidia, Scipio, the conqueror of Spain, became the terror of Carthage. Convinced that his object was to perform such exploits in Africa as their commander had executed in Italy, the Carthaginians recalled Hannibal, who had been sixteen years absent. Appearing upon his native soil, Hannibal took command of the troops. The attempts of the Africans at reconciliation proving abortive, a battle ensued in which the Romans under Scipio were victorious. Carthage again sued for peace, which was granted to her upon condition of paying ten thousand talents of silver into the Roman treasury in fifty years, of surrendering her ships and elephants, and of not making war in or out of Africa without the consent of Rome. Thus was peace restored after seventeen years spent in war.

In the contest just terminated, Philip, king of Macedonia, had favored the Carthaginians; Attalus, king of Pergamus, the Romans. Soon after its conclusion word was sent to Rome that Philip was tampering with the

---

* Livy, Bks. XXIII. to XXX., inclusive.

states of Attalus. War was commenced against Philip (A.M. 3807), and he was stripped of all his power in Greece and Asia.* Antiochus, king of Syria, insisting upon his right to portions of Thrace which he asserted his grandfather Seleucus had conquered from Lysimachus, whom he had slain in battle, as also to the cities of Ionia and Ætolia, the Romans declared their intention to maintain the rights not only of Grecians in Greece, but of those settled in Asia.† Hannibal, who had fled from Carthage to the court of Antiochus, took advantage of these disputes and finally led the king into an open rupture with Rome. But his advice being disregarded, the Syrian with a small force entered Greece, sustained by the Ætolians. The Romans shortly expelled him, and the Ætolians were obliged to sue for peace. Scipio, surnamed Asiaticus, with his brother Africanus, first invaded Asia, and with Eumenes, king of Pergamus, conquered Antiochus, compelling him to sue for peace, which was granted to him upon ceding to Rome all the countries west of Mount Taurus. Macedonia was subjected to a still deeper humiliation in the time of Perseus, son to Philip, when war was declared against it, because the monarch had violated the terms of the treaty made with his father. After some delay the contest was closed by Lucius Æmilius Paulus, when the kingdom was reduced to a Roman province.‡ A territorial dispute between Masinissa and Carthage led to a war between them. This occurrence and the vast naval preparations of the latter were considered breaches of treaty by Rome, and induced the third Punic war (A.M. 3858), which ended

---

* Livy, Bks. XXXI. to XXXIII. Justin, Bks. XVI., XXIV., XXV. Plut. Demetrius.

† Livy, Bks. XXXIV. to XXXVII. Jus., Bk. XXXI. Dio., Frag. Bk. XXVI.

‡ Livy, Bks. XXXVIII. to XLV. Justin, Bk. XXXIII.

in the destruction of Carthage. About the same time Achaia was reduced and Corinth demolished. The possessions of the king of Pergamus fell to the lot of Rome by the dying bequest of Attalus.*

Rome, possessed of the best portions of the world, began to feel the fatal influences of luxury. An effort to limit the amount of property held by the citizens, according to ancient law, made successively by the two Gracchi, proving a failure, its authors suffered death. These domestic troubles gave place in the public mind to Numidian affairs. The injustice of Jugurtha led him to grasp a sceptre left by the deceased king of that country between himself and his two cousins. One of the brothers he killed; the other he expelled from the kingdom. The cause of the fugitive was embraced by the Roman senate, and a war commenced; which, though at first unsuccessful, eventually terminated in a complete triumph under Caius Marius.† An equally good fortune marked the operations of this general against the Teutons, Ambrogians, and Cimbrians. Marius, in order to procure the consulship a fourth time, aided in the enactment of an agrarian law and actually distributed money among the people. Domestic feuds were revived. The senate tried to destroy the equestrian order. Drusus, the plebeian tribune, intending to favor the former, held out to the people the hope of pecuniary aid; to the allies and the Italian states, the freedom of the city. In this manner the tribune procured the passage of agrarian and corn laws; got the senate an equal jurisdiction in criminal matters with the equestrian order; but not being able to perform his promise to the allies and states, his life paid the forfeit. Civil war ensued, which, after raging many years, was

---

* Livy, Bk. XLVI., etc. Justin, Bk. XXXVI. ch. iv.
† Livy's Fragments. Sallust's Jug. War.

terminated by Lucius Sylla, in the submission of most of the states.*

Sulpicius, the tribune, procured the recall of many banished persons; the distribution of newly-created citizens and the sons of citizens among the tribes; and the appointment of Marius to the command against Mithridates, king of Pontus. The consuls Pompey and Sylla opposed these measures. In revenge for their opposition, the tribune killed Quintus, the son of one consul and the son-in-law of the other. Sylla raised a force, expelled Marius and Sulpicius from the city, but was himself soon expelled by Octavius, his colleague, and the tribunes. In his exile Sylla was reconciled to Marius. Alluring the Italian states to their cause by the promise of the freedom of the city, they regained possession of Rome. The most abandoned barbarities marked their sway. Marius soon died, but Sylla survived to triumph over Mithridates, recover Bithynia, regain Cappadocia, and obtain possession of supreme power, which he prostituted to still more wicked purposes than had disgraced the days of his joint dominion.† Shortly after the death of Sylla (A.M. 3927), Quintus Sertorius, who had been proscribed by him, raised a war in Spain. Mithridates stirred up commotions in the East. Pompey is entitled to the credit of having suppressed both these formidable rebellions. These foreign disturbances were scarcely over when Catiline shook Rome to its centre by a conspiracy which had for its object the overthrow of the commonwealth. It was fortunately detected and defeated by Cicero, the consul. A revolution nevertheless took place. Power was seized by Cæsar, Crassus, and Pompey.

---

* Livy, Fragments of Bks. LXXI. to LXXVI. Dio. Frag.

† Justin, Bk. XLIII. ch. v. Livy, Fragments of Bks. XC. to CII. Sallust, Con. of Catiline. Cæs. Com. Livy's Fragments. Dio. Frag., Bk. XXXVII.

Gaul and Germany were assigned to Cæsar; Spain to Pompey; Syria and the Parthian war to Crassus. In the eastern expedition Crassus lost his life. Cæsar vanquished the Germans who had invaded Gaul; passed the Rhine; and penetrating Britain, reduced a portion of it. Such remarkable success excited the jealousy of Pompey. A law was therefore passed by his influence declaring that Cæsar should give up his command and return home, when he presented himself for the consulship. Specious as this measure appeared, Cæsar, regarding it as a mere trap, refused to comply unless Pompey would also resign his command. A civil war ensued, which was concluded by Cæsar's triumph at Pharsalia. Pompey fled to Egypt, where he was slain and his partisans finally destroyed. Rome, by the genius of Cæsar, subdued Egypt, Gaul, Pontus, Africa, and Spain. These vast accessions of power conferring an unbounded popularity upon their author, he was declared perpetual dictator. But in this dangerous elevation Cæsar was soon assailed. The plebeian tribunes charged him with aiming at royalty. The accusation was repelled by the dictator, and the tribunes were ejected from their office. A conspiracy ensued, and Cæsar was assassinated in the senate-house.* Mark Antony, the consul, attempting to punish the murderers of Cæsar, brought upon himself the indignation of the senate.† A civil war ensued, in which he was overpowered by his enemies, who were commanded by Pansa, Hirtius, and Octavianus, nephew of the departed conqueror as well as heir to his name and fortune. Soon reconciled, however, to Antony by the intervention of Lepidus, the master of horse under Julius, Octavianus and his two friends took command of public affairs. Burning with revenge, the nephew commenced a dreadful proscrip-

---

* Eu., VI.   † Eu., VII. 1–3.

tion among the enemies of his uncle. Brutus and Cassius, the chief conspirators in the assassination of Cæsar, rallied their friends, and an engagement ensued at Philippi in Macedonia which was fatal to the lives of the leaders and the hopes of the party by which they had been sustained.

Leaving Antony to take care of the provinces beyond sea, Octavianus returned to Rome. The veterans were rewarded by a liberal distribution of money. Complaints followed from those whose property was taxed to make the donation. Lucius Antoninus headed a sedition which was countenanced by Fulvia, the wife of Antony the triumvir. It was, however, suppressed; but upon a second attempt she was repudiated by her husband, who married Octavia, the sister of Octavianus. The movement of young Pompey in the East met a similar fate with these seditions in the capital, and Lepidus, who was connected with it, was deprived of his share in the government, though his life was spared. Triumphant over the Japidæ, Dalmatians, and Pannonians, Octavianus passed into Epirus to oppose Antony, who, captivated with the charms of Cleopatra, the Egyptian queen, had divorced Octavia, and, protected by a powerful military force, refused either to appear at Rome or to resign his office in the triumvirate. Brought to a naval engagement at Actium, he was vanquished, and both husband and wife in despair destroyed their lives. Thus was Octavianus left in the sole possession of power; which he managed so adroitly as to secure to himself and to transmit to his successors the sceptre of the greatest empire ever established.

In reflecting upon the affairs of the empires that have passed in review, the mind is impressed with the significance of the imagery used by Daniel, the captive prophet at Babylon.* Although he spoke centuries before most of these powers existed (A.M. 3397), their distinctive characteristics are in conformity to his words. The Assyrians established the first and the most opulent empire of ancient times: which is appropriately represented as gold. The Medes and Persians erected the next empire, which was less wealthy and a narrower domain than the former: which is described as silver, a metal not as valuable as gold. The Macedonians created the third empire; they were a poor people, and Alexander, their leader, gave no consistency to his conquests, and they were soon broken in pieces: that empire is most strikingly denominated brass, a metal of less value than either gold or silver and of great brittleness, and of which the armor of Alexander's Greek soldiers was composed. The Romans, a virtuous, brave, and enlightened people, after centuries of effort succeeded in founding the fourth empire, which was the most powerful one that ever existed: it is portrayed as iron, the strongest of all metals. It broke "in pieces and bruised" all that preceded it.

Clearly as the distinctive characteristics of empires in all ages are pointed out by Daniel, he is no less precise in describing their succession in all periods of time. This he portrays figuratively by the image of the human body. Imperial power was to be vested at one time in "the head of gold," at another time in "the breasts of silver," again in "the belly and thighs of brass," then in "the legs of iron," and lastly in the "feet part of iron and part of clay." But in no instance was the unity of the body to be impaired. How remarkably true has this always proved! The kingdoms that comprised the Assyrian Empire were

---

* Dan. ii.

the basis of Medo-Persian power, which passed into the hands of Alexander and his generals simply as trustees for the Romans, and being blended with their possessions formed but one empire, until it was divided into the East and the West; in the last of which its authority was revived by Charlemagne. Is not therefore the union of the members in the human body the most appropriate representation of the succession of empires during all ages?

How amazing is the description of Daniel when considered in the order of time! It was uttered over a century before the accession of Cyrus, called by name, in the prophecy of Isaiah (xlv. 1), as the deliverer of the Jews from Babylonian captivity; it was over two centuries anterior to the time of Alexander the Great; near six centuries before the rise of the Roman Empire; about one thousand years before its division: and over fourteen centuries prior to the time of Charlemagne!

Daniel's declarations as to the characteristics and succession of empires have proved no more prophetic than the words of Noah as to their direction, uttered over three centuries and a half (A.M. 1684) before the first empire was founded. The sententious passage* of the antediluvian indicates Asia as the primitive seat of empire; the descendants of Shem as its founders; the subordination of all Ham's children in Africa; the western course of Japheth's sons; their extensive settlements in Shem's possessions, and their final absorption of the domains of both their brothers. Have not subsequent events verified this prophecy to the letter? Shem's descendants founded in Asia the first empire (A.M. 2040), and afterwards extended their power to Africa (A.M. 3474) in the time of Cambyses. The

---

*Gen. ix. 24-27. Scott's Com. Newton's Dissertations on the Prophecies, pp. 1-25; Dis., i. 13, 14.

Greeks, a portion of Japheth's children, made such vast and permanent settlements in Asia that the western part was called after them, Ionia. Finally, the Romans, sprung from the blood of Japheth, erected their imperial standard throughout all the west, and being "enlarged" as no people ever were before or since their time, they encompassed the three continents of Asia, Africa, and Europe and reigned supreme all over the world!

The course of empires in all ages is described by the antediluvian prophet: "And Noah awoke from his wine, and knew what his younger son had done unto him. And he said, Cursed be Canaan; a servant of servants shall he be unto his brethren. And he said, Blessed be the Lord God of Shem; and Canaan shall be his servant. God shall enlarge Japheth, and he shall dwell in the tents of Shem; and Canaan shall be his servant." (Genesis ix. 24–27.)

The foreshadowings of Daniel and Noah embrace all time, but are no less impressive and explicit, though grander, than those of Isaiah and Jeremiah:

"Thou, O king, sawest, and behold a great image. This great image, whose brightness was excellent, stood before thee; and the form thereof was terrible. The image's head was of fine gold, his breast and his arms of silver, his belly and his thighs of brass, his legs of iron, his feet part of iron and part of clay." (Dan. ii. 31–33.) "This is the dream; and we will tell the interpretation before the king. Thou, O king, art a king of kings: for the God of heaven hath given thee a kingdom, power, and strength, and glory. And wheresoever the children of men dwell, the beasts of the field and the fowls of the heaven hath he given into thine hand, and hath made thee ruler over them all. Thou art this head of gold. And after thee shall arise another kingdom inferior to thee, and another third kingdom of brass, which shall bear rule over all the earth. And the fourth kingdom shall be strong as iron: forasmuch as iron breaketh in pieces and subdueth all things: and as iron that breaketh all these, shall it break in pieces and bruise." (vs. 36–40.)

Daniel afterwards speaks in detail of the great powers predicted in his interpretation of the king's dream.

Chap. vii. 3, 4: "And four great beasts came up from the sea, diverse one from another. The first was like a lion, and had eagle's wings: I beheld till the wings thereof were plucked, and it was lifted up from the earth, and made stand upon the feet as a man, and a man's heart was given to it."

The ambition of the Chaldeans attempted to make Babylon as great as Nineveh had been under the Assyrians, before its lion heart was destroyed and its wings plucked; but it was only "lifted up from the earth, and made to stand upon its feet as a man," and only had the heart of a man; that is to say, it became simply a local tyrant, never attained imperial power, and finally fell before the arms of the Medes and Persians.

Chap. vii. 5: "And behold another beast, a second, like to a bear, and it raised up itself on one side, and it had three ribs in the mouth of it between the teeth of it: and they said thus unto it, Arise, devour much flesh."

The conquests of the Medes and Persians were mainly on their own side—to the west of their dominions, as if within their reach or between their teeth. They subdued Lydia, Babylon, and Egypt. They aimed at "devouring much flesh," and attempted to conquer Thrace, Macedonia, and Greece, and thus produced national combinations which finally crushed them.

Chap. vii. 6: "After this I beheld, and lo another, like a leopard, which had upon the back of it four wings of a fowl; the beast had also four heads; and dominion was given to it."

The Western nations, particularly the Greeks, were infuriated by the incursions and cruelty of the Medes and Persians. Alexander the Great, as the leader and avenger of the former, pounced on the latter as a leopard, and his conquests were rapid beyond a parallel; but after his death his vast dominions fell into four divisions.

What follows renders the predictions about these powers still plainer.

Chap. viii. 3: "Then I lifted up mine eyes, and saw, and, behold, there stood before the river a ram which had two horns: and the two horns were high; but one was higher than the other, and the higher came up last. I saw the ram pushing westward, and northward, and southward; so that no beasts might stand before him, neither was there any that could deliver out of his hand; but he did according to his will, and became great."

The diadems of the kings of Persia were like a ram's head, "and rams' heads with horns, one higher and the other lower, are still to be seen on the pillars at Persepolis" (Scott's comment on this place). This indicates that the Persians were more renowned than the Medes, as well as that in the division of power after the Babylonish conquest, if not from the overthrow of Astyages, Darius the Mede should take precedence of his nephew Cyrus the Persian, who after his uncle's death succeeded to sole power.

Chap. viii. 4: "I saw the ram pushing westward, and northward, and southward; so that no beasts might stand before him, neither was there any that could deliver out of his hand; but he did according to his will, and became great."

Cyrus conquered Lydia to the west, and Herodotus says he fell in his attempts on the Massagetæ at the north; while Cambyses, his son, subdued Egypt.

Chap. viii. 5–8: "And as I was considering, behold,

a he-goat came from the west on the face of the whole earth, and touched not the ground : and the goat had a notable horn between his eyes. And he came to the ram that had two horns, which I had seen standing before the river, and ran unto him in the fury of his power. And I saw him come close unto the ram, and he was moved with choler against him, and smote the ram, and brake his two horns : and there was no power in the ram to stand before him, but he cast him down to the ground and stamped upon him : and there was none that could deliver the ram out of his hand. Therefore the he-goat waxed very great: and when he was strong, the great horn was broken ; and for it came up four notable ones toward the four winds of heaven."

The Macedonians were called the "goat's people," and a goat was the national emblem. After Alexander united their power with the Greeks and thus obtained strength for his work, or, as the prophet says, " had a notable horn between his eyes," he passed with such rapidity from the west in assailing the Medo-Persian power that he scarcely seemed to "touch the ground," and ran upon his foe with such fury as to cast him down to the ground, by which overthrow he was completely disheartened ; so that the after-battles of Alexander were but stamping down the adversary. Hence the Macedonian passed forward to universal empire in half a score of years, but which was suddenly broken by his death, and his vast dominions divided among his four great generals—Cassander in Macedon and Greece ; Lysimachus in Thrace and the countries on the Hellespont and Bosphorus ; Ptolemy in Egypt, Libya, Arabia, Syria, and Palestine ; and Seleucus in Chaldea, Persia, and the East.

Imperial Rome finally subdued the kingdoms which had composed pre-existing empires, and swayed the destinies of the world ; thus verifying the words of Daniel concerning the fourth development of empire, which was to be as "a beast dreadful and terrible, and strong exceedingly; and it had great iron teeth: it devoured and brake in pieces, and stamped the residue with the feet of it" (Dan. vii. 7).

The after-periods of Roman Empire; its division into the Eastern and Western branches, and the overthrow of the latter by the northern nations; and its attempted mixture with them, as well as the fate of the former by the followers of Mohammed, are announced in the words of the prophet to the ancient king:

"And whereas thou sawest the feet and toes, part of potters' clay, and part of iron, the kingdom shall be divided; but there shall be in it of the strength of the iron, forasmuch as thou sawest the iron mixed with miry clay. And as the toes of the feet were part of iron, and part of clay, so the kingdom shall be partly strong, and partly broken. And whereas thou sawest iron mixed with miry clay, they shall mingle themselves with the seed of men: but they shall not cleave one to another, even as iron is not mixed with clay." (Dan. ii. 41–43.)

"The two consuls by whom the Romans were long governed, and the Eastern and Western Empires into which their dominions were at length divided, might be denoted by the two legs and feet on which the image stood; and the ten toes into which the feet divided represented the ten kingdoms into which at length the whole empire was broken. The civil wars which weakened the state, and the conjunction of the Romans with the conquered nations, and afterwards with the Goths, Vandals, and other barbarians who subverted the empire, is denoted by the compounding of the iron with the potters' clay, which cannot unite or strengthen each other." (Scott in loc.)

CHAPTER V.

THE STATE OF SOCIETY IN ALL EMPIRES TO THE COMMENCEMENT OF THE CHRISTIAN ERA.—THE INCARNATION.—THE APOCALYPSE.

It is impossible to understand the history of empires without considering the condition of their inhabitants, as well as the genius of their projectors. In conducting this inquiry, the safest mode is to master undisputed facts before attempting to comprehend the ingenious refinements of the commentators. The succeeding details are presented as an auxiliary in the application of this suggestion.

The Egyptians claim to be considered the parents of science and the framers of good government.* Whether this pre-eminence is accorded to them or not, an impartial mind will admit the excellence of many of their institutions and attainments.

The government of Egypt was regal; but the reflecting and moral tendency of the people imposed upon it such restraints as rendered it less oppressive there than in some other portions of the world. The leading feature in the system was the strict subordination of the king to immemorial custom. In other nations the will of the monarch was regarded as the standard of civil right and wrong. The king of Egypt, on the contrary, no matter how venerable, how powerful, how ancient the dynasty from which he arose, was considered as first in obligation to maintain the laws, by submitting to them himself and by enforcing their execution on all classes of society. The

---

* Dio. Sic., Bk. I. ch. i., vi., vii. Her., Euterpe.

better to prepare him for this work, he was subjected to a rigorous probation in early life. Nor was he allowed, when he came to the throne, to depart from the rules of his pupilage. Diet was calculated with a strict regard to the subjection of passion and the sway of reason. At break of day the king was required to be present at the chamber of state, where he examined the communications which claimed immediate attention. After the performance of this duty, the monarch and ministers repaired to the temple, witnessed the services of the altar, and offered petitions to Heaven for the blessings of a calm temper, a sense of right, and an appreciation of those virtues that adorn and a hatred of those vices which debase the head of a nation. The administration of justice was committed to thirty judges, who were commissioned by the king. Ample revenues were provided for these functionaries so as to preserve them from corruption and to enable them to devote their time exclusively to public affairs. The causes brought before the court were submitted in writing.

Egyptian laws present many remarkable features. Deliberate murder was treated as the highest offence of which man can be guilty. The perjurer was punished with death, like the murderer. He who neglected or refused to aid a fellow-being attacked by the hand of violence was liable to severe punishment. Local magistrates were bound to keep a register of all persons within their precincts. Debts were only payable out of the debtor's goods; his body being regarded as the property of the public, was not liable, on this account, to imprisonment. Adulteration of the coin, making false money, contriving false weights, counterfeiting seals, forging deeds, razing public records, were punished by the loss of the culprit's hands. Adultery and rape were followed by mutilation and stripes. Parents who killed their children were compelled to hug their dead bodies for three nights and days; but children who killed their parents were laid upon thorns, tortured, and then burnt alive. Age was respected, as indicating experience and knowledge.

Notwithstanding the excellent features of some of these laws, this ancient nation allowed a man, if not a priest, to have many wives, and compelled its people to worship many gods. No objects of worship were presented but those which addressed the senses. The sun, called Osiris, and the moon, styled Isis, were their two chief gods; which together with the quickening efficacy, the heat, the dryness, the moisture, and the air existing in the physical world, personified under the names of Jupiter, Vulcan, Matera, Oceana, and Minerva, composed the celestial divinities. Begotten by these were a throng of terrestrial gods too tedious for enumeration, but who in reality were only men rendered immortal by their wisdom or benevolence. Besides, divine regard was had for a countless catalogue of animals, such as the ox, the dog, the wolf, the hawk, the crocodile, and the cat. In the Egyptian mythology are found the elements from which most of the heathen nations formed their religious systems.

Nothing is more remarkable in the customs of this people than the manner in which they treated the dead. A solemn inquisition was held upon the past actions of the deceased. If it was determined that the conduct of the deceased had been, in the main, bad, the rite of common burial was refused; but if, on the contrary, it was decided to have been good, it was decreed. So exceptionless was this rule in its application that even kings were not above its operation.

Artificers, husbandmen, and shepherds were the ordinary classes among the Egyptians. The attention of the nation had been directed in the earliest periods to the improvement of the soil. The Nile abounded in works conducive to the welfare of the people. This river is subject to periodical inundations, from which the adjacent land derives great fertility. Public authority directed these to be ascertained; notice to be given of them throughout the country; and the inhabitants were thus enabled to form accurate calculations as to the forthcoming harvest. The fecundity of the soil was proverbial. Three or four different crops were raised in the same year. The first consisted of lettuce and cucumbers, the next of corn, and after the harvest was gathered several kinds of pulse were produced. A communication from the Red Sea to the Mediterranean, opened by a canal, afforded an ample channel of transportation for the products of the citizens, and furnished the readiest opportunity for improving the state of the surrounding country.

The army numbered about four hundred thousand men for the peace establishment. The Egyptians, however, were by no means a warlike people. When centuries old they could not, in recounting the events of their history, point to any military achievements except those which the memory of Sesostris recalled. Still this people for ages governed the refined portions of the world and exerted an influence which neither Cyrus nor Cæsar ever attained: and to this hour he who contemplates the pyramids, the obelisks, the temples, the palaces, the labyrinth, recognizes much that serves to explain the extraction of the exact sciences.

Carthage, the great African metropolis, was settled by a colony from the far-famed city of Tyre. The system of religion established by its settlers was pagan. Among the most famous of their deities was the goddess Cælestus, or the moon, and Saturn. The former was invoked in times of calamity, particularly during periods of drought; while the latter, noticed in the Sacred Scriptures under the name Moloch, was the divinity propitiated by the dying shrieks of innocent infants.* Horrible as are the details of this ceremony, the Carthaginians were considered a people of profound wisdom. Their constitution was regarded by Aristotle as a model in politics; and for five centuries the citizens were not disturbed by sedition nor oppressed by tyranny. Two officers called saffetes, chosen annually, were invested with the administration. To these belonged the convocation of the senate, the proposal to it of such measures as the public good required, and the collection of the votes of the senators. What number composed the senate is not known. Its members were chosen from that class which was considered most likely to conserve the public interests. Its decisions were ascertained by majorities; but if there was a division, an appeal lay from their authority to the people in their assemblies. This troublesome and expensive process was rarely adopted, the power of both the senate and the executive being sufficiently guarded by what was denominated the Tribunal of the Hundred. Eventually, when wealth and luxury increased, factions became powerful, the balance of the system was destroyed, and the establishment precipitated into anarchy. Two glaring defects have been noticed in the African government. The one was the multiplicity of offices which one man was permitted to exercise; the other was the necessity for wealth in order to take part in any public service.

The basis of commerce has in all ages been the command of the Eastern trade.† King David, the founder of Jewish greatness, having conquered the land of Edom, obtained

---

* Justin, Bk. XVIII. ch. iii. to vii.; Bk. XIX. Polybius, Bk. VI. ch. ii.

† Prideaux's Con., Bk. I. pp. 118–122. Rob. Hist. Am., Vol. I. ch. i.

control over the coast of the Red Sea. Two ports, Elath and Esion-geber, were seized and the trade of the Indies secured. Solomon improved upon the work of his father; the gold, silver, ivory, and precious stuffs of Ophir and Tarshish fell into the possession of his people, and they obtained command of the trade of the world. It was retained by them until the Syrians snatched it away in the reign of Ahaz. Tyre afterwards became the possessor of the Eastern monopoly. She enjoyed it, under the patronage of the Persian princes, down to the time that the Ptolemies prevailed in Egypt. Myos-Hormos, founded by these monarchs on the western side of the Red Sea, then became the mart of Eastern produce.

Commerce was the absorbing occupation of the Carthaginians. They traversed the Mediterranean Sea and passed beyond the straits in its pursuit. From Egypt they obtained flax, paper, and corn; from India, by way of the Red Sea, spices, frankincense, perfumes, gold, pearls, and precious stones; from their parent-land, Tyre and Phœnicia, purple, scarlet, costly furniture, tapestry, rich stuffs, and works of exquisite fabric, which they bore to the western world. Here they were exchanged for iron, tin, lead, and copper, which were disposed of at immense profits on the return to the East. In the course of commercial speculations among the Spaniards, the Carthaginians discovered them to be ignorant of the precious metals which were concealed in their soil. Taking advantage of this ignorance, some articles of trifling value were passed upon the Spanish people in exchange for their lands, which placed extensive gold and silver mines at the command of Carthage.

The military power of the African capital was considerable. Her strength, however, in this respect consisted more in her wealth and maritime knowledge than in her soldiers, though she could boast of having produced in

Hannibal one of the ablest commanders the world ever saw. The bulk of her armies was composed of mercenary troops. Numidia furnished her with cavalry; the Balearic Isles with practised slingers; an unconquerable infantry came from Spain; Genoa and Gaul swelled her ranks with bold and powerful troops; and Greece supplied her with its invincible phalanx.

In the pursuit of money the Carthaginians neglected the sciences. Education among them was confined to the knowledge of reading, writing, arithmetic, and bookkeeping. Their libraries, though extensive, were arrayed in so much pomp that none ventured to disturb them; and they boast of no men of letters except Hannibal and Mago, Hasdrubal and Terence.

Monarchy was established in the Eastern Empire in its most stringent form.* A body consisting of seven councillors was the only curb upon the emperor. It is true the judiciary was guarded with great caution and became a protection to the people. Commissions were issued only to persons of fifty years of age, well skilled in the laws, and of good reputation for talents and integrity. After the judge was appointed he was still guarded in the exercise of his functions by the dread of a disgraceful punishment in case he proved false to the trust reposed in him.

Three remarkable usages existed among the Persians. Although they inflicted capital punishment, no one was subjected to it for the first offence. In estimating crime, they acted upon the principle that if the offender's merits exceeded his demerits he was not the subject of condemnation. The accused in all cases was brought face to face with his adversary, and had the fullest opportunity to prepare for his defence.

---

* Her., Clio. Dio., Bk. II. ch. iii. Xen., In. Cyrus, Bk. VIII.

Cyrus not only knew how to conquer, but he understood how to govern. The empire was divided into provinces, each of which was placed under a governor called a satrap. A supervisory power was exercised over all of them by the emperor in person; or, if that was impossible, it was reposed in some person of tried character, who in the discharge of his duties travelled from province to province. The viceroy did not suppose he could acquit himself to his master by merely attending to the acts done by the satraps, but carefully reported the condition of the subjects in every department, suggesting the improvements desired or needed in commerce, agriculture, and the arts. The execution of a system so vast in its operations induced the emperor to establish regular communications by posts and couriers.

Cyrus brought the military art to the highest perfection. Youth was the time at which he commenced making a soldier. At twenty years of age persons were permitted to enter the army. None were compelled to serve after arriving at the fiftieth year. From the vast body of those fit to bear arms the monarch selected ten thousand on account of their superior physical powers, who were in constant attendance upon his person. This guard was decorated in a style of extravagance which distinguished it from the troops that composed the army. It was also peculiar in its name, being called the Immortals, from the fact that its number was never diminished; a successor being instantly added upon the death of any of its members. The armor of a soldier consisted of a sabre or dagger, which was suspended from the right side, and of two javelins, one of which was used to fling and the other in close fight. A cuirass composed of brass covered the body. Some doubt exists as to whether the Persians used helmets; but it is quite certain they used shields of enormous size. Chariots armed with scythes, cumbersome but destructive instruments of warfare, were much improved by Cyrus. Walled cities and towns presented great obstacles to surmount, upon the ancient principles of warfare. Four methods were then known. A complete enclosure was formed, so as to force the place into terms by the horrors of famine. The tediousness and expense of this process gave rise to the invention of scaling-ladders. A large number of these being raised at the same time, a sufficient force was elevated to make an entrance into the place besieged. But a counter-movement being got up in the erection of towers above the walls, from which the assailants were checked, a scheme was adopted to balance this advantage by raising movable towers. These dangerous and uncertain inventions gave place to the battering-ram, by which a breach was made in the walls and through it the besiegers entered. Equally successful was the other process of undermining the foundation of the structure attacked, in consequence of which it was demolished or prepared for immediate overthrow by the application of the ram.

Very imperfect information is communicated of the state of the arts in the ancient Eastern empires, except what is afforded of their skill in architecture by the works already noticed. Music, it may be fairly inferred from many customs which existed among them, had made considerable progress. The healing art was gradually perfected by a curious but correct process. Patients who were laboring under disease were put in some conspicuous place. If any one passed who had seen a similar case and knew a remedy, he communicated his knowledge. Upon the success of the prescription it was recorded, and thus was established the system of medicine so far as known in the East. Astronomy led nearly all the Asiatics into judicial astrology, by which they professed to declare the fate of every person. Not only were they guilty of this misapplication of what they knew, but a sin more gross was committed by them in worshipping the sun, which they knew ought not to be the object of devotion. These charges, which apply to all the ancients, induce the candid mind to admit and admire the truth contained in the laconic expression of the apostle Paul that "when they knew God, they glorified him not as God, neither were thankful; but became vain in their imaginations, and their foolish heart was darkened" (Rom. i. 21).

The condition of Athens and Sparta affords a key to the state of all the republics of Greece.* Monarchical power, which had been exercised at Sparta from time immemorial by two kings, was reformed by Lycurgus, who flourished about A.M. 3120. A senate was constituted by him composed of twenty-eight members taken from the venerable and learned of the community. The kings presided in this body, but their influence was rendered almost nugatory by their bickerings and the jealousy of the senators. This tribunal in the course of time became dangerous, and the ephori were instituted as a guard and check to both kings and senators. These officers were five in number, and held the trust reposed in them only for a year. An appeal lay to the popular assemblies from the decision of the senate. After all the nicety with which this political machine was balanced, the Spartans were indebted to their system of education for the decorum and order that marked the transaction of their public affairs. The domestic economy of Lycurgus expanded the moral energies of the people. Labor was made respectable, indolence rendered contemptible. Poverty was held in high esteem, as indicating

---

* Her., Ter. Xenophon's At. and Sp. Reps. Jus., Bk. II. ch. vi. to ix.; Bk. III. ch. iii. Dio. Sic., Bk. V. ch. i.

honesty and as calculated to improve the social virtues. Commercial pursuits were regulated by law, and gold and silver money gave place to a currency of iron.

A reformation was effected also in Athens, by Solon, about A.M. 3426. The senate, whose numbers at times had risen as high as from two to three hundred, was improved by a fairer representation of the four classes into which the people were divided. A balance against the excesses of its power was instituted in the Areopagus. The tenure of the archons, who held the judicial power, was reduced, and from being officers for life they were finally subjected to annual change. Popular assemblies were elevated to their proper position. Ceasing to be the instruments of demagogues, they became the means of providing for the common weal. Notice being duly circulated, apprised every one of the exact object of their convocation. After sacrifices and invocation of the gods, the president propounded distinctly the object of the convention, which was canvassed by speakers on both sides of the question. The vote was ascertained by counting the extended hands of the multitude. If the measure was approved by a majority it was reduced to writing and twice read aloud, when it was put to a final vote.

Gymnastic exercises were fashionable among the Athenian youth. Dancing and the feats of the palæstra were considered healthful. Still more attention was paid to the development of the mental faculties. The course of study embraced poetry, eloquence, philosophy, and mathematics. The works of Plato and Aristotle communicate an idea of the thorough character of Grecian learning. The Spartans did not devote an equal attention to the attainment of science. So steadily were these capitals divided that war appears to have been the only common result at which they ever arrived. The reason for this disunion can be traced in the tempers and habits of the two people. The Athenians were quick in perception, volatile in disposition, frank in manners, generous in habits, ambitious in desires. The Spartans were calculating in temper, deliberate in action, plodding in pursuit, expansive in views, unchangeable in purpose.

Notwithstanding their perfection in science and glory in arms, the Grecians adhered to a system of religion which merely enjoined the observance of feasts and the consultation of oracles, the conducting of games and the display of scenic representations. Their three great feasts were the Panatheneia, those of Bacchus, and Eleusis. The first was in honor of Minerva, the tutelary goddess of Athens, and was divided into the greater and lesser; the latter celebrated yearly, the former every fourth year. The exercises consisted in racing, feats of strength, and contests for the prizes of music and poetry, followed by a procession of persons from all classes and of all ages. The Bacchanalian orgies were divided like the former, and in their celebration were not dissimilar from them. They took place in the open field about autumn. Such was their effect upon public morals that during their continuance Plato says he has seen the whole population of Athens inebriated. The Eleusinian feasts were styled, by way of pre-eminence, the Mysteries. These were divided like the former, the one being celebrated in August, the other in November. Mythology assigns as their origin that when Pluto had carried away Proserpine, the daughter of Ceres, the mother came to Eleusis in search of the daughter, and finding the country distressed by a famine, she invented the culture of corn and taught the people the principles of humanity. In addition to the grandeur with which they were celebrated during the space of nine days, they were attended with rites which a becoming sense of decorum has buried in oblivion. Many cities of Greece were famous for their oracles, but none was so much consulted as that at Delphi. The Grecian games were the Olympic, celebrated at Olympia every four years, in honor of Jupiter Olympicus; the Pythian, at Delphi every four years, sacred to Apollo Pythius, who killed the serpent Python; the Nemæan, at Nemæa, instituted in memory of Hercules, who slew the lion in the Nemæan forest, solemnized every two years; and the Isthmian, on the Isthmus of Corinth, in honor of Neptune, which occurred every four years. In all these games the feats were those of strength or racing, and the prize was a wreath of wild olive, laurel, or parsley: thus simple to indicate that honorable ambition alone should be the motive to great actions. Tragic or comic representations were in repute, and are considered by the most dispassionate writers to have been very destructive to the interests of Greece.

The ordinary revenue of the Attic republic was derived from a tax on the silver-mines, agricultural pursuits, the sale of woods, the operations of commerce, and on the powers in alliance with or under the protection of the commonwealth. A tax was levied upon the citizen in great emergencies. Whenever a fine was imposed and collected it replenished the common treasury.

The Romans were divided by Romulus into three tribes, which were ranged in ten portions called curiæ.*
The first were increased from time to time as the population demanded; the latter remained unchanged. Each curia was directed by an officer, over all of whom presided a chief. One thousand foot-soldiers and one hundred horse were furnished by each tribe. The revenue arising

---

* Adam's and Kennett's Roman Antiquities. Livy. Polybius, Book VI.

from this organization was applied to the service of religion, the king's use, and the wants of the curiæ. The nation was distinguished in the early ages by the patrician and plebeian ranks; in later times a third order was constituted, called the equestrian, which sprang from the horsemen furnished by the tribes.

The senate was composed of one man from each tribe and three from each curia. It was increased and diminished from time to time, rising under Julius Cæsar to nine hundred; sinking in the reign of Augustus to six hundred. Rank and wealth were indispensable to the attainment of senatorial honors. Senators were distinguished as well by their dress as the places which they occupied on religious solemnities and at scenic displays. The senate, though not possessed of the law-making power independent of the popular assemblies, was supreme in its decrees on religion, the finances, the provinces, ambassadors, public triumphs, the treatment of common enemies, mitigating the severity or absolving from the obligation of law, postponing popular convocations, and controlling the conduct of the citizens in case of public danger or calamity. The tribunes of the people controlled senatorial action simply by their veto. Each plebeian was bound to choose a patrician, who was compelled to advance his interests and guard his rights: and thus was created the relation of patron and client. The nation was portioned into clans, and these clans into families. Hence the more important citizens had three names; the first arising from some peculiarity, the second derived from his clan, and the third from his family. Some kinds of criminals and prisoners of war were made slaves. The power of the master was so absolute as to extend even to the life of the slave. An alleviation for the misery of this condition was provided by law in the process of emancipation.

After the abolition of regal power, the executive and judicial functions were reposed in the consuls, who were elected by the people. Their military duties calling them often from the capital, the administration of justice was committed to officers called prætors. While the empire was confined to Italy only two prætors were chosen, but as it extended its limits the number was increased. The censors supervised the registration of the citizens, the valuation of property, and the imposition of taxes. When first created, they were two in number and served for five years. That period was subsequently abridged, and the powers of these officers so increased as to embrace a general purview of public morals and public works. Upon the ædiles devolved the duty of taking care of the theatres, baths, temples, roads, sewers, and the buildings of the city, as well as of inspecting the produce in the markets, guarding the citizens against frauds from false measures and weights, limiting the expense of funerals, restraining the avarice of usurers, abating nuisances, and protecting religion. The quæstors collected and disbursed public moneys. Minor officers existed, who respectively supervised the condition of slaves and prisons, controlled the operations of the mint, protected property from fire, attended to the streets by day and guarded the city by night. Great emergencies gave rise to other officers, the principal of which was a dictator, created by the magistrates alone. So jealous were the citizens of this functionary that his power was limited to a duration of six months; nor did it extend to the treasury without senatorial or popular sanction, and was so restrained that he could not go out of Italy or ride on horseback without the citizens' consent. The provinces were controlled at first by prætors; afterwards pro-consuls and pro-prætors, united with quæstors and lieutenants, were invested with the rule. A horde of underlings were attached to the magistrates, such as clerks and lictors, who executed their orders and protected their persons.

The laws by which the empire was governed were contained in the Twelve Tables.* These treat of lawsuits, thefts and robberies, loans and the rights of the creditor over the debtor, parents of families, inheritances and guardianship, property and possession, trespasses and damages, estates in the country, rights of the people, funerals and solemnities relating to the dead, matters of religion, marriages and the rights of the husband. Plain as was this system of jurisprudence, ingenious construction in the course of time buried it under a multiplicity of forms. The connection of patron and client, originally established for the best of reasons, was perverted to the worst of purposes. So completely technical did the advice of the former become, when transformed into the quibbling lawyer, that the latter was deprived of all the advantage which the relation was designed to confer. The general features of Roman jurisprudence may be briefly defined. Personal injuries and infractions of public law occupied the time of the judiciary. There was a wisdom which marked the Roman mode of proceeding in the first class of cases which might be imitated with advantage by all nations. It was incumbent on a complainant to commune, or, at all events, to attempt a communion, with his adversary before he embroiled him in a lawsuit. Should the monition which this preliminary implied prove unavailing, the prætor issued his writ. Upon the appearance of the parties, a body of persons were selected, which, being qualified according to legal solemnity, heard and determined the case. The award being returned to the

---

* 1 Kent's Com., sec. 23. Adam's Rom. Antiq., pp. 352-9.

prætor, the case was under his control, unless removed for the correction of error to a higher tribunal. Offenders against public law in early times were tried at a popular forum; but at later periods they were disposed of by the prætors, assisted by a jury of citizens. The punishments of criminals were imprisonment and bonds, scourging and mutilation, infamy and banishment, slavery and death.

Religion was established and supported by the state. The priests were selected from distinguished families. Their number varied with the times; at one period being as low as four, and rising in the reign of Sylla to fifteen. A chief was chosen from among them, who, until Crassus was invested with the high-priesthood, was not allowed to go beyond the bounds of Italy. Beside this college, which directed the sacred concerns of the republic, there were three other religious offices. The augurs pretended to predict events by the appearance of celestial bodies, the flight of birds, accidental occurrences, and the inspection of the entrails of the victims at the sacrifices. The quindecemviri had the custody of the Sibylline books, which were asserted to be of divine origin and to unfold the destiny of Rome. The septemviri prepared the sacred feasts, games, and processions.

Objects of worship were divided into the higher and the inferior deities. The former were twelve in number; the latter increased with such rapidity that eventually the Pantheon groaned beneath their weight. Devotion consisted in prayers, vows, and sacrifices.

The year originally consisted of ten months, named as at present from the month of March. Numa added the months of January and February, making the year contain three hundred and fifty-five days, which exceeded the Grecian computation one day. A difference followed between lunar and solar calculation of ten days, five hours, and forty-nine minutes. Provision was made against this discrepancy by an extraordinary month which was attached to every other year. The intercalating was left to the priests, who, despite their sacred vows, frequently arranged time to serve the purposes of ambition. Julius Cæsar determined to destroy this chance for fraud. Sosigenes, his astronomer, matured the present arrangement into months and years, which has undergone but two changes. Pope Gregory in the year 1582 deducted ten days between the fourth and fifteenth of October, so as to make the civil correspond with the solar year. A similar excision of eleven days between the second and fourteenth of September was made in the year 1752 in England. In the reign of the emperors, the creation of weeks was adopted from the Hebrews, the original division of the months having been into calends, so called from the annunciation of a new moon by the priests; ides, being the thirteenth day or the dividing period, nearly, of the month; and nones, which reckoned nine days from the last time or the middle of the month. The days of the week derived their respective names from the planets, and were subjected to two divisions; the first, styled the civil, from midnight to midnight; the natural, from sunrise to sunset. The night was distinguished by three watches.

Festivals occurred every month. During their continuance a partial or entire suspension of business prevailed. In the opinion of the Romans, this time was religiously employed in witnessing the displays of the circus, the contests of gladiators, and the mimicries of the drama.

Sacrifices were prevalent throughout the world from the remotest periods of antiquity. Animals were mostly the victims laid on the altar; but among many nations human beings were devoted. The reason ordinarily assigned in ancient times for the institution was that its observance procured the divine favor; upon what principle or for what reason, the wisest of the pagan philosophers do not pretend to tell.* But that on which the oracles of the old world were dumb becomes plain under the teachings of Revelation. The direction of this unerring guide points by Abel's offering to the perfect work which the "woman's seed" was to accomplish. Abel's faith led him to abandon all human works as a ground of justification before God; and notwithstanding Cain's rage was incurred by disavowing his way of salvation by works, the protomartyr willingly yielded his life in defence of the truth of God. Noah reproclaimed the same doctrine by the sacrifice he offered soon after the waters of the flood subsided.† The patriarch of an apostate and the parent of a believing world may have supposed that the way of salvation would not again be subverted by his descendants. Five centuries, however, scarcely passed before men were so corrupt that the sole mode by which the agent in the introduction of sin and the promised one by whom it was to be destroyed were presented to mankind was by idols of gold in the Temple of Belus.‡ The Jews were the only people who offered sacrifices under proper views of their nature. But even among them the masses were ignorant of the spirituality of their own institutions. A remnant nevertheless saw in them a foreshadowing of a mighty offering that was to be made for sin. To this end pointed the ceremonials of Moses and the predictions of Isaiah.§

What was the divine purpose in allowing ages to intervene between the publication of the promise of salvation and the

---

* Her., Calliope, 61, 62. Livy, Bks. XXXIV., LV.; Bk. XXXIX. ch. viii.–xviii. Xen. Soc., Bk. IV. ch. iv.

† Gen. iii. 14, 15; iv. 2–8; viii. 20.

‡ Dio. Sic., B. II. ch. i.

§ Lev. Is. liii. Luke xxiii. 9. John xviii. 14; xix. 16–18.

period of its performance no human power has ever discovered. All that can be said is, "Even so, Father; for so it seemed good in thy sight" (Luke x. 21). Still it must be admitted that the most proper time for the completion of this scheme of grace was when the nations of the world were in the best state for receiving the tidings of it. Under the sway of the two first Roman emperors the facilities for intercommunication were greater than at any preceding period. The advent of the Lord Jesus Christ, therefore, on the first occasion of this description was emphatically "in the fulness of the time" (Gal. iv. 4). As the antitype was manifested, sacrificial offerings, which formed the type, began to disappear and finally vanished, just as the brightest star of the firmament ceases to be seen when the sun arises. The work of redemption begun in Eden by a promise, and continued through the Mosaic age of symbols, by a miracle was at last consummated on Calvary, when its author, having offered " the one sacrifice for sin, forever sat down at the right hand of God " (Heb. x. 12).

The language of prophecy on this subject is very plain.

Isaiah liii. 4-9: " Surely he hath borne our griefs, and carried our sorrows: yet we did esteem him stricken, smitten of God, and afflicted. But he was wounded for our transgressions, he was bruised for our iniquities: the chastisement of our peace was upon him; and with his stripes we are healed. All we like sheep have gone astray; we have turned every one to his own way; and the Lord hath laid on him the iniquity of us all. He was oppressed, and he was afflicted, yet he opened not his mouth: He is brought as a lamb to the slaughter, and as a sheep before her shearers is dumb, so he openeth not his mouth. He was taken from prison and from judgment: and who shall declare his generation? for he was cut off out of the land of the living: for the transgression of my people was he stricken. And he made his grave with the wicked, and with the rich in his death; because he had done no violence, neither was any deceit in his mouth."

Luke xxiii. 9: "Then he [Herod] questioned with him in many words; but he answered him nothing."

John xviii., 14: "Now Caiaphas was he, which gave counsel to the Jews, that it was expedient that one man should die for the people." V. 40: "Then cried they all again, Not this man, but Barabbas." Ch. xix. 16–18: "And they took Jesus, and led him away. And he bearing his cross went forth into a place called the place of a skull, which is called in the Hebrew Golgotha: where they crucified him, and two others with him, on either side one."

Matt. xxvii. 13, 14: "Then said Pilate unto him, Hearest thou not how many things they witness against Thee? And he answered him to never a word; insomuch that the governor marvelled greatly." V. 27–31: "Then the soldiers of the governor took Jesus into the common hall, and gathered unto him the whole band of soldiers. And they stripped him, and put on him a scarlet robe. And when they had platted a crown of thorns, they put it upon his head, and a reed in his right hand: and they bowed the knee before him, and mocked him, saying, Hail, King of the Jews! And they spit upon him, and took the reed, and smote him on the head. And after that they had mocked him, they took the robe off from him, and put his own raiment on him, and led him away to crucify him." V. 57–60: "When the even was come, there came a rich man of Arimathea, named Joseph, who also was Jesus' disciple: he went to Pilate, and begged the body of Jesus. Then Pilate commanded the body to be delivered. And when Joseph had taken the body, he wrapped it in a clean linen cloth, and laid it in his own new tomb, which he had hewn out in the rock: and he rolled a great stone to the door of the sepulchre, and departed."

A kingdom founded against human expectations and without man's instrumentality was the result of this wonderful display of mercy and power. The work is the burden of prophecy under the former and under the present dispensation (Dan. ii. 34, 35, 44, 45; Rev. iv.–xxi.). Daniel is, in ancient times, to the great outlines of empires and Christianity what John is, in subsequent times, to the details of both during the Christian era.*

The sublime imagery and lofty style of the "Revelation" invite every person of taste and refinement to a perusal of it. Impartial reflection on its contents will detect facts in its figures which form such striking coincidences with the events of history as will stamp the work a divine prediction of the general course of occurrences from the early ages of Christianity to the "restitution of all things."

Without noting the discordant opinions of commentators upon minor parts or unfulfilled portions of the Apocalypse, a brief review of its accomplished predictions is appropriate in this place.

The despotism and downfall of the Roman Empire and its paganism are distinctly foretold in the Revelation of St. John.† No sooner did the heralds of Christianity proclaim it to the nations than the princes of imperial Rome arrayed themselves in opposition to it. Bloody persecutions followed throughout three centuries. Still the divine truths of Christ made rapid progress among the people of Asia Minor, Greece, Macedonia, Illyricum, Italy, Rome,

---

* Scott's Com., Introd. to Dan.   Newton on Pro., Dis. 13.
† Rev. vi. 9–17.

Spain, and the African states.* This astonishing revolution in the religious sentiments of a hundred and twenty millions of people resulted in the utter overthrow of the Roman system of faith in the fore part of the fourth century (A.D. 325), when Constantine the Great established Christianity and selected Constantinople as the seat of imperial authority. Whatever doubts had existed as to the inspiration of John now vanished from the Christian world, and this remarkable verification of his utterances placed his claims as a prophet beyond dispute.

Rev. vi. 9-17: "And when he had opened the fifth seal, I saw under the altar the souls of them that were slain for the word of God, and for the testimony which they held: and they cried with a loud voice, saying, How long, O Lord, holy and true, dost thou not judge and avenge our blood on them that dwell on the earth? And white robes were given unto every one of them; and it was said unto them, that they should rest yet for a little season, until their fellow-servants also and their brethren, that should be killed as they were, should be fulfilled. And I beheld when he had opened the sixth seal, and, lo, there was a great earthquake; and the sun became black as sackcloth of hair, and the moon became as blood; and the stars of heaven fell unto the earth, even as a fig-tree casteth her untimely figs, when she is shaken of a mighty wind: and the heaven departed as a scroll when it is rolled together; and every mountain and island were moved out of their places. And the kings of the earth, and the great men, and the rich men, and the chief captains, and the mighty men, and every bondman, and every freeman, hid themselves in the dens and in the rocks of the mountains."

---

* Newton, Dis. 24.

What language can more aptly portray the vengeance of Heaven inflicted by the terrible wars between Licinius and Constantine on imperial pagan Rome for its bloody persecutions of the early Christians?

The apostasy in the Christian Church from the principles of Christ, and the rise of a new empire, embracing the ten nations of Europe existing at the overthrow of Rome, as its prop and support, are predicted in the Apocalypse.

In order to gratify its lust for power, the Church of Rome destroyed the simplicity of the gospel and substituted in its place unscriptural dogmas, pompous ceremonies, and immoral practices.* The Eastern Church it is true was less faulty in this respect than the Western, but both are justly chargeable with departing from the teachings of Christ. At Rome was set up the most despotic ecclesiastical establishment that has ever oppressed the world, and it derived all its power from the protection of Charlemagne, the first emperor of the West. The hierarchy of Rome for ages claimed the right to release subjects from their oaths of allegiance to their princes, and laid nations under interdicts which closed their churches and cut off the people at large from the use of the sacraments and the rites of burial. In later times it was as persecuting as it was formerly despotic. What numbers of Lollards were burnt in England! What multitudes of Huguenots perished in France! What scores of Reformers suffered in Germany, the Low Countries, and Sweden!† During the Duke of Alva's administration of five years and six months in the Netherlands he put to death eighteen thousand

---

*Rev. xiii. 1 Tim. iv. 1–3. Thes. ii. 1–10. Montesquieu's Rise and Fall of Rom. Emp., ch. xxii. pp. 282–5. Hume's Hist. of Eng., Vol. I. pp. 455–6. New., Dis. 22–26.

†See Chapters XVI., XVII. Machiavel's History of Florence., Bk. I. p. 6.

persons for no reason but their opposition to the hierarchy of Rome.*

There is the best reason to believe that if the real number of those who have been cruelly murdered during the Christian era on account of their religious opinions could be ascertained, it would appear that the multitude martyred by ignorant pagans and misguided Protestants would dwindle into insignificance when compared with the countless throng put to an ignominious death for resisting the tyranny of the pope or disputing the dogmas of the Roman Catholic Church.

As imperial affairs are traced in the succeeding pages they will afford the strongest evidence that John wrote by the spirit of prophecy.

Two quotations will explain the mode of calculating prophetical time. Numbers xiv. 34: "After the number of the days in which ye searched the land, even forty days, each day for a year, shall ye bear your iniquities, even forty years." Leviticus xxv. 8: "And thou shalt number seven sabbaths of years unto thee, seven times seven years; and the space of the seven sabbaths of years shall be unto thee forty and nine years."

1 Tim. iv. 1-3: "Now the Spirit speaketh expressly, that in the latter times some shall depart from the faith, giving heed to seducing spirits, and doctrines of devils; speaking lies in hypocrisy; having their conscience seared with a hot iron; forbidding to marry, and commanding to abstain from meats, which God hath created to be received with thanksgiving of them which believe and know the truth."

2 Thes. ii. 1-4: "Now we beseech you, brethren, by the coming of our Lord Jesus Christ, and by our gather-

---

* Watson's Philip II., Vol. I. p. 212.

ing together unto him, that ye be not soon shaken in mind, or be troubled, neither by spirit, nor by word, nor by letter as from us, as that the day of Christ is at hand. Let no man deceive you by any means: for that day shall not come, except there come a falling away first, and that man of sin be revealed, the son of perdition; who opposeth and exalteth himself above all that is called God, or that is worshipped; so that he as God sitteth in the temple of God, shewing himself that he is God."

Rev. xvii. 15: "The waters which thou sawest . . . are peoples, and multitudes, and nations, and tongues."

Rev. xiii. 1: "And I stood upon the sand of the sea, and saw a beast rise up out of the sea, having seven heads and ten horns, and upon his horns ten crowns, and upon his heads the name of blasphemy." "The seven heads and ten horns" are the well-known marks of the Roman Empire; the former alluding to the seven hills on which Rome was built, as well as to the seven forms of government which successively prevailed there, to wit, that of kings, consuls, dictators, decemvirs, military tribunes, emperors, popes; and the latter signifying the ten kingdoms into which the Roman Empire was divided upon its downfall.

These ten kingdoms are thus enumerated by Sir Isaac Newton (Obs. on Dan., ch. vi. p. 47; Dis., p. 210), namely: (1) the kingdom of the Vandals and Alans in Spain and Africa; (2) the kingdom of the Suevians in Spain; (3) the kingdom of the Visigoths; (4) the kingdom of the Alans in Gallia; (5) the kingdom of the Burgundians; (6) the kingdom of the Franks; (7) the kingdom of the Britons; (8) the kingdom of the Huns; (9) the kingdom of the Lombards; (10) the kingdom of Ravenna.

V. 2: "And the beast which I saw was like unto a

leopard, and his feet were as the feet of a bear, and his mouth as the mouth of a lion: and the dragon gave him his power, and his seat, and great authority." Papal Rome succeeded to the power and place of Imperial Rome.

V. 3: "And I saw one of his heads as it were wounded to death; and his deadly wound was healed: and all the world wondered after the beast." The imperial power of papal Rome "was wounded" by the invasion of the Goths and northern nations, but Charlemagne by his power and victories "healed the wound," re-established imperial authority in the West, and gave the popedom control over Europe, which held its kingdoms in spiritual bondage until the Reformation: so that during that period of time "they worshipped the dragon which gave power unto the beast: and they worshipped the beast, saying, Who is like unto the beast? who is able to make war with him? And there was given unto him a mouth speaking great things and blasphemies; and power was given unto him to continue forty and two months. And he opened his mouth in blasphemy against God, to blaspheme his name, and his tabernacle, and them that dwelt in heaven. And it was given unto him to make war with the saints, and to overcome them: and power was given him over all kindreds, and tongues, and nations. And all that dwell upon the earth shall worship him, whose names are not written in the book of life of the Lamb slain, from the foundation of the world." (V. 4-8.)

V. 11-14: "And I beheld another beast coming up out of the earth; and he had two horns like a lamb" (the regular and secular clergy of the papal hierarchy), "and he spake as a dragon" (that is, with the power to command). "And he exerciseth all the power of the first beast before him, and causeth the earth and them which dwell therein to worship the first beast, whose deadly wound was healed.

And he doeth great wonders, so that he maketh fire come down from heaven on the earth in the sight of men, and deceiveth them that dwell on the earth by the means of those miracles which he had power to do in the sight of the beast; saying to them that dwell on the earth, that they should make an image to the beast, which had the wound by a sword, and did live." The pope is the idol of the Church, represents the whole power of the hierarchy, or " beast," and is the head of all authority, temporal and spiritual. He is nothing more than a private man till the corrupted clergy, represented by the cardinals, choose him to be pope; when he is arrayed in pontifical robes, crowned, and placed upon the altar, and the cardinals come and kiss his feet, which ceremony is called adoration : thus life is given to the " image of the beast," that " it should both speak, and cause that as many as would not worship the image of the beast should be killed. And he causeth all, both small and great, rich and poor, free and bond, to receive a mark in their right hand, or in their foreheads. And that no man might buy or sell, save he that had the mark, or the name of the beast, or the number of his name." (Verses 15–17.)

The extinction of the Roman Empire, both in the West and the East,—the former by the barbarians of the North, the latter by the followers of Mahomet,—is positively announced in the Revelation.* When the Revelation of John appeared, the Romans had no more reason to dread the Northern barbarians than the people of the United States now have to fear the numerous tribes of Indians which are scattered on their western frontiers. In the course of years, however, those people began to pillage in small bands. Large bodies of armed men then roamed

---

* Rev. viii.

at will through various portions of the empire. At last encroachments were made upon the imperial domains by regular settlements. Open war soon ensued. Vast armies came into deadly conflict. The loss of life on both sides was terrific. The barbarians were taught the mode of Roman warfare by these contests. As luxury indisposed the Roman to enter the army, its ranks were filled by these barbarians. Having thus obtained skill and knowledge by the gradual advancements of years, they were able, as will be seen, at the commencement of the sixth century to sack Rome, settle Italy, and sit themselves down in Gaul, Spain, and the African states.

The case is still stronger in regard to the Mahometans.* When the Apocalypse was first published these people were not in existence. Mahomet was not born till nearly six centuries afterwards. The Eastern world, however, soon glowed with his fanaticism. A portion of his followers from the distant East slowly extended their domain towards the West. Notwithstanding many events tending to retard their progress, their ambition to compass the Roman states steadily increased with revolving years. The best portion of Asia Minor coming into their possession, they pushed forward their schemes with astonishing resolution, and in the middle of the fifteenth century Constantinople, it will be seen, fell into their hands.

Rev. viii. 7: "And the first angel sounded, and there followed hail and fire mingled with blood, and they were cast upon the earth: and the third part of trees was burnt up, and all green grass was burnt up." "On the decease of Theodosius, A.D. 395," says Gibbon, "the northern cloud, which had been so long gathering, discharged itself." "After spreading desolation through the

---

* Rev. ix.

provinces by fire and sword," remarks Scott, "the Goths, under Alaric, took and plundered Rome, A.D. 410, with circumstances of barbarity corresponding to the emblems used in this verse."

V. 8: "And the second angel sounded, and as it were a great mountain burning with fire was cast into the sea; and the third part of the creatures which were and had life, died; and the third part of the ships were destroyed." "A great burning mountain" is emblematic of a mighty destructive warrior. After Alaric had finished his depredation, Attila with a vast army of Huns ravaged the empire during the space of fourteen years. He called himself "the scourge of God and the terror of mankind," and no man ever better merited that title.

V. 10: "And the third angel sounded, and there fell a great star from heaven, burning as it were a lamp, and it fell upon the third part of the rivers, and upon the fountains of waters."

V. 11: "And the name of the star is called Wormwood: and the third part of the waters became wormwood; and many men died of the waters, because they were bitter." After Attila's barbarities, Genseric with three hundred thousand Vandals, and Moors from Africa, took Rome, and abandoned it to the lust and cruelty of his troops. For some years it gasped as it were for breath, when its existence as an imperial city was terminated A.D. 566, and it became a dukedom, tributary to the exarch of Ravenna. All which is beautifully set forth in verse 12: "And the fourth angel sounded, and the third part of the sun was smitten, and the third part of the moon, and the third part of the stars; so as the third part of them was darkened, and the day shone not for a third part of it, and the night likewise." And thus terminated the sovereign powers of the western division of the Roman Empire, which are portrayed by the figurative language of the prophet.

Rev. ix. 1: "And the fifth angel sounded, and I saw a star fall from heaven unto the earth: and to him was given the key of the bottomless pit. And he opened the bottomless pit; and there arose a smoke of a great furnace; and the sun and the air were darkened by reason of the smoke of the pit." The corrupt practices of the so-called Christian Church, both in the West and East, in the worship of images, saints, and angels, prayers for the dead, devotion paid to relics, monastic life interfering with matrimony, and the whole round of their superstitious observances, prepared the way for Mahomet—that is, "darkened the air by reason of the smoke of the pit."

V. 3–5: "And there came out of the smoke locusts upon the earth: and unto them was given power, as the scorpions of the earth have power. And it was commanded that they should not hurt the grass of the earth, neither any green thing, neither any tree; but only those men which have not the seal of God in their foreheads. And to them it was given that they should not kill them, but that they should be tormented five months: and their torment was as the torment of a scorpion when he striketh a man." When Yezed was marching with his army to invade Syria, Abubekeer charged him with this among other orders: "Destroy no palm-trees, nor burn any fields of corn; cut down no fruit-trees, nor do any mischief to cattle only such as you kill to eat." (Ockley's His. of Sar., 94.) The Saracens were only able to torment and kill the subjects of the Roman Empire, they could not destroy it as a political body; and this is all they ever did, and that only for the period of five prophetical months, each month embracing thirty days, and each day denoting a year: which is the exact time these roaming destroyers pillaged the world, namely, from A.D. 612 to A.D. 762, being one hundred and fifty years, when Bagdad was built and they became a settled nation.

Rev. ix. 13–15: "And the sixth angel sounded, and I heard a voice from the four horns of the golden altar which is before God, saying to the sixth angel which had the trumpet, Loose the four angels which are in the great river Euphrates. And the four angels were loosed, which were prepared for an hour, and a day, and a month, and a year, for to slay the third part of men." When the Turks supplanted the Saracens, they founded four kingdoms or sultanies in Persia and the regions bordering on the Euphrates. They were hemmed in here till after the Crusades were abandoned by the Western Christians, when they broke out and made terrible havoc among the inhabitants of that part of the world which had constituted the Roman Empire, and in the year A.D. 1453 took Constantinople and terminated the empire forever. The time of their conquests is fixed at 391 years and 15 days in prophetic language. Now their first conquest, according to their historian, Cantemir, took place A.D. 1281, and their last 1672; which makes the period mentioned in verse 15.

The revival of science and the reformation of religion are set forth by John. The practical result of the politico-ecclesiastical despotism of Rome and the new Empire of the West was to lower the standard of learning in Europe.* In the course of a few years science ceased to exist among the masses, and finally vanished from society altogether. In some of the best-populated countries of the Franks it was a rare thing to find a person who could read and write. If a man possessed this capacity, he was in many countries shielded from the penal effect of violated law, under the

---

* Rev. xiv.–xx. Is. ii. 1–4; xi.

plea of what was called "the benefit of clergy"—that is, his ability to act as a clerk.* Nobles and kings were in the same condition, as is evinced by the fact that numerous public documents—Magna Charta, for instance, in England—contain the marks and not the signatures of the parties to them. This deplorable state of ignorance reached its height about the latter part of the ninth century. From that period it will be discovered that a succession of causes began to influence society that produced a complete revolution in its intellectual state.† The result was an exact completion of John's prediction.

It is not astonishing that as men became well informed they should become tired of the superstitious observances of Romanism. A total religious change was for this reason very soon the common demand of intelligent people throughout Europe. Rome saw and could not avert, but sought to postpone, her doom. It was in vain, however, she endeavored to delude her sons and subjects. They became imperative in their demands. When she refused to yield to them, they boldly left her bosom, erected the standard of truth upon a new foundation, and bid defiance to her rage.

Events have been looking in this direction for the last three centuries. Within the present century the course they have taken shows that this result is inevitable. What does the mission spirit mean which has been roused up in Protestant Christendom? How stupendous have been its results in lands of ignorance and idolatry! Should it produce the same effects during the next half-century which it has done during the last half-century, where will be a country in which the Gospel of Jesus will not be received? In that case must not "the glory of the Lord fill the

---

* Black's Comts., Vol. I. p. 367. † Dan. xii. 4.

whole earth"? When four fifths of a prophecy have been verified,* no one can reasonably doubt that what remains unfulfilled will in time become accomplished fact: and the final conquest of the world to Christianity is certain.

Rev. xiv. 6–8: "And I saw another angel fly in the midst of heaven, having the everlasting gospel to preach unto them that dwell on the earth, and to every nation, and kindred, and tongue, and people, saying with a loud voice, Fear God, and give glory to him for the hour of his judgment is come: and worship him that made heaven, and earth, and the sea, and the fountains of waters. And there followed another angel, saying, Babylon is fallen, is fallen, that great city, because she made all nations drink of the wine of the wrath of her fornication."

Rev. xv. 2, 3: "And I saw as it were a sea of glass mingled with fire: and them that had gotten the victory over the beast, and over his image, and over his mark, and over the number of his name; stand on the sea of glass, having the harps of God. And they sing the song of Moses the servant of God, and the song of the Lamb, saying, Great and marvellous are thy works, Lord God Almighty; just and true are thy ways, thou King of saints."

Rev. xvi. 17–20: "And there came a great voice out of the temple of heaven, from the throne, saying, It is done. And there were voices, and thunders, and lightnings; and there was a great earthquake, such as was not since men were upon the earth, so mighty an earthquake, and so great. And the great city was divided into three parts, and the cities of the nations fell: and great Babylon" (so-called mystically; meaning papal Rome) "came in remembrance before God, to give unto her the cup of the

---

* Rev. xx. 1–4. Is. liii. Numb. xiv. 21. Dan. ii. 44, 45. Ps. lxxxii. 8.

wine of the fierceness of his wrath. And every island fled away, and the mountains were not found."

Rev. xvii. 12-14: "And the ten horns which thou sawest are ten kings, which have received no kingdom as yet; but receive power as kings one hour with the beast" (or at the hour). "These have one mind, and shall give their power and strength unto the beast. These shall make war with the Lamb, and the Lamb shall overcome them: for he is Lord of lords, and King of kings."

Rev. xviii. 1, 2: "And another angel came down from heaven, having great power; and the earth was lightened with his glory. And he cried mightily, saying, Babylon the great is fallen, is fallen, and is become the habitation of devils, and the hold of every foul spirit, and a cage of every unclean and hateful bird."

Rev. xix. 20: "And the beast was taken, and with him the false prophet that wrought miracles before him, with which he deceived them that had received the mark of the beast, and them that worshipped his image. These both were cast alive into a lake of fire burning with brimstone."

Numbers xiv. 21: "Truly as I live, all the earth shall be filled with the glory of the Lord."

Ps. lxxxii. 8: "Arise, O God, judge the earth: for thou shalt inherit all nations."

Dan. ii. 34, 35: "Thou sawest till that a stone was cut out without hands, which smote the image upon his feet that were of iron and clay, and brake them to pieces. Then was the iron, the clay, the brass, the silver, and the gold, broken to pieces together, and became like the chaff of the summer threshing-floors; and the wind carried them away, that no place was found for them: and the stone that smote the image became a great mountain, and filled the whole earth."

Verses 44, 45: And in the days of these kings shall the

God of heaven set up a kingdom, which shall never be destroyed: and the kingdom shall not be left to other people, but it shall break in pieces and consume all these kingdoms, and it shall stand for ever. Forasmuch as thou sawest that the stone was cut out of the mountain without hands, and that it brake in pieces the iron, the brass, the clay, the silver, and the gold; the great God hath made known to the king what shall come to pass hereafter: and the dream is certain, and the interpretation thereof sure."

Ps. ii. 1–9: " Why do the heathen rage, and the people imagine a vain thing? The kings of the earth set themselves, and the rulers take counsel together against the Lord, and against his anointed, saying, Let us break their bonds asunder, and cast away their cords from us. He that sitteth in the heavens shall laugh: the Lord shall have them in derision. Then shall he speak unto them in his wrath, and vex them in his sore displeasure. Yet have I set my king upon my holy hill of Zion. I will declare the decree: the Lord hath said unto me, Thou art my Son; this day have I begotten thee. Ask of me, and I shall give thee the heathen for thine inheritance, and the uttermost parts of the earth for thy possession. Thou shalt break them with a rod of iron; thou shalt dash them in pieces like a potter's vessel."

CHAPTER VI.

THE EMPIRE OF THE ROMANS TO THE TRIUMPH OF AURELIAN OVER THE GOTHS.

Upon the death of Octavianus (A.D. 14), entitled by the senate Augustus Cæsar, his son-in-law Tiberius began a reign which, during a period of twenty-three years, was productive of little but evil.* Caligula, though only four years in power, exceeded his predecessor in vice;† nor was the sway of Claudius, which continued for thirteen years, of much more public benefit.‡ Nero, the next in the purple, was a monster of iniquity. The murder of his wife and mother, the sacrifice of Seneca and many illustrious citizens, the firing of Rome, and a train of other wrongs united the senate, the army, and the people, in the space of four years, in a combination to crush a wretch who had become intolerable. Galba, Otho, and Vitellius rose and fell successively in eighteen months; each being elevated by the favor or destroyed by the fury of the army. The empire obtained a chief worthy of its former glory in Vespasian, who, throughout a reign of nine years, was not less distinguished for wisdom as a legislator than for courage as a soldier. Titus, pursuing the course of his father, obtained in an eminent degree the esteem of his subjects; but the atrocities of Domitian, his brother, would have been seriously detrimental to the common good had not the hand of violence soon terminated his existence.§ Nerva obtained the sceptre at an advanced age, and finding himself too feeble for the conduct of affairs, manifested the wisdom next to ruling well in selecting Trajan as his associate, who did not cease to be popular when he came to the sole possession of sovereignty.‖ Hadrian (A.D. 117), his successor, visited in person all the provinces, patronized the arts, reformed the laws, and established strict military discipline. Lucius, his only male issue, was recommended by the emperor to the regard of Antoninus Pius and Marcus Antoninus, whom he finally declared his successors.

---

* An. Tac., 1–6.   † Eu., 7.
‡ An. Tac., 11–16.   His. Tac.   His. Aug., Vol. I.
§ Suet., in loc.   ‖ Eu., 8, 9.   His. Aug. Ner. Per.

The indulgence of Marcus to his faithless wife Faustina was the source of the evils which scourged the world in the reign of his son Commodus. Most auspicious circumstances surrounded the emperor when he came to power. The fate of predecessors afforded ample lessons of the folly of vice and of the excellence of virtue. On the one hand was an approving senate, on the other a happy people. The wealth of the Antonines was at his command, and to obtain their glory it was only necessary to imitate their virtues. A false step involved the reign in disgrace. The disposition with which the emperor's mother had imbued him gave a taste for vain company. Idle persons were recalled from whom his father had separated him by their exile. The counsel of these companions prevailed against that of the wise ministers of the former reign. The war beyond the Danube was abandoned for the ease of licentious Rome. Commodus entered the capital amidst much festivity. Perhaps the expression of feeling on this occasion might have induced him to follow the steps of his virtuous predecessors had it not been for the occurrence of a perplexing event. His sister, the widow of Lucius Verus, formed a conspiracy to take his life. The agent by whom she was to execute her plan attacked her brother as he was returning to the palace through a long portico, and rushing on him with a drawn sword, exclaimed, "The senate sends you this!" The assassin was prevented from executing his purpose, and secured by the guards. The emperor from this time manifested a bitter hatred for the senate; slaying many of the best members of that body, as well as those who mourned their loss. Among the most remarkable of these sufferers were the Quintilian brothers, whose fortunes and feelings had been singularly united in life, and who were spared the pang of being divided in death. Perennis, the principal minister, suspected of aspiring to the sceptre, fell a victim to royal wrath. Cleander, a Phrygian by birth and formerly a slave, succeeded Perennis. Peculation soon filled the coffers of this favorite. At the suggestion of the emperor he consented to appropriate much of his fortune in building public baths at Rome. This measure was mutually adopted by king and minister as a sort of propitiation for tyranny and extortion. It did not, however, effect that object. A scarcity of corn occurring, the populace were roused against the administration. A multitude rushed to the palace, demanding a reparation of wrongs. The prætorian guards were directed to disperse it, but the sedition was so well organized as to render their attacks ineffective. As a last expedient, Commodus ordered the bloody head of Cleander to be cast among the people. The execution of this horrid command allayed the insurrection. The emperor nevertheless did not seize this favorable moment to reform his government or life. On the contrary, his crimes increased to such fearful enormity that he was shortly afterwards slain by the domestics of the palace. Pertinax, the præfect of the city, was declared emperor by the senate. During a reign of only eighty-six days a salutary system of reform was commenced in the state and army. The new regulations excited the fury of the soldiers, a band of whom repaired to the palace and demanded a sight of the emperor. On his approach, he reminded them of his innocence and their oath; but, bent upon effecting their purpose, one of them struck the fatal blow, and Pertinax fell dead at his feet.

The prætorian guards exposed the crown to sale.[*] Didius Julianus, a rich senator and a vain old man, urged and flattered by his domestics and family, made the highest

---

[*] Zos., 1. His. Aug. in loc., Vol. II. p. 135.

bid and was elected by this portion of the army. The servile senate confirmed the choice, and Julianus assumed the purple. The Roman army consisted of nine legions abroad: three in Syria, commanded by Pescennius Niger; three in Britain, under Clodius Albinus; and three in Pannonia, at the head of which was Septimius Severus. The elevation of Julianus offended all these chiefs. Niger first raised the standard of rebellion, and was declared emperor by his troops. He might have succeeded if he had not wasted the summer season in idle pleasures at Antioch. Severus being much nearer to the capital, marched immediately there, having been declared emperor by his troops. The celerity of his movements is almost incredible. Within the space of fifteen days he was not only in Rome, but was invested with the purple without having drawn a sword. Julianus was condemned and executed. Civil war ensued, but was terminated by the uncommon talent of Severus in two engagements. One took place in the defiles of Cilicia, where Niger was totally defeated; the other at Lyons, which determined the prospects of Albinus by giving to Severus a complete victory. Both the disappointed generals were slain. The first object of the emperor's desire was the destruction of the prætorian guards, to serve the purpose of which body an army three times as large was created. The humiliation of the senate was next attempted; and in accomplishing it over forty of its members were slain, as well as some of the most honorable citizens of Rome. Thus fortified in power, the sovereign sought to corrupt the minds of men by promulgating sentiments on imperial prerogative which, while they acknowledged his right to do anything he pleased, enjoined on the subject the duties of passive obedience and non-resistance. The empress was not a pattern of chastity, though she was a patroness of the arts and sciences. She was the second wife of Severus. The fruit of the union was Caracalla and Geta. These brothers from infancy manifested implacable hatred for each other; which, together with the unfavorable reports concerning their mother, form an adequate explanation for the discontent of Severus. Seeking an antidote for his cares in the camp, he commenced an expedition against Caledonia. In the prosecution of this perilous plan, his queen and her two sons accompanied the emperor. The Roman arms were successful, but the sovereign died whilst engaged in the expedition. Caracalla and Geta were immediately declared emperors by the army. Upon returning home they celebrated the funeral of their parent with divine honors. Jealousy, however, still continued to rankle in their bosoms. Under pretence of settling all differences, Caracalla sought an interview with his brother. While the conference was proceeding, some of the guards of Caracalla rushed upon Geta with drawn swords and despatched him, nothing daunted at the intrepid but ineffectual attempt of his mother to shield his person by interposing her own. Thus was Caracalla left in the sole possession of the purple. A fratricide could but prove the worst of tyrants. Papinian, the prætorian præfect, a lawyer of great distinction, fell a victim to his revenge because he would not justify the murder of Geta. The whole empire felt his despotism; the affections of the people were alienated, and the general relaxation of military discipline destroyed the only remaining fastness of the emperor's strength. The language of an African magician, at this critical juncture, directed the anxious and agitated minds of the citizens to Macrinus, the prætorian præfect, as their next emperor. The magician was seized, and when brought before the supreme judicial tribunal of Rome persisted in his prediction. All the gloomy feelings of Caracalla were excited. Macrinus, in defence of his own life, was compelled to plot the ruin of his sovereign. He effected it through the instrumentality of Martialis, who, from having been refused the rank of a centurion, was keenly sensible to the suggestions of revenge.

Macrinus succeeded to the purple amid the murmurs of both senate and army. A sister of the empress Julia had been driven from the court (now located in Antioch) to Emesa. She had two daughters, Soæmias and Mammæa, who were widows and each had one son. Bassianus, the son of the former, was high-priest of the Temple of the Sun. A large number of troops were stationed there, whose discontents at the rigid discipline of Macrinus were encouraged by the priest and his relations, until they broke out into open rebellion. The emperor mustered all his forces to compel submission; but risking the fate of empire in one battle, his hopes and army were defeated, and his rival was proclaimed sovereign under the name of Elagabalus. This reign was weak and wicked. The grandmother of the emperor persuaded him to declare Alexander Severus, the son of Mammæa, a Cæsar. Both, in the space of about fifteen years, were succeeded by Maximin, a Thracian wrestler, who was denounced by the senate and resisted by their favorites the Gordians, Maximus, and Balbinus. Gordian III. eventually came to power. Without doing anything of importance, he was supplanted by Philip, called the Arab.* A throne gained by perfidy was soon lost by the fears of its possessor. An insurrectionary movement in Mœsia, which had resulted in the elevation of Macrinus, a subaltern, to imperial honors, induced Philip, instead of suppressing it with promptness, to communicate the whole matter to the senate. Decius treated the affair with ridicule. The task of quelling it

---

*Zos., 1. Aug. His., Vol. II. p. 574, etc.

was committed to him. In attempting to execute his commission, the troops dropped their favorite and proclaimed their judge emperor. The dread of violence or the love of glory induced Decius to accept the honor, and he maintained his cause by the defeat and death of his adversary in battle. The senate confirmed the title of the victorious general. Scarcely, however, had Decius mounted the throne before he was called to the camp by a Gothic irruption upon Dacia. War was prosecuted with vigor. The armies finally joined battle at a small town in Mœsia called Forum Terebronii, where the Romans were defeated and Decius slain. The fickle army, which abandoned the issue of Decius for Æmilianus, the conqueror of the Goths, soon tumbled him from the throne to make place for Valerian, a new favorite.

The enemies of Rome at this period were the Franks, the Alemanni, the Goths, and the Persians. The Franks invaded Gaul, ravaged Spain, and passed over into Africa. The Alemanni laid waste Gaul and made an unsuccessful attempt on Rome. The Goths took a different direction; subduing the Cimmerian Bosphorus, they besieged and captured Trebizond, plundered the cities of Bithynia, passed the Thracian Bosphrous and Hellespont, entered the Ægean, ravaged Greece, took Athens, and then became divided, some going into the Roman service and others, retreating, forced their way through Asia to the Ukraine. The Persians having defeated and imprisoned Valerian, swept the eastern provinces. Amidst these calamities abroad and the convulsions produced at home by the efforts of nineteen pretenders to power, Gallienus, associated by his father in the government, resigned himself to inglorious ease at Rome. At last the approach of Aureolus at the head of the Danubian forces incited him to an effort, in which the libels of his besieged adversary directed the arms of his own men against his life. Before his death he nominated Claudius as his successor. Confirmed in power, the emperor subdued the rebels, slew Aureolus, and in a mild manner effected a reform in the army. The Goths meantime repaired their losses, and with an army of three hundred thousand men invaded the empire. Claudius met them near Naissus, a city of Dardania, and after a desperate struggle they were defeated with a loss of fifty thousand men. Aurelian was nominated as his successor by the sovereign, who died shortly after this signal victory. Though defeated, the Goths were not destroyed. Rallying their scattered forces, a battle was again fought with the Romans, which was bloody yet not decisive. A peace ensued which yielded Dacia to the barbarians, and secured a free market to the Romans. Zenobia, the queen of Palmyra, who had raised the arm of rebellion against imperial power, together with Firmius, who had pursued the same course in Egypt, were both subdued by Aurelian. The dreadful catalogue of ills, war, famine, and pestilence which had prevailed during the gloomy period of twenty-five years, sweeping in its course at least the fourth part of the human family, was now distinguished by the death of the emperor at the hands of the army.

In reviewing this terrible period, the mind is irresistibly impelled to contemplate the remarkable words of the Apocalypse, written two centuries before the occurrence of the events which distinguished it.*

Rev. vi. 8. "And I looked, and behold a pale horse: and his name that sat on him was Death, and hell followed with him. And power was given unto them over the fourth part of the earth, to kill with sword, and with hunger, and with death, and with the beasts of the earth."

---

* Gibbons' Decline and Fall, Vol. II. p. 159. Rev. vi. 8.

CHAPTER VII.

THE EMPIRE OF THE ROMANS TO ITS EXTINGUISHMENT IN THE WEST.

The turpitude of Aurelian's murder awed the legions to such an extent that they pressed the senate to name a successor. Tacitus, a veteran of nearly fourscore, descended from the historian, was selected. The cares of government proving too much for his constitution, he soon died. Florianus, his brother, seized the sceptre; but being slain by the soldiery in less than three months, Probus ascended the throne. Energy marked the course of this emperor. Internal commotions were quelled, Germanic inroads were stayed and prevented by the establishment of a line of forts from the Rhine to the Danube, and salutary reforms were adopted both in the state and army. In fact, Probus was ahead of the times and hence fell a victim to the rage of the legions: so certain an enemy has a standing army always proved to human progress. As quick to relent as to err, the blood-stained soldiery clad in the purple Carus, the friend and præfect of the murdered monarch. A Sarmatian war was successfully concluded, and a Persian one projected, in which the monarch perished. The army forthwith abandoned the expedition in the East on the death of Carus, to settle the strife about his successor.

Diocletian took the prize, and succeeded in securing it by a victory over Carinus, the son of the deceased monarch.* Still the emperor thought he possessed more than his own

---

*Zos., Bk. II. Oro., Bk. VI. ch. xxx.-xxxviii. Aug. His. in loc., Vol. II.

hands could hold. Accordingly, a distribution of the empire took place. Constantius received Spain and Britain; the Illyrian provinces were given to Galerius; Italy and Africa were committed to Maximian; and Thrace, Egypt, and Asia were taken by Diocletian. The city of Rome ceased to be the capital of the empire. Desperate as was the struggle for freedom, the imperial arms triumphed in Gaul and Britain, in Egypt and the African states. The contest with Persia was more severe; yet the defeated and disgraced Galerius at last humbled that proud power and secured the Araxes as the eastern boundary of the empire. Politically dead as Rome was, she witnessed the triumph of all and the resignation of two of the emperors. The retirement of Diocletian and Maximian devolved the sovereignty on Constantius and Galerius. But for dissensions fomented at Rome by Maxentius, the son of the retired emperor Maximian, and the succession of Constantine on the death of his father Constantius, the sceptre would have come to the sole possession of Galerius. As events happened, the empire, instead of being controlled by one person, fell under the direction of six. In the west reigned Maximian, Maxentius, and Constantine; in the east, Licinius, Maximin, and Galerius. Death removing Maximian and Galerius, only one obstacle remained to impede the progress of Constantine in the west. A hard-fought battle at Turin, the capture of Verona, and the overthrow and death of his adversary quickly established him at Rome. Licinius was the brother-in-law and ally of the western conqueror, Maximin his enemy and the friend of the defeated Maxentius. The destruction of the latter by the former made the two brothers masters of the empire. Their friendship, however, was but of short duration. Secret suspicions created bitter jealousies, and in less than a year open war ensued. The two battles of Cibilis and

Mardia settled little more than the superior military skill of Constantine. A peace was proclaimed, which proved to be only the calm that precedes the storm. The war was renewed, and three of the most memorable battles were fought that ever stained the annals of any times. The first was that of Hadrianople, in which the loss of Licinius was near thirty-four thousand; the second was at the siege of Byzantium, in which the fleet of Licinius was totally routed by Crispus, the talented son of Constantine, and thirty vessels were destroyed and five thousand men were slain; the last the battle of Chrysopolis, in which Licinius lost twenty-five thousand men. Thus ended the awful contest by which Constantine was made the sole sovereign of the entire Roman Empire, which as a pagan power departed "as a scroll when it is rolled together."* The master of the world, nevertheless, could not secure domestic comfort, as he did the sceptre. There was a root of bitterness in his house which produced pestiferous fruits. Crispus was the son of a former wife and stood in the way of the three sons of the present spouse. A quarrel followed which destroyed for life the comfort of the emperor, and successively the lives of son and stepmother: and thus did exalted place in this instance, as it ever does, prove itself the twin-sister of miseries which never haunt the dwellings of virtuous obscurity.

Upon the death of Constantine, the bishop of Nicomedia produced a scroll which he alleged was executed by the emperor shortly before his death, in which he strongly asserted he had been poisoned by his brothers. This was a sufficient pretext for an indiscriminate slaughter of the Flavian family. None of the race of Constantine escaped except Gallus and Julian, two sons of his brother Constan-

---

* See Chapter V. Rev. vi. 9–17.

tius. The empire was divided between the sons of the deceased emperor: Constantine taking Constantinople, Constantius Thrace and the East, and Constans Italy, France or Gaul, and western Illyricum. The East was immediately scourged with a Persian war, the West with a wrangle between the two brothers as to their shares of their father's dominions. The adherents of Constans slew Constantine; the friends of Magnentius, now proclaimed emperor, in turn killed Constans. Constantius made preparations to destroy his adversary, and, meeting him at Mursa, a battle was fought in which the imperial arms triumphed, after the loss on both sides of one hundred thousand men. By this bloody process did Constantius obtain an empire which he had not the ability by himself to govern. Gallus, his cousin, was accordingly created a Cæsar, and commenced at Antioch an administration which was marked with cruelties that finally led to his recall and execution. The Gallic provinces were then committed to Julian.*
Relieved as the emperor thus was from a portion of the cares of government, he soon found himself involved in troubles of no ordinary character from the East. The Persian king had merely stayed the war, at the commencement of this reign, in consequence of a foreign inroad on his dominions. His own concerns being now settled, he threatened Constantius with a renewal of hostilities unless he yielded both Armenia and Mesopotamia. On the refusal of these terms, war was commenced in its most fearful form. Fire, outrage, slaughter marked the steps of the Persians, and an unusual success attended their arms from the sack of Amida to the siege of Bezabde. Nor did the presence of Constantius at the head of the army produce any change for the better. All was disaster and death. Not

---

* Zos., Bk. III.   Am. Mar., Bk. XIV.   Aug. His., Vol. III.

less than sixty thousand Romans were consigned to hopeless captivity, to say nothing of those that fell in actual service. These accumulated misfortunes might have induced the empire to conclude dishonorable terms of peace, had it not been cheered by the news of Julian's successes in the West. Young and unused to arms as was the Cæsar when placed in command, he notwithstanding displayed a coolness and courage which at once excited the confidence of his friends and the dread of his enemies. With a comparatively small force, such were his skill and perseverance that he effectually repelled all the Northern hordes, liberated twenty thousand captives, and thrice carried the Roman eagle in triumph beyond the Rhine. Nor were the victories of Julian all of which he could boast. Gaul underwent a reformation quite as important to her citizens as the conquest of their foes. The judiciary was purged, exaction was banished, personal liberty was protected, the laws rendered supreme. Popular as the career of the young hero rendered him with the masses, it kindled a flame of jealousy in the bosom of the emperor which no sense of policy could repress. Accordingly he determined to destroy the Cæsar by withdrawing his legions, under the pretext of employing them to save the fortunes of the empire in the East. Stung to the quick at parting with their general, the veteran hosts reared the standard of rebellion and proclaimed him emperor. After some ineffectual negotiation both parties prepared to settle the controversy by arms. The death of Constantius prevented the effusion of blood, and Julian was acknowledged emperor.

The preparations Julian had made to maintain his sceptre enabled him readily to assert its authority in the East. Persia was invaded, and a bitter retaliation meted to her for outrages on the Roman provinces. The arts of a traitor nevertheless defeated the wise plans of the emperor and prematurely produced his disaster and death. Jovian, the first of the domestics, was invested with the purple; a truce for thirty years concluded, and the expedition abandoned. The death of the emperor was as sudden as his elevation. Sallust, the venerable præfect, and his son were successively offered the sceptre; the father declined on account of age, the son because of youth. Valentinian was finally selected, and associated his brother Valens in the administration:* the first reserving the West as his dominion, the latter taking as his the East. Valentinian was passionate yet liberal. Valens was cowardly and proscriptive. Both did much for the cause of education, protected the empire from Persian inroads, and checked the lawless desires of Alemanni and Burgundian, of Saxon and Goth. After the death of Valentinian and the accession of his sons Gratian and Valentinian II., it was impossible to restrain the Goths, driven as they were to madness by the exactions of the Roman governors. A fearful struggle commenced, in which the armies were brought to battle near Hadrianople, where the emperor Valens was defeated and Slain. Theodosius, who was raised to the throne of the East, pursued a different course with the barbarians. Fomenting their domestic feuds, he attached some of their leaders to his interests, weakened their adversaries, and eventually prepared all for the influence of royal gold and goodness. It was not, however, for lack of courage that the emperor resorted to management. When the brother of his benefactor, Gratian, was threatened with ruin through a rebellion headed by Maximus, Theodosius collected a powerful army, gained a signal victory at Æmona, settled his friend in power, and only bore away as his

---

* Zos., Bk. IV. Am. Mar., Bks. XXX., XXXI. Dan. ii. 41–43. Ante, Chapter V.

portion of the spoils the fair sister of Valentinian, a willingly won wife. After the assassination of Valentinian the emperor of the East gained the possessions of his wife's father by a desperate battle on the plains of Aquileia.

The sons of Theodosius, on the death of their father, shared his empire:* Arcadius reigning in the East, Honorius in the West. Force and fraud had long restrained the Northern nations. The time had now arrived when they were to sweep the Western Empire from existence. But one man remained who could stay their progress, and that was the blood-stained commander Stilicho, whose life was soon destroyed, as his influence with the emperor was totally undermined. The fall and death of this personage was the signal for action with the barbarians. Alaric, their leader, marshalled his myriad multitudes, which poured down like an avalanche on Rome. Reduced to the lowest condition, starved and sick, the citizens procured the withdrawal of their enemies by the payment of five thousand pieces of gold, thirty thousand pounds of silver, four thousand robes of silk, three thousand pieces of fine scarlet cloth, and three thousandweight of pepper. Under the pretence of procuring a permanent peace, the artful Alaric hovered about in the plains of Tuscany. Satisfied with no proposition, as soon as the season allowed he again invested Rome. Without hope from Honorius, and expecting relief from a new sovereign, the people elevated Attalus. The siege was raised; it was, however, but for a moment. Attalus was quickly despoiled of the purple; Honorius, re-enforced and safe at Ravenna, bid defiance to his enemies. Alaric again fell

---

*Zos., Bks. V., VI. Pro. Van. War, Bk. I. Aug. Hist. in loc. Rev. viii. 11, 12.

on Rome, entered the Salarian gate at the dead of night by the treason of slaves, and for six days his forces pillaged at will, sparing nothing but the temples. The death of the Gothic chief and the accession of his kinsman Adolphus restored peace; yet the Empire in the West had received a mortal blow. Like a girdled tree it had still life in the roots, which might germinate; but the boughs and foliage could bloom no more forever.

On the death of Honorius his widow Placida became regent for his son Valentinian III., who was too young to hold the sceptre. A bloody struggle followed between her generals, Ætius and Boniface, which resulted in the dismemberment of Africa and the settlement of the Vandals in that country. Pretending to believe there existed an agreement between the Eastern and Western Empires to regain Africa, Genseric, the leader of the Vandals, incited Attila, king of the Huns, to an attack on both empires.* It was a desolating and barbarous war, which was terminated by the dreadful battle of Chalons (A.D. 451). Shortly after Ætius had conquered the barbarians, Valentinian, in a passion, slew him. In turn the emperor was despatched by the domestics of the general. Maximus was declared emperor. This brutal cruelty to the widow of the murdered monarch forced her in despair to call on the Vandals for aid. Landing quickly on the shores of Italy, they subjected Rome to a sack which far exceeded in enormity that of the Goths. Rid of their oppressors, the Romans raised Avitus to the purple. This transient and feeble reign gave place to that of the manly Majorian, whose vigorous efforts at general reformation, resistance of the barbarians, and the recaption of Africa were not appreciated by his effeminate countrymen. A treaty with the

---

* Jornandes' Goth. Hist., ch. xxxiv.-1.

East, to restrain the Vandals, placed Anthemius on the throne, from which Libius Severus was hurled. The failure of this scheme forced him to yield the sceptre to Olybius, the favorite of the Gothic Count Ricimer, who was now at the head of the barbarian band that again humbled the pride of Rome. Death removing both, Julius Nepos held the sceptre, under the auspices of the East, till it was snatched from him by the hovering hordes of barbarians under the promptings of the traitor Orestes. Romulus Augustulus was the pageant set up by these freebooters. Odoacer promised more plunder, received the crown, was acknowledged king of Italy by the East, and reigned in quiet up the time (A.D. 493) that Theodoric established the kingdom of the Ostrogoths.*

The ten races of people or nations existing in Europe at the overthrow of the Roman power in the West were the same as ultimately composed the Empire of the Franks.† Before entering on this history, the affairs of the East claim attention.

CHAPTER VIII.

THE EMPIRE OF THE ROMANS TO ITS EXTINCTION IN THE EAST BY THE OTTOMANS.

ARCADIUS died at an early age.‡ The regency was devolved on his sister Pulcheria during the minority of her brother Theodosius. On the death of the prince,

---

* Pro. Goth. War, Bk. I. ch. i., ii. Rev. viii.
† Malte-Brun., Bk. XCVI.
‡ Aug. His. in loc., Vol. IV. New. Dis., 18.

the sister took the sceptre. Marcian, a senator of sixty years of age, became the husband of the queen, and administered the government with ability. A revolution would have determined the succession on the death of the emperor, had not the influence of one great family been sufficient to secure it for their chief steward. Thus was Leo raised to the throne. Many years were spent in fruitless efforts to regain the West. Dying without issue and his infant grandson of the same name not long surviving, Basiliscus, the brother-in-law of Leo, obtained the throne. A change in the sentiments of court-circles quickly expelled the monarch and put in his place Zeno, the son-in-law of Leo. Barbarian inroads and civil feuds distracted the reign. The widow of Zeno married Anastasius, on whose death Justin, the commander of the guards, at an advanced age obtained the purple. Grossly ignorant of even the rudiments of learning, the sovereign managed to conduct public affairs through the talents of his nephew Justinian, who was invested with royalty four months before his uncle's death. The hopes which the Eastern court had long entertained in regard to the Western possessions were fully realized in this reign.[*] Gelimer, the Vandal king, was led a captive to Constantinople by Belisarius, and Africa completely reduced. The Goths shared a similar fate in Italy. The heir to the throne of Theodoric was his infant grandson. Offended at the refined education which his mother was giving him, the Goths charged her with the foulest conspiracies and demanded the person of their young king. In her distress she sought the protection of Justinian. Though her life was destroyed, the forces of the emperor under Belisarius invaded Italy, captured Naples, and taking possession of Rome, held it with

---

[*] Pro. Wars.

an army of five thousand in despite of one hundred and fifty thousand Gothic assailants. Notwithstanding the jealousies created by Narses, a new favorite of the emperor, and the irruption of the Lombards, the Romans reduced the kingdom of the Goths to the walls of Ravenna, which fell before the arms of Belisarius. Merit is not the sole motive that prompts the favors of rulers. There is often an undercurrent set in motion by sinister agents that regulates the affairs of states. Belisarius was the conqueror of Italy, but he was recalled without fault and Narses advanced to his honors. The Goths were not insensible of the change, and, rallying under Totila, recovered many of their lost holds and pitched their camp near Rome. All eyes were turned to Belisarius, who was reinvested with the command, forced his way into Rome, and maintained the imperial supremacy by three hard-fought battles. Again the hoary veteran was robbed of the reward of his labors, and spent the remainder of his days in obscurity, while Narses enjoyed the royal favor in the government of Italy. Justinian survived Belisarius only eight months. Justin II., a nephew of Justinian, was elected emperor by the senate.* Unfit from the loss of health for the discharge of public duties, the emperor chose as his associate Tiberius, the chief of the guards. Throughout his reign Tiberius strove to imitate the virtues of the Antonines. On his deathbed the emperor bestowed his purple and his daughter on Maurice, who reigned twenty years a pattern of reason and virtue. The conflict between the power of the empire and the progress of the Lombards in Italy, as well as the old factions of the Greens and Blues, embarrassed the court. Phocas, elevated by the soldiery, espoused the cause of the Greens, created sedition over the

---

* Aug. His. in loc., Vol. IV.

city, and procured the death of Maurice and all his family. Power won by such heartless cruelty could not long be retained. Heraclius, son of the African exarch, soon landed, expelled the tyrant, and received the sceptre. War raged in the East at the accession of the emperor, and for twelve years his efforts to suppress it were fruitless. From this cause, as well as from the stealthy attack of the Scythians on the capital, the emperor was reduced to despair, and tried the clemency of Chosroes, king of Persia. "When the emperor abjures his crucified god and embraces the worship of the sun, I will give him peace," was the infidel's profane reply. Six' years war moderated this wicked demand to a tribute from the empire annually of a thousand talents of gold, as many talents of silver, a thousand silk robes, a thousand horses, and a thousand virgins. Heraclius, gathering energy from despair, before the first instalment was due pitched his camp near the spot where Alexander vanquished Darius. The Persian army was defeated, and in three years the Romans triumphed beyond the Tigris. Determined to regain his power, the Persian levied a large army, but was utterly frustrated by the arts and arms of the emperor. Again did Chosroes rally. A bloody battle at Nineveh sealed his doom, and settled the war for the remainder of the reign. By the will of Heraclius his sons were declared heirs of the empire. Constantine, the eldest, was believed to have been murdered by his stepmother.* She and her son were debarred from power, and Constans II. and Theodosius, the children of the despatched monarch, raised to the throne. The former slew his brother and was himself killed by his domestics; and his eldest son, Constantine IV., received the purple. Justinian II. was the son and suc-

---

* Aug. His. in loc., Vol. IV.

cessor of the last monarch. Cold-blooded villainy expelled him from a throne which though he regained by an alliance with the Tartars, he was eventually compelled to yield to his rival, Philippicus. Two years brought Anastaaius II. to the sceptre: a less time Theodosius III., and not much longer Leo III. Theological disputes in regard to the use of images in divine worship agitated this and the reign of Constantine V. Leo IV. was the son of the last emperor. He did little else than fix the succession of his son Constantine. Severity to the Armenian guards and domestic strifes destroyed the emperor and transferred his crown to his mother Irene. Nicephorus, the royal treasurer, subverted the queen, seized her throne, and being shortly afterwards slain in a Bulgarian war, his son Saturacius obtained a palace, from which he was quickly expelled by the arts of his kinsman Michael. Leo V. supplanted the emperor, and was overthrown himself by Michael the Stammerer, who in a few years left his throne to Theophilus; after whom was Michael, the last of the Isaurian dynasty. Vice so belittles its subject that he becomes an easy prey to his assailant. Michael was debauched and despotic, and Basil the Macedonian was not only protected in destroying him, but was rewarded with a crown. The reign of Basil was glorious; he repelled the Saracens, restored the finances, and reformed the laws. After a reign of near twenty years he was succeeded by his sons Leo and Alexander. Constantine, the son of the former, and his mother Zoe eventually came to the throne. A regency, with its crimes and cruelties, distracted the nation for years. Romanus got the sceptre by causing his father Constantine to be poisoned. A swift retribution followed. His guilty widow Theophano married Nicephorus Phocas, whom she sacrificed to please her gallant John Zimisces. Secure in power, John banished the murderess of three kings. Still the emperor was little better than his abandoned wife, and, though brave and successful against the Saracens, he was murdered for his oppressions by the domestics of the palace. The children of Romanus, Basil and Constantine, enjoyed a transient power. Zoe, the daughter of the latter, was married, by order of council, to Romanus Argyrus, now elevated to the throne. The queen poisoned her husband and put in his place Michael the chamberlain.

An unchaste woman is as fickle as she is treacherous. Michael, the nephew, soon enjoyed the smile of Zoe and the throne of his uncle, but lost both by his ingratitude and cruelty. The death of Zoe and her husband Constantine X. cast the sceptre on her sister Theodora, who before her death nominated Michael VI., who closed the Basilian dynasty. Isaac Comnenus was chosen emperor; bad health compelling his abdication, Constantine Ducas assumed power for the purpose of securing it to his sons. The marriage of the widow, however, with Romanus Diogenes expelled the sons of the deceased king and raised the new husband to the throne. The emperor was overpowered by the Turks and his sceptre finally fell into the hands of Nicephorus, who was at last forced to yield to the popularity of his general Alexius, the son of John Comnenus. During a long reign Alexius repelled the Normans on the West, the Turks on the East, and maintaining his authority at home, left his sceptre to his son John, whose life was no less heroically spent than that of his father. Manuel, the brother of the last emperor, heired the throne and did not disgrace the dynasty. On the death of Manuel, his minor son Alexius and his mother were left in power. Andronicus, a son of Isaac Comnenus, taking advantage of the times, seized the crown and slew Alexius and his mother. Determined to sate his vengeance on his adversaries, he condemned to death Isaac Angelus, a descendant of Alexius I. The emperor's cruelties reacted on himself. Isaac fled to the temple from the executioner; was proclaimed emperor; and committed Andronicus to torture and death. Isaac's power vanished before the ambition of his brother Alexius, who was rapidly followed by Alexius, son of Isaac II.; whose title was overruled by a popular election that elevated Alexius Ducas.

Upon the promise of submitting the Eastern to the Romish Church and the payment of two hundred thousand marks of silver, Alexius IV. procured the aid of the leaders of the fourth crusade.* A sharp contest ensued, in which Ducas being overpowered, fled, and Isaac and his son Alexius were proclaimed emperors. Fear induced the emperors to desire the stay of the Latins for one year. Before that time arrived, Isaac became jealous of his son and the people of the strangers. Alexius was deserted by citizens and allies, and both he and his father were put to death. Ducas was again invested with the purple. The Latins demanded fifty thousand pounds of gold and submission to the Roman see; which being refused, they commenced operations and reduced the city. The victors settled among themselves the division of the spoils. Over one fourth of the Eastern Empire was retained for the emperor, the balance divided among the French and Venetians. Baldwin Count of Flanders was finally elected emperor, Ducas slain, and Alexius III. exiled. The emperor shortly afterwards was overpowered in a Bulgarian war, and his brother Henry became monarch. On his death the title fell to Peter of Courtenay, his brother-in-law. Attempting to recover Durazzo, he was taken prisoner and died.

---

* See Chapter XI., after. Aug. His., Vol. VI. pp. 271, 689; Vol. VII. pp. 430, 526. Malte-Brun's Geo., Vol. IV. Bk. XCVI. pp. 44–56.

Robert, the son of Peter, ascended the throne, and by his mismanagement lost the Asiatic provinces, and by his vices lost his life. John of Brienne, though on the throne merely until Baldwin, the son of Peter, should come to age, proved himself a hero. Michael Palæologus, king of Epirus, however, succeeded in expelling Baldwin and the Latin succession of emperors, as well as in establishing his own authority. Andronicus, his son, followed him on the throne ; but was supplanted by his grandson Andronicus, whose vices carried him off when his son John was only nine years old. The regency was imposed on John Cantacazune, who strengthened his power by the aid of the Turks, but in the end was compelled to yield to his ward. A bitter and protracted altercation occurred between the emperor and his son Andronicus, in which they were successively raised to the sceptre and finally settled the matter by John and his son Manuel taking the capital and Andronicus all the rest of the empire. Manuel succeeded during his reign in keeping the Ottomans at bay by a boast of his ability to procure help from the West. Constantine Palæologus, his brother, was not so fortunate. The first act of rebellion on the part of the Ottomans was in refusing the tribute ; the next in the erection of a fortress on the European side of the Bosphorus, about five miles from the capital. The emperor remonstrated, the sultan threatened ; negotiations were unavailing ; Constantinople was invested by sea and by land, and in fifty-three days fell into the hands of the Ottomans.

CHAPTER IX.

THE CONDITION OF THE EMPIRE OF THE ROMANS FROM THE AGE OF AUGUSTUS CÆSAR TO ITS OVERTHROW BY THE OTTOMANS.

The Empire of the Romans at its most prosperous period embraced Spain, Gaul, Britain, Italy, Rhætia, Noricum, Pannonia, Dalmatia, Mœsia, Dacia, Thrace, Macedonia, Greece, Asia Minor, Syria, Phœnicia, Palestine, Egypt, Africa, and the islands of the Mediterranean.* In breadth from the wall of Antoninus and the northern limits of Dacia to Mount Atlas and the tropic of Cancer it was nearly two thousand miles, and in length from the Atlantic to the Euphrates upwards of three thousand miles, and contained a population of one hundred and twenty millions. This widely extended dominion was preserved in a state of subordination by an army consisting of thirty legions, distributed throughout the provinces: three in Britain, on the Danube and Rhine sixteen, upon the Euphrates eight, and one each to Egypt, Africa, and Spain.† A legion consisted of a body of infantry, cavalry, light-armed troops called auxiliaries, besides the various attendants on baggage. The infantry, which constituted the strength of the legion, was divided into ten cohorts and fifty-five companies. Each of the former was commanded by a tribune, and each of the latter by a centurion. The first cohort, upon which devolved the honor of carrying the eagle, contained eleven hundred and five soldiers of the most approved character.

---

* Butler's Geo. Clas. Pol., Bk. VI. ex.
† Vegetius, B. II. ch. iv.   Jos. Bel., B. III. ch. v.

Each of the other cohorts numbered five hundred and fifty-five men. The arms of the soldiers were a helmet with a lofty crest, a breastplate or coat of mail, greaves for their legs, and on their left arm a buckler four feet in length and two and a half in breadth, formed of light wood covered with bull's hide and strengthened with plates of brass. The most effective weapon was a heavy spear, about six feet long, which terminated in a triangular point of steel eighteen inches in length. A short two-edged sword was used in close contest. The legion, when drawn up in battle array, stood eight deep, leaving a distance of three feet between the ranks, so that ample room was afforded for every description of military movements. A body of cavalry consisting of ten troops was assigned to each legion. The first, numbering one hundred and thirty-two men, was attached to the first cohort, and the others, consisting each of sixty-six men, were appointed respectively to the remaining nine cohorts. A helmet, an oblong shield, light boots, and a coat of mail arrayed the person of each horseman, and his action was made desperately effective upon the enemy either by a javelin or a broadsword. The auxiliaries and attendants increased the total number of the imperial legion to twelve thousand. Ten engines of the larger and fifty-five of the smaller size were assigned to each legion for the purpose of assaults on walls, towers, and forts.

The construction of a Roman camp is worthy of consideration. The spot where it was to be cast being cleared by the pioneers, the tents were pitched on either sides of broad streets, towering above which, in the centre, were erected the quarters of the general. The whole of the square occupied seven hundred yards, and was surrounded by a rampart twelve feet high, formed of wood and earth, encircled by a ditch as many feet broad. Extensive as these preparations were, no sooner was the camp ordered to be left than all the tents were struck with incredible celerity. The empire did not consider the strength of its military establishment to consist in its numbers. The strictest discipline was constantly enforced. Every mode of trial was practised which could fit the soldier for the toils of a campaign or the dangers of a battle. This course was pursued in peace and in war. A field of battle differed from a field of exercise only by the effusion of blood. The naval preparations were not very extensive, being suggested and limited almost entirely by the desire to suppress piratical outrage and to preserve the commerce of the Mediterranean. Competent fleets were placed at Ravenna on the Adriatic, at Misenum in the Bay of Naples, at Fregus on the coast of Provence, on the Euxine, upon the sea between Gaul and Britain, and upon the Rhine and Danube.

The scheme of government established by Augustus Cæsar was an absolute monarchy, disguised by the forms of a commonwealth.* By craft and cunning the subtle tyrant united in his person the consular and tribunitian powers, and modelled the senate according to his own will. Securing an unexampled popularity with the army, the emperor governed the Roman world by himself and his submissive lieutenants. The revenues were placed upon a new basis. In addition to the income from the provinces, which was not far short of twenty millions of pounds sterling, three new and distinct modes of taxation were created; one falling on commerce, another on sales in markets or by auction, and the last on legacies and inheritances.

The age of the Antonines abounded sufficiently in mild laws and useful arts to have reconciled, if not to have attached, the people to the sway of the emperors. The invid-

---

* Aug. His. in loc. Tac. Arn. 13. 31,

ious distinction which formerly existed between the citizens of Rome and Italy was now succeeded by the liberal policy of admitting the inhabitants of the latter to the freedom of the imperial city. The conquests of the empire were also elevated by royal grants of distinguished privileges.* The benignity of imperial power was extended to that large and depressed portion of society which by the accidents of battle or birth had fallen into a state of slavery. The oppressions to which this unfortunate class of beings had been long subject were mitigated in the reigns of Hadrian and the Antonines by taking the power of life and death from the hands of the master and vesting it in the magistrates, by abolishing subterraneous prisons, and by directing, upon a complaint of intolerable treatment, the slave to be delivered from bonds or to be transferred to a less cruel master. A process of manumission was also enacted. The slave, however, was not permitted to acquire any other than the rights of a denizen by his liberation; being cautiously excluded from all civil or military honors. The marks of a servile origin were not obliterated until the third or fourth generation.

The state of the arts is presented by the existence at Rome of the Coliseum, the baths of Titus, the Claudian portico, the temples dedicated to the goddess of peace and the genius of the capital, to say nothing of the curious library attached to the former, and the forum of Trajan, the column of which has withstood the ravages of time. The same spirit for elegant improvement pervaded the provinces, and, supplied with ample incentive by royal munificence, amphitheatres, temples, porticos, triumphal arches, baths, and aqueducts were constructed in every part of the empire. Besides the eleven hundred and ninety-

---

* Tac. An., 11, 23, 24. Aug. His. in loc.

seven cities of Italy, the attention is attracted by the splendor of Verona, Padua, Milan, Ravenna, as well as by the increasing greatness of York, Bath, London, in Britain, and the twelve hundred Gallic cities of the southern provinces alone, all of which imitated the elegance of the common capital. Nor were the three hundred and sixty cities of Spain, the three hundred of Africa, and the five hundred of Asia to be considered as holding an inferior rank, since among them all were to be found the clearest evidences of advancement in art and science. These cities were all connected with each other and the capital by public highways formed of the most durable materials, by means of which intelligence of every description was conveyed from and to the most distant parts of the empire by regular posts established under imperial authority. Opportunity for similar intercourse was also presented by sea. Italy, though destitute of safe harbors, was by industry and skill made to abound in them. An instance of this is presented in the formation of the port of Ostia, situate at the mouth of the Tiber. A comparatively perfect navigation being opened, a brisk interchange in the various articles of agriculture and manufacture was created. A desire for luxuries was enkindled, which was amply gratified by means of ships which brought the products of India to Myos-Hermos, a port of Egypt on the Red Sea, and thence they were conveyed by land to Alexandria for distribution among the provinces or in the capital.

The division of power was not the most important change introduced in the reign of Diocletian.* The royal residences of the emperors were removed from Rome: that of Diocletian to Nicomedia; that of Maximian to Milan:

---

* Aug. His. Dioc. Zos., Bk. II. Notitia Dignitatum, at the end of Theodosian Code. Gib. Decline and Fall, ch. xvii.

which was a fatal blow to the exemptions the people of Rome and Italy had enjoyed, the sway of the guards and the power of the senators. The ministers now became the principal advisers of the emperors. Thus delivered from the restraints of the senate, the emperors possessed all the prerogatives of the most absolute kings. In order to establish firmly these new assumptions of authority the pomp of a Persian court was introduced. Such was the state of affairs when Constantine came to the possession of the sceptre and fixed his capital at Constantinople. The changes made by him were rather those suggested by prudential considerations than by a spirit of innovation. The magistracy were subjected to three divisions: the illustrious, the respectable, and the honorable. The last was composed of such as were possessed of senatorial dignity; the respectable included all those who were entitled to a superior rank; and the illustrious consisted of persons preeminent for their stations who were obeyed or venerated by the two subordinate classes. The consuls and patricians, the prætorian præfects, with the præfects of Rome and Constantinople, the masters-general of cavalry and infantry, and the seven ministers of the palace, were embraced in this division. The first two were possessed of a rank more connected with honor than power. The præfects, after the destruction of the prætorian guards, were elevated to civil jurisdiction. The military and civil administration being thus separated, the generals of cavalry and infantry were created. The seven ministers of the palace consisted of a chamberlain, whose duty it was to attend the emperor in his hours of state or amusement; of the master of offices, upon whom devolved the administration of public affairs; of the quæstor, whose province it was to form and deliver the imperial edicts; of the public and private treasurers, whose names indicate their duties; and of the two counts of the domestics, under whose control respectively were placed the bands of cavalry and infantry which guarded the person of the sovereign. The communication between the new capital, to which Constantine had given his name, and the various parts of the empire was facilitated by the construction of roads and the institution of posts. For the more speedy transmission of royal messages two or three hundred agents were employed. The expenses of the government were immense. In addition to the excise and customs, a direct tax was laid on the landed interest of the citizen. Surveyors were sent into all the provinces, who measured the lands, reported their quality, and estimated their value from the average produce of five years. The number of slaves and cattle were also returned. The proprietor was bound upon oath to make a full disclosure of his affairs; elusion or prevarication was treated as a capital crime. A large proportion of the tribute was paid in current gold coin; the balance was discharged by delivering to the commissioners of the revenue articles of produce in such quantities as the annual indication of the emperor determined. The tax on trade was collected by a mode excessively severe. Without regard to the ability of the debtor, his person was considered as the representative of the property assessed, and was liable to imprisonment, although deprived of his valuables, after the imposition was made, by means beyond his control. Another source of income was from an exaction denominated the coronary gold. Originally this was a voluntary offering made by the allies of the republic in gratitude for protection or deliverance consequent upon the Roman arms, or by the cities of Italy to grace the triumph of a victorious general. But eventually it became an exaction, and was so considerable as to amount from Rome alone to the sum of sixteen hundred pounds of gold, which was nearly equal to sixty-four thousand pounds sterling. The occasion upon which it was demanded now ceased to be that of a triumph, and arose whenever the emperor announced his accession, consulship, birth of a son, the creation of a Cæsar, a victory over the barbarians, or any other great event.

Without giving the details of the time or cause of Constantine's conversion, suffice it to say, after his victory over Licinius he immediately distributed letters throughout the empire in which he exhorted his subjects to pursue the example of their sovereign in embracing the sacred truths of Christianity. The sincerity of this profession was evinced in the subsequent conduct of the sovereign. Desirous to bring the entire force of imperial influence to bear upon the object of its adoption, he eventually established the Christian Church in the full enjoyment of its rites and ceremonies, as well as in the possession of a competent share of property; while he elevated to the most distinguished posts of honor and emolument her professed sons and disciples. A change so important naturally suggests a reflection upon the previous condition of the Christians. It was not long after the ascension of their Divine Master that his followers were pursued with malignant cruelty by the emperors. Considering the sentiments and morals inculcated by Christianity, as well as the vaunted liberality of polytheism, it is hard to find any reason for this conduct independent of the conclusions of ignorance, the promptings of prejudice, and the pride of power. The flame of persecution was first lighted by Nero, who, charging upon the Christians the crime of having fired the capital, inflicted on their persons the most severe punishments his native cruelty could invent. This, however, was confined to Rome alone. A more extensive scheme of operation was reserved for the time of Trajan, who in his directions to Pliny nicely graduates the amount of evidence necessary to fasten upon individuals the offence of Christianity, and suggests the punishment. A similar policy was pursued by Severus towards the close of his reign. The distracted Church then enjoyed peace until the reign of Decius, who during his short sway waged against it a war of extermination. Valerian followed his footsteps; but under Gallienus commenced a period of quiet which continued for the space of forty years. The scene was changed by the edict of Diocletian. Persecution raged with unexampled severity throughout the western provinces, Italy, Africa, Illyricum, and the East. It is impossible to ascertain with certainty the number that suffered during these perilous times; yet it must have been considerable, even admitting the obscure and contradictory accounts of contemporary historians. Convinced at last of the folly of attempting to force men's consciences on the subject of religion, Galerius, the worst of persecutors, proclaimed a toleration which was never materially invaded by imperial authority.*

Reversing the course of his father, Constantius bestowed the royal favors on Arius and his followers. The great advocate of orthodoxy became the object of the emperor's vengeance, and, thrice exiled from his see, the bold, intrepid, and incorruptible Athanasius sought and obtained a home among the hospitable Trinitarians of the West. The aversion of Constantius would appear to have been more vindictive against polytheism than was that of his father. There is still preserved a royal edict which inflicted upon the misguided votaries of this system the punishment of death, and the confiscation of their goods to the public use after their execution. If the emperor's object was to enlighten the

---

*Tac. An., 15, 38–44. Mos. Ch. His., 1st to 4th cent. Sozomen, Bk. III. ch. xviii. Rev. vi. 12–17. Eusebius, Ch. His. Gib. Decline and Fall, in loc.

minds of this portion of his benighted subjects, the principles of our Lord Jesus Christ would have taught that the course he pursued was calculated to thwart his purpose and promote the triumph of his apostate kinsman. The accession of Julian opened a new scene to the empire.*
Though educated in the principles of Christianity, he subsequently adopted the maxims of Grecian philosophy. The native enthusiasm of his mind, the perilous circumstances of his life, and the unbroken succession of good fortunes which had crowned his career previous to his imperial elevation, infused into his character an unhappy inclination to disregard the ordinary proprieties in dress and living. Still the impartial mind has the amplest reason for approbation in considering the wise regulations which the emperor established when he came into possession of the royal household. The numerous and useless trains of domestics and dependants which had accumulated in the palace at Constantinople, for no other purpose than to enjoy a princely grandeur by administering to imperial wants which they created, were at once deprived of their ignominious occupations and immense revenues. The avowed attachment of Julian to pagan superstition induced its votaries to hope he would pursue a similar policy to that of Galerius. They were, however, disappointed. Either craft or humanity inclined the emperor to the wiser course of a toleration of all forms of religion. Nevertheless the patronage of the court was enjoyed exclusively by the ancient superstition. The temples of polytheism were thrown open, its worshippers emboldened by honors and rewards, and its altars drenched with the blood of sacrifice. The palace and its gardens were filled with the statues of gods, while the emperor manifested his devotion by blowing the

---

* Sozomen, Bk. V. ch. ii. Am. Mar., Bks. XXII., XXIII.

fire, bringing the wood, and slaughtering the victims at the altar in the presence of priests and people. Determined to re-establish a declining religion, Julian attacked the Christian cause in a learned dissertation which was disseminated throughout the empire, excluded Christians from teaching grammar and rhetoric, interdicted them from all public offices, and to afford a practical proof of the falsity of their faith he made a powerful effort to rebuild the temple at Jerusalem and to restore the Jews to the Holy Land, their dispersion being conclusive evidence of the truth of prophecy. The bold enterprise was not sufficient to sustain a cause whose claims to credence had already proved insufficient with the discriminating and serious. A signal overthrow was connected with the work at Jerusalem, which indicated the power and presence of God too clearly to be denied.* Its announcement filled every Christian heart with honest joy, and produced in every pagan bosom the involuntary conviction of the utter hopelessness of polytheism. Contrary to expectation, the reign of Jovian brought universal toleration, which even the tyranny of Valentinian did not assume to interrupt, though the weakness of Valens led him to display his partiality for the sect of Arians by persecuting the orthodox. The choice of Gratian determined the fate of the two great sects which divided the faith and fears of Christendom. The downfall of both Arianism and pagan superstition properly dates from the time of the first Theodosius.

The increasing power of the barbarians and the influence of luxury occasioned a general relaxation of military discipline, as well as an universal corruption of manners.† A supersti-

---

*Am. Mar., Bk. XXIII. ch. i. Rev. vi.
† Mos. Ch. Hist., 4th to 12th cent. Aug. Hist., Theod. Ar. Hon. Rev. xiii. 2 Thes. ii. 1–12. New. Dis., 17–23.

tion more flagrant than that of paganism was introduced into the Roman world in the reign of Arcadius and Honorius. Martyrs, both fabulous and real, became the objects of homage; the relics of saints were carefully collected, sacredly preserved, and sincerely venerated. The policy of the now corrupted churchmen was to engage the attention of those whose prepossessions were in favor of the splendid display of paganism by an accurate assimilation of Christian worship to the forms of the ancient temples. Shrewd and fortunate as was this movement, candor must compel the confession that it involved Christianity in a condition equally destructive to its purity and pristine simplicity. Thus committed, its professors were under a sort of necessity to continue their appeals to the favor and their courtesies to the prejudices of a corrupted age. This step must be regarded as rather the legitimate result of gradual defection than the motion of temporary expediency. The time of its occurrence was in a generation ripened by a succession of events for the reign of a debasing superstition. The monastic life, which had taken its rise more than a century previous in Egypt, proved itself a potent instrument in the full development of this era. Under the favor of ecclesiastics an extensive degree of popularity had been given to it, and in the course of events an ignorant and credulous age had been disposed to look on it as the surest passport to divine favor and a certain cure for those evils which the want of true piety rendered intolerable. Lured by motives of this description, an immense number of persons forsook the active duties of life to find a shelter and a home within the walls of a monastery. Though composed of individuals from every class of society, the tenants of these abodes were subjected to the strictest rules of government. Their dress, their diet, their labor, and even their devotions were so regulated as to secure a character for unparalleled sanctity. The visions of these enthusiasts soon came to be regarded as inspiration. The power of working miracles was attributed to them. The gratitude of a credulous world daily increased their authority and possessions, until the last remnants of science were swept from the distracted empire, and the word of God, as contained in the Sacred Scriptures, ceased to be the rule of faith and practice to the church. Such an overgrown power was a convenient refuge for Justinian when his profusions and oppressions had weaned from him the hearts of his subjects. Hence his absorbing object was to secure the interest and affection of the clergy. Splendid temples were erected to flatter their pride, to further their devotions, and to fasten their power upon the community. The laws themselves were made subservient to this end, and no inconsiderable portion of that system of jurisprudence which it is the honor and glory of Justinian to have established carefully provides for the rights, marks out the jurisdiction, and secures the emoluments of the Church.*

The Christian Church was rent asunder in the forepart of the eighth century by conflicting opinions among its members as to the use of images in divine worship.† The emperor, Leo III., excluded them from the services of the sanctuary. Gregory, the bishop of Rome, refused to comply with the decree. The rebellion of the pontiff exposed him at once to the indignation of the emperor and the cupidity of the Lombards. Thinking to avert the former, he plotted the destruction of the latter by uniting

---

* Procopius de Edif.
† Rus. Mod. Eu., p. 36. Diac., Bk. VI. Kol. Ger., ch. xvi., xvii. Aug. Hist., Vol. V. ch. lxxxix.-xcii. New. Dis., 14, 22, 23. Malte-Brun, Bk. CXXXV. 1 Tim. iv. 2, 3. Rev. xiii.

with the Venetians against them. Though successful by this means in restoring Ravenna to the emperor, he failed in regaining his favor. The new exarch was therefore directed to enforce the decree against the use of images in divine worship, and to procure the seizure or asasssination of Gregory's person. The harshness of the order rendered the people of Rome obstinate in their idolatry, and their rebellion elevated a priest to temporal powers which the arms of Charles Martel, Pepin, his successors, and the sword of Charlemagne found it profitable to maintain. Thus originated the popedom, the sources of whose power in all subsequent times were the cunning of its clergy, the despotism of its chief, the splendor of its temple-service, and the suppleness of its ethics. By corrupt leagues with princes, whose titles to their sceptres were weak, it has enslaved nations, "spoken great things and blasphemies, done great wonders," and killed those that disputed its authority (Rev. xviii. 5, 13, 14). In its train followed superstition, with all its mystic mummeries. The height of its dominion was the depth of human degradation. Its present state affords no idea of what it was at that period. The Reformation, which sprang from the bosom of papal power and was begotten by its errors and exactions, breaking the charm of its influence, intellectual emancipation and evangelical enlightenment spread throughout the world and elevated the condition of the people of every land, papal, Protestant, and pagan, to the existing standard of perfection.

The voluptuous Roman, though able at an exorbitant price to number among his luxuries the article of silk, was until the reign of Justinian compelled to procure it from the distant regions of India. At this period, by imperial efforts, the rearing of the worm and the fabrication of the article commenced within the empire.* Its progress to perfection was of course slow. The emperor having secured the favor of the Ethiopians of Abyssinia by treaty, procured their instrumentality in obtaining the eggs from whence the worm could be raised. The easy virtue of these traders suggested to them a plan of accomplishing the object of their royal patron. Having entered India with an apparently amicable intention, they succeeded in concealing the eggs of the worm in a hollow cane and bore back in triumph to their own land the long-sought prize. The eggs were hatched in the course of time by the artificial heat of dung; the worms were fed upon the leaves of the mulberry; butterflies enough to propagate the race were secured, and a sufficient number of trees were planted to provide nourishment for the rising race. Thus Justinian obtained the means of at once administering to his own avarice and the vitiated taste of his subjects. Notwithstanding, the government was unpopular and the citizens were rent asunder by the distractions of contending parties. Either the matrimonial or ministerial connections of the sovereign had induced him to depart from the strict economy of some of his immediate predecessors. To sustain the magnificence of this estate and to support the profitless wars in which the empire was involved, resort was made to the most burdensome taxes. Upon the farmer was imposed the annona, or supply of corn for the capital and army, which was graduated in its amount according to the wants of the needy monarch. The orial tribute, which was levied on the prætorian præfect, was no less burdensome to the people, inasmuch as the discretion of that officer dictated the source from whence it was to be collected. Monopolies in trade, the former objects of

---

* Pro. Goth. War, Bk. IV. ch. x.

Roman hatred, were also created with no sparing hand by the emperor; which, by reason of the check they gave to the competition of the industrious mechanic, served as an oppressive burden to the enterprise, ambition, and skill of the laboring classes of society. The court was the scene of a nefarious traffic in honors and offices, and the connivance of both emperor and empress to the disgraceful act is established by undoubted evidence. Yet, with the proceeds of this immense revenue, the empire beheld unpaid soldiers begging bread, and unrewarded armies wasting away amid the wars of Italy and Persia. It required the talents of a Justinian to control popular disaffections like these. Still the emperor succeeded in the perilous work, and has left to posterity two imperishable monuments of his genius: the one, the splendid edifices with which he decorated his capital; the other, the code of laws by which the rights and persons of his subjects were guarded and governed.

The devotion of Justinian to the hierarchy was faithfully imitated by his successors. During all the after-dynasties of the empire, to its very conclusion, sectarian dogmas divided and distracted the state. Princes lost or gained the sceptre as they happened to adhere to the unpopular or side with the ascendant party. The long, angry, and fluctuating controversy about the use of images in divine worship which poured its bitter streams throughout the empire served to illustrate the extent of ecclesiastical influence, to display the weakness as well as the wickedness of our common nature, to sow the seeds of discord between the churches of Rome and Constantinople, and to complete the apostasy of both from the faith of Christ.

The sovereignty of the empire was measurably retrieved by the valor and talents of Heraclius. During the most fortunate of the successive dynasties the widest extent of dominion stretched from the Tigris to the neighborhood of the ancient capital; but by far the greatest portion of them extended their sway no further than from the Danube to Peloponnesus, and from Belgrade to Nice, Trebizond, and the Meander, and at times were contracted within more circumscribed limits. Thus reduced as was the empire from its former dimensions, it still contained a greater amount of population and wealth than the largest kingdom of modern Europe. Its capital was unsurpassed in the splendor of its edifices and the riches of its inhabitants. Though the Grecian superstition enervated the minds of the Byzantine citizens from the days of Justinian, they were nevertheless the most ingenious and industrious of all the nations of the earth. A lucrative trade was conducted by the mariners of the Peloponnesus, who exchanged for the gold of the capital their country's produce, fine linens and woollens, carpets and silks of the most exquisite colors. Commerce was encouraged by a law exempting all the sailors of the Peloponnesus and the workmen in parchment and purple from much taxation to which others were liable. Greece alone until the twelfth century was possessed of the worm from which silk is taken, and of the individuals who understood the rearing of the insect and the fabrication of the article. After that period this invaluable possession was transferred to Sicily, and thence introduced into the European countries. As did Greece, so did all the provinces furnish revenue to the sovereign, which was increased to an immense amount by the various sums levied on shops, taverns, markets, and foreign trade. No authority on which much reliance can be placed fixes the total of these various items, although some fair conjecture as to it may be formed by adverting to the surplus in the vaults of Basil after the discharge of national liabilities, which was no less than two hundred thousand pounds of gold, or above eight millions sterling. The discretion or caprice of the reigning monarch applied such portions of the income as were necessary to the enlargement or decoration of the royal buildings in the capital. These were constructed upon a principle of profusion vastly exceeding any precedent which Eastern luxury afforded. Gold, silver, marble, and precious gems were the materials with which the degenerate successors of Constantine beautified their royal residences. The pride which suggested such apologies for greatness naturally dictated a course of living and a train of distinctions equally unbecoming Roman emperors. Pleasure constituted the sole object of their pursuit, and to this end their summer and winter abodes were exquisitely adapted.

The princes of the blood were respectively styled Despot or Lord, Sebastocrator, Cæsar, Panhypersebastor, and Protosebastos, which were useless names that could only gratify the vanity of their gaudy possessors. The substantial functions of government were exercised by the protovestiare, who presided over the wardrobe; the logothete, the supreme guardian of the laws and revenues, assisted by the eparch or præfect of the city; the first secretary and the keepers of the privy seal, archives, and purple ink, with which the royal signature was made; the lieutenant of the great domestics, whose supervision pervaded the stables, cavalry, and hunting-train of the monarch; and the Great Duke, to whom was committed the command of the navy. To these pompous names, by which the emperor was concealed from his subjects, was added a pernicious Persian custom, first introduced by Diocletian. Whenever audience was given to any one, his costly presents being first received, he fell prostrate and kissed the feet of the emperor, who, clad in his purple buskins and glittering diadem, condescended to look on the suppliant from his massive throne, guarded as it was by roaring lions of gold. A display equally as puerile but less disgusting was presented on the stated and extraordinary processions of the monarch. These were announced by heralds the night before they took place. The streets were carefully cleansed, flowers strewed on the pavements, and silk hangings were tastefully arranged and suspended from the windows and balconies. At every convenient station the ear was greeted with the sweetest notes of the most select musicians.

The naval power of the empire was of great importance. The fleet for the reduction of Crete amounted to nearly two hundred vessels, and had on board not far from fifty thousand men. The galleys were of light structure, yet remarkably manageable, and were rendered very effective by means of the Greek fire and the control of skilful officers. Towards the period under review, the study and use of the Greek language were revived, though the emperor and people adhered to the name of Romans. Genius, however, was not awakened from its long slumber, nor was national taste aroused. The conquest of the Latins opened the sources of information to the subjects of the empire. Whether any passion but that of avarice was excited is problematical. The arts and sciences remained stationary from this period to the final destruction of the capital. The learned, though familiar with the noblest models of ancient greatness and not ignorant of the then modern attainments, were satisfied with the contemplation of the one and the report of the other, without making an effort to imitate or exceed either. Such supineness characterized all classes, even to the hour that the crescent glittered upon the walls of Constantinople and the last emperor lost more by the listlessness of his subjects than by the valor of the Ottomans.*

---

* Gib. Decline and Fall, ch. liii. Montesqieu's Rise and Fall of Rom. Emp., ch. xxii. pp. 282-5.

CHAPTER X.

THE EMPIRE OF THE SARACENS, TURKS, AND OTTOMANS FROM ITS RISE TO THE PRESENT TIMES.

ORDINARY events are often the occasion of the most astonishing results. Mohammed, of respectable parentage, declaiming unsuccessfully against the religion of Mecca, fled with a few followers to Medina, a neighboring town. As far astray from the truth as the idolaters whom they denounced, the self-constituted prophet and his companions would have now fallen into contempt had they not kindled a feud between their new protectors and their old enemies which, in the end, enabled them to subdue not only Mecca but Arabia. Thus was established the Empire of the Saracens, arising at first like "the smoke of a great furnace," and in the short space of ten years overcasting the Eastern Hemisphere. On the death of Mohammed, Ali, the husband of his daughter Fatima, must have succeeded to the sceptre but for the arts of Ayesha, his mother-in-law. Warm dissensions ensued which threatened to nip the new religion in its bud. The disinterested proposition of Omar to devolve the chiefship on Abubeker prevailing, the excitements were allayed.*
In two years Abubeker died, and Omar became khalif. Old strifes revived with renewed fury. So high were they carried that Omar fell by the dagger of an assassin, in the

---

* Elmakin's His. Sar. Em. Ockley's His. Sar. Rev. ix. 2–19. Augustan His., Vol. VII. pp. 468, 526, 683, 733. Newton's Dis., 2, 24.

tenth year of his reign. Six electors, of whom Ali was one, chose Othman, the late secretary of Mohammed, to the vacant throne. The extreme age of the khalif incapacitated him for power; his subjects becoming discontented, appealed to arms, and Othman, overpowered at Medina, fell clasping the Koran to his bosom. Popular feeling turned in favor of Ali, and he obtained a long-sought sceptre. The daring spirit of youth still swelled the bosom of the old khalif. Ample opportunity was soon presented for its display. Telha and Zobeir, two formidable chiefs, rebelled. The courage of Ali was irresistible; the enemy was defeated, the rebels were slain. No sooner was this faction crushed than a more powerful foe appeared in Moawiyah, son of Aboo Sofian, who declared himself khalif and the avenger of Othman. Ali met the usurper in the plain of Seffin, where, after a successful contest of one hundred and ten days, he would have proved victor had not his mutinous troops lost him the prize. This was but the beginning of his misfortunes. Three enthusiasts meeting in the temple of Mecca agreed that the only cure for the disorders of church and state was the destruction of Ali, Moawiyah, and Amroo his ally. Each chose his victim, poisoned his arrow, and repaired to the place of destination. None was successful save he who had plotted the death of Ali.

Moawiyah became khalif, and removed the seat of empire to Damascus. During the times of the first four khalifs the victorious arms of the Saracens extended from the deserts of Arabia to the banks of the Oxus and Indus, the shores of the Euxine and Caspian. The Nile watered their dominions; Africa, Cyprus, and Rhodes submitted to their champions. The house of Ommiyah continued almost a century in power. During this period Saracen sway was extended from the Atlantic to India; Africa and

Spain were completely subjugated; and nothing but the arm of Charles Martel prevented Europe from its grasp. Notwithstanding this extensive range of foreign conquest, the Ommiyades were never able to establish their throne in the affections of the people. The family of Mohammed were still regarded as rightfully entitled to the power of their ancestor. These consisted of two branches—the Fatimites, or the descendants of Ali by Fatima; the Abbasides, or children of Abbas, the uncle of Mohammed. The former were defective in talent; the latter were possessed of every quality that could enable them to hold the sceptre of a mighty empire. Persia soon resounded with the conflicts of the Ommiyades and Abbasides; the former displayed the white banner, the latter unfurled the black. Upon the destruction of Ibrahim, the chief of the house of Abbas, his brothers Saffah and Almanzor fled to Cufa, where Saffah was proclaimed khalif. The Ommiyade chief, Mervan II., collected a large army, and meeting the hosts of his rival on the banks of the Zab, a battle was fought which resulted in the success of the Abbasides. Mervan escaped to Egypt, and in a second engagement at Busir, on the banks of the Nile, the event was fatal to his sceptre and life. Saffah, established on the throne, detroyed all the house of Ommiyah except one youth, by name Abd-er-rahman, who fled to Africa and was afterwards elevated in Spain. The first of the Abbasides did not reign long. Almanzor, who succeeded, removed the royal residence to the banks of the Tigris, where were laid the foundations of the far-famed Bagdad (A.D. 762). Mohadi recovered the domains which the powers of Constantinople had wrested from the Saracens during the civil commotions. Haroon, at the head of a large army, dictated his own terms to Irene. In the subsequent reign of Haroon-el-Rasheed the Just, the Grecian territory was subjected to greater inroads and the treasury of Bagdad was enriched by the gold of the imperial city. Al Maroon performed no deeds of martial daring, yet his fame has proved more enduring than that of his father by reason of the encouragement he extended to scientific pursuits. Saracenic rule, however, had reached its utmost limits. Spain, Africa, Syria, were one after another dismembered. Motassem, the eighth of the house of Abbas, to fortify himself against ruin formed the plan of creating a body-guard from the warlike bands of Turks beyond the Jihon. Fifty thousand of these people were accordingly collected about the royal residence at Bagdad. On the death of Motassem they were treated with cruelty by his son Motawakkel, whom they murdered at the suggestion of his son Mostauser. The unnatural son felt the punishment of his vices in the ceaseless pangs of a chiding conscience, which soon cut short his days. Rid of their rulers, the guards bestowed the vacant throne on the weak Mosteyoo, uncle to the wicked Mostauser, merely for the purpose of obtaining the right to nominate their own commander. Completely dominant, the haughty Turks committed every outrage on the khalifs; beating them with clubs, dragging them by the feet, exposing their half-naked persons to the piercing rays of the sun. Such enormities could not fail to effect the ruin or rouse the resistance of the khalifate. The latter proved to be the result. Mohtadi Billah made an effort to regain his power. Seizing the commander of the guards, he directed him to be decapitated in the palace. As the Turks rushed round the royal dwelling, the bloody head of their chief was thrown into their midst. Enraged by the act, the veteran bands forced their way into the building and satisfied their revenge by the sacrifice of their sovereign. Intent upon the object in the accomplishment of which his brother fell a martyr, Moktader resolved to destroy his military enemies. Under the specious plea of protecting the frontiers of the empire, the guards were removed. This policy afforded a temporary relief to the royal resident of Bagdad; but the disease that preyed on his political power was incurable, and the defection of kingdom after kingdom finally eventuated in the downfall of the Saracens and the exaltation of the Turks (A.D. 1055).

Toghrul Beg, the Turkish chief, was the terror of the Romans, the conqueror of Bagdad, and the lord of all Mohammedans. Alp Arslan came to power on the death of his uncle Toghrul. The invasion of the Roman dominions was more terrific than ever; penetrating Phrygia and carrying captive Romanus Diogenes, the emperor. The passion of Malek Shah, the son and successor of Alp, sought gratification in nobler scenes than those of blood and conquest. The advancement of men of genius and the promotion of learning were the great objects of the reign. The ambition of the sovereign, however, was too exalted for the taste of his subjects. Scenes of violence ensued. The vizier was murdered, and the monarch did not long survive. The empire was shaken to its centre by the conflicts of Malek's sons. Defections were wide-spread and rapidly successive. Eventually the great irruption of the Moguls extinguished the house of Seljook (A.D. 1278). Amidst the changes consequent on these revolutions, Suleiman, one of the bravest of the Turkish tribes, with fifty thousand of his countrymen, left Khorassen, to seek a settlement in Armenia. After a stay of some years, the chief in returning home was drowned in the Euphrates, and his followers dispersed. Ortoghrul, with a portion of his father's forces, in removing from their temporary residence on the mountains of Erzeroom through the dominions of Ala-ed-deen, the sultan of Iconium, approached two armies in battle. Nobly siding with the weaker force, the fugitive chieftain turned the victory in its favor. The grateful sultan bestowed on his generous ally and his people extensive pasture-grounds in the ancient Phrygia Epictetos.* Among these valleys and mountains the Ottoman power began first to thrive under the fostering care of Osman, son of Ortoghrul, who established a kingdom in Bithynia, of which he made Prusa, at the foot of the Mysian Olympus, the capital. Orchan, the second of this line, added to his patrimony by arms much of Lesser Asia, and secured the prospects of his crown by the establishment of a corps styled janizaries. The work of the father was well applied by his son and successor Amurath, who extended the national boundaries by the conquest of Adrianople, the purchase of Hamid, and the acquisition of the larger part of Kermain by marriage. Bajazet, who inherited the sceptre, stained the commencement of his reign by the murder of his only brother; but the foulness of the act was forgotten by his subjects in the contemplation of the glory which he won at Nicopolis as the victor over the combined forces of Christian Europe. Constantinople was now the prize which fired the ambition of the Ottomans. The approach of the Tartars, under Timoor, diverted their attention (A.D. 1402). The fatal field of Angora was at once the salvation of the capital and the confusion of its enemies. The wisdom of Mohammed I., however, retrieved public affairs. Moorad II. manifested still greater capacity than his father, extending the Ottoman sway to nearly all the possessions of the Greek emperors. Mohammed II. finished the work and seized the throne of the Cæsars. Bayezeed succeeded to a sceptre which he held peacefully for thirty years, and would have enjoyed through life had

---

* Cantemir's His. of the Othman Empire. Aug. His., Vol. VII. p. 474.

not a wicked son snatched it from his grasp. The heartless Selim was a wretch of a day; yet he was the father of Suleiman, whose encouragement of learning and extent of conquest have won him the title of the magnificent and great, and under whose sway the empire of the Ottomans attained its summit (A.D. 1565). The time of declension commences from this bright period, just as the rising cloud eclipses the splendor of a meridian sun. The succeeding sultans have acted a secondary part in the affairs of the world; a detailed account, therefore, of their reigns would be prematurely anticipating the events of greater empires.

In the image of Daniel "the gold" is not more descriptive of the Assyrian, "the silver" of the Medo-Persian, "the brass" of the Grecian, "the iron" of the sole, and "the two legs partly of clay and partly of iron," of the divided supremacy of the Roman Empire, than are "the ten toes" of the ten nations or races * from which was to spring the empire that should be the chief stay of "the man of sin" and "the locusts" of that power which should sweep from existence the last remnant of the empire of the Romans in the East.† The visions of John, the victim of Cæsar, are just as remarkable as those of Daniel, the captive of Cyrus. Both in connection form a beautiful outline of human actions from the time of Ninus to the consummation of that grand scheme of divine love for the accomplishment of which God has shaped events in all ages, though in perfect harmony with human responsibility, and will continue in the same manner to control the doings of future generations until the race of Adam shall be reclaimed from the dominion of sin, and Jesus Christ, their deliverer, reign King of nations, as he is and ever has been "King of saints"!

---

* Malte-Brun's Geo. Bk. XCVI. New. Dis., 14.   † Rev. ix. 4-21.

CHAPTER XI.

THE NEUSTRIAN DIVISION OF THE EMPIRE OF THE FRANKS TO THE DEATH OF LOUIS XII.

CLOVIS destroyed the power of the Romans and Visigoths in Gaul, and founded on their ruins the Empire of the Franks.* The acquisitions of the father were divided among his four sons: Thierry took that part which lies between the Rhine and the Meuse, having Metz as its capital; Childebert was king of Paris; Clodonmir, of Orleans; Clotaire, of Soissons. Bloody dissensions ensued which resulted in the sole succession of Clotaire. A second quadruple division on the death of the king was followed by similar results. Justice and generosity exalted the character of Clotaire II. Dagobert, his son, however, disgraced and terminated his reign and life by his vices. The twelve succeeding kings were pageants; the mayors of the palace held the power. Pepin Heristal, Duke of Austrasia, ruled France for twenty-eight years. Charles Martel, descended from the deceased duke, was the idol of his country and the protector of Europe. Pepin, the son of the departed hero, became actually sovereign. Charles and Carloman were the sons of the late king. The latter died soon after his father. The former became sole sovereign. In the space of thirty years Charles extended his arms to Italy, Germany, and Spain; was universally acknowledged Emperor of the West (A.D. 800); "and gave his power and his seat and

---

* Lardner's Cabinet Cyclopædia (History: France). Vol. I. ch. i.-iv. Aug. Hist., Vol, V. in loc.

great authority" to the Roman hierarchy. His successors followed in his footsteps. In the course of time ignorance and superstition triumphed and the lights of Christianity and science were almost extinguished in Europe; the pope being considered the principle of unity to its kingdoms, a denial of which incurred death. (Rev. xiii. New., p. 546. Chapter V., ante.) Louis, the son and successor of Charlemagne, at the outset of his reign offended the clergy by attempting a reformation, and pleased his children by dividing with them his power and dominions. The wrath of the one and the ingratitude of the other followed the king through a life of care and change. The old cause of quarrel, the division of the empire, continued to agitate the reign of Lothario, who, though beaten at Fontenay, was able soon to raise an army sufficiently formidable to extort from his adversaries a treaty by which the sceptre of his father and all the countries between the Rhone and Alps, the Meuse and Rhine, fell to his lot, while his brother Charles took Aquitaine and Neustria, and his brother Louis Germany. The constitutions of Mersen shortly after confirmed the imperial sceptre to the children of Lothario. Divisions of power and dominion created contentions. Perpetual wars followed for over a century, when the Carlovingian dynasty yielded to the popularity of Hugh Capet. In eight years Robert the second of this line succeeded to the sceptre, which after a reign marked by no important events came to the possession of his son Henry I. The sway of this king was quite as inglorious as that of his father. Philip the son of Henry was a minor at his father's death. Baldwin Earl of Flanders became the guardian of the prince, discharged his duties with fidelity and, dying, left Philip at fifteen years of age in possession of the throne. The Council of Clermont distinguishes this period (A.D. 1095). The famous plan of a crusade having for its object the recovery of the Holy Land originated in this body. Peter the Hermit in his pilgrimage to "the Sepulchre" had encountered great difficulties. Europe was roused by his declamations against the Turks. The more experienced leaders were Hugh Count of Vermandois, Robert Duke of Normandy, Godfrey Prince of Brabant, and Stephen Count of Blois. Fearing that the greatness of the forces would defeat their purpose, the generals persuaded Peter, at the head of an undisciplined multitude of three hundred thousand men, to set out by land for Palestine. In the course of their journey they were almost entirely destroyed. Twenty thousand got to Constantinople. The emperor furnished them vessels to cross the Bosphorus. In Asia they were slaughtered by the Turks. (Rev. ix. 14-18.) Godfrey and his companions had better success. Nice and Antioch were taken, Jerusalem conquered, and their leader became its king. Propitious as was the commencement of the life of Philip, his subsequent days were disturbed by the contentions of the nobles. Louis VI., his son, was more fortunate. A war with England gave popularity to his rule and roused national emulation. The monarch having acquired sufficient strength to curb the ambition of the nobles, effectually accomplished this object by creating the commons and establishing courts of appeal.

An unmixed cup of calamity falls to the lot of few mortals; Louis VII., however, was one of that few. In the commencement of his reign the town of Vitri was taken and burned. Thirteen hundred persons lost their lives in a church which was fired. So deeply did the event affect the king that he made immense preparation for a crusade to the Holy Land. Defeat and the loss of his wife's affections followed in rapid succession. Philip Augustus, his son, united his arms with Richard I. of England in the holy wars which proved so calamitous to his father. Deserting his ally, he returned home and attempted designs on Britain; which in the reign of John, Richard's successor, added the continental possessions of the English to the French crown. The battle of Bouvines gave Philip a victory over the Flemish and German forces and secured his dominions for the future. Louis VIII., the son of Philip, had neither the talents nor courage of his father. He lived and died in an effort to subdue the Albigenses, a pious people in the south of France who had excited the indignation of the pope by opposing his temporal authority. His son, Louis IX., a minor twelve years old, took the crown under the regency of his mother, Blanche of Castile. When possessed of power the king prepared to enter the wars of Palestine. On arriving in Egypt, Damietta fell into his hands. One half the troops died by sickness; the survivors were defeated by the soldan of Egypt at Mansourah, where the king's brother was killed and Louis taken prisoner. Damietta was besieged and returned to the Mohammedans by the French upon the liberation of their king. One thousand pieces of gold were paid for the other prisoners. On his return to France, the disorders of the state presented a wide field for the action of a wisdom which Louis proved to possess. The most delicate subjects were managed with profound ability. The right of appeal from the decisions of the courts was confirmed; private wars, the bane and offspring of feudal anarchy, were prohibited; judicial proof substituted for that by duel; and France rescued from the exactions of Rome. The greatest and best men are liable to error. The close of Louis' reign presents an incident which detracts from his merits. Charles, the king's brother, by color of a grant from England, and aided by the pope, managed to obtain the crown of Sicily and publicly executed Conradine and his uncle. Louis sanctioned this enormity. Not disheartened by the result of the former crusade, the king raised a new force against the Turks. Supposing he could make a convert of the chief of Tunis, he landed upon the shores of Africa. The Moslem rejected Christianity. The French were seized with the epidemic, which destroyed among its numerous victims the king and his son. Philip III., the son and successor of Louis, recovered, maintaining the field against his enemies, and returning home with the shattered troops. Sicilian affairs had tarnished the memory of his father, and they ruined the prospects of the son.

Philip IV. is known by his quarrel with the pope and his persecution of the Templars. Boniface VIII. forbid the clergy to give pecuniary aid to the king without his consent. Philip in return interdicted the clergy from sending money abroad without royal permission. Bernard Saisseti was deputed as the pope's legate to the court of France. The conduct and pretensions of the nuncio in the presence of the king led to his delivery to his metropolitan, the archbishop of Narbonne. The pope issued a bull declaring his authority over the kings and kingdoms of the earth, and citing the French clergy to repair to Rome. A French archdeacon carried the bull to Philip, commanding him under pain of excommunication to acknowledge the sovereignty of Boniface. The king ordered the bull to be thrown into the fire, and forbid the clergy from departing the realm. Forty ecclesiastics, however, went to Rome, and their temporalities were seized by the royal agents. The states-general were assembled. The cities were for the first time allowed a representation in this body. The sovereignty of Philip was acknowledged and the pope's claim disallowed. De Dagoret was immediately sent into Italy to raise troops, and a league formed with the family of Colonna. An army was marshalled under Dagoret and Colonna, who surprised the pope at Anagni. Arrayed in his official robes, the pontiff stood before his conquerors. Colonna demanded of him the renunciation of his office. "I am pope, and will die pope," replied Boniface. The conduct of the general and the reply of the pope so affected the citizens that they rose and rescued the captive. Boniface survived these indignities but a few days, when Clement V. succeeded and revoked the objectionable acts of his predecessor.

The Knights Templars constituted a society which originated in the enthusiasm of the crusades. Philip, charging on it a connection with seditious movements in Paris, ordered all the Templars in France to be imprisoned. Many were put to the rack, while others perished. Fifty-four Templars were burned as relapsed heretics. John De Molay, the grand master of the order, and another officer were conducted to a scaffold before the church of Notre Dame at Paris, and a pardon being offered to them upon confession, the reward of their fortitude in refusing was the flames. Thus was the order suppressed and its property placed at the disposal of the crown.

Louis X., the son of Philip IV., began his reign by killing his prime minister and confiscating his property. The two succeeding reigns of Philip V. and Charles IV. were short and unimportant. The direct male line failing in the last, Philip of Valois, cousin-german to Charles, came to the sceptre. Disturbances in Brittany involved him in war with England. The British arms well-nigh proved fatal to him at Cressy,* where firearms were first used. Calais was snatched from him. Nothing but a truce brought relief. John, his successor, was still more unfortunate. The conspiracy of the king of Navarre shook the throne at the commencement of the reign. The battle of

---

*Lard., ch. iv. pp. 81, 82. Kol. Ger., p. 243.

Poictiers soon followed, when the French were defeated and the king made prisoner. Another truce restored John to his country. The states-general were assembled.* Instead of giving supplies, they demanded a limitation of the royal prerogative and the freedom of the king of Navarre. Faction spread havoc on every side. Domestic discord, however, in this instance proved a national blessing. The English landed; the country was so desolated that they could not subsist. The treaty of Bretigni was therefore concluded, by which John was to pay three millions of crowns of gold for his ransom, Edward to surrender all claim to Normandy, Maine, Touraine, and Anjou; in exchange for which he was to receive Poitou, Saintonge, l'Angenois, Perigord, the Limousin, Quercy, Rovergue, l'Angoumois, Calais, Guisnes, Montreuil, and the county of Pontieu. John obtained his liberty and returned to France; but not being able to meet the demands of the treaty, he went back to England, where he died about one year afterwards. Charles V., his son, became sovereign. Ridding himself of the king of Navarre and the banditti which had infested the nation, Charles asserted his claim to the English provinces on the continent. Hostilities were again commenced. A singular reverse of fortune attended the arms of Britain. France fell under the government of a minor on the death of Charles V. The infancy of the king did not prove as disastrous as his subsequent insanity. Taking advantage of this melancholy event, the Dukes of Orleans and Burgundy arrayed parties in the deadliest forms of hostility. The murder of the former lighted the flames of civil war. In rapid succession followed the victories of the invading English, until France, crippled by the enormities of her sons and pursued by the

---

* Froissart.

arms of her enemies, was compelled to conclude the treaty of Troye (A.D. 1420),* by which the crown of France was transferred to the house of Lancaster. Notwithstanding this act, Charles VII., the son of the last king, came to the throne on the death of his father, Charles VI. The British marshalled their forces to effect the treaty. Charles, defeated at Verneuil and besieged at Orleans, concluded to seek refuge in Languedoc. A remarkable incident changed the face of affairs. In the village of Domremi lived a female, Joan d'Arc, the servant at an inn, who having heard of the many feats of courage displayed by her countrymen, and being deeply affected by the distress of the king, was fired by the daring enthusiasm of attempting to relieve her prostrate country. In her constant reflections on the subject she mistook the impulses of passion for the emotions of inspiration. Repairing to the governor of her native province, Joan announced her heavenly mission. That functionary, struck with the singularity of the occurrence, perceived what use could be made of it, and accordingly sent the maid to the court at Chinon. Introduced to the king, Joan offered in the name of God to raise the siege of Orleans and to conduct the sovereign to Rheims to be crowned and anointed. The only demand she made was the possession of a particular sword in the church of St. Catherine de Fierbois. Charles, to test the firmness of the novel petitioner, pretended to doubt her representations. In order, however, to settle the subject, the whole matter was referred to an assembly of divines and a jury of matrons. The former pronounced her mission supernatural, the latter declared her an unspotted virgin, while parliament attested her inspiration. Equipped for her work, Joan was received by the inhabitants and garrison of

---

* De Comines.

Orleans as a celestial deliverer, and, to the astonishment of the world, not only succeeded in routing the British in many desperate engagements, but finally raised the siege of the city. At the head of twelve thousand men, the martial virgin actually passed through the country fortified by the enemy's garrisons, and arriving at Rheims, verified her mission in the crowning and anointing of the king. Although the English went through the same ceremony as to Henry VI., the pretended king under the treaty of Troye, succeeded in taking prisoner and executing Joan, still they could not stem the torrent of popular delusion which had concentrated all the energies of the French. The British cause was ruined; the French regained all their possessions except Calais, and Charles VII. was left in undisputed possession of the sceptre. Louis XI.* was the opposite of his father. Ministers of mature judgment gave place to men of degraded character. The nobles, deprived of their rights, openly rebelled. To allay their vengeance, the king gave them terms which he avoided by the decision of the states-general. The Duke of Burgundy was not so easily ensnared. Seizing Louis, Burgundy compelled him to perform all his promises. On the death of Louis XI., his son Charles VIII., a youth fourteen years of age, took the sceptre under the guardianship of his sister. Intent upon asserting his title to the kingdom of Naples, the king, when arrived at age, settled his domestic concerns and invaded Italy. Great success attended his march; but a league between Germany, Spain, and the Italian states stripped him of all his conquests. Louis XII. was equally as unfortunate as his father in Italy, and would have suffered sorely from the invasion of the English king and German emperor had not the season of the year com-

---

* Lr., Vol. I. ch. v.-x.; Vol. II. ch. i.-iii.

pelled them to withdraw. Notwithstanding his misfortunes, Louis was beloved by his subjects. A single fact in his life unfolds his character. Being told that his economy had been ridiculed, the king observed, "I had rather my people should smile at my parsimony than weep at their own oppressions."

CHAPTER XII.

THE NEUSTRIAN DIVISION OF THE EMPIRE OF THE FRANKS TO THE ACCESSION OF LOUIS XIV.

FRANCIS I., the son-in-law of the late king, came to the throne.* The first object of his ambition, the recovery of Milan, he effected by one of the bloodiest battles of modern times at Marignano. Foiled in his attempt to obtain the sceptre of the German Empire, the king became the implacable enemy of the emperor of Germany, Charles V. Desolating wars ensued in rapid succession. Francis restored John d'Albert to the kingdom of Navarre, and encouraged the Duke of Bouillon to invade Luxembourg. Charles repaired both injuries, but sustained a defeat at Mezières in attempting to retaliate by an invasion of France. These events, together with the unfortunate assault of the French king on the Low Countries, caused a league between the emperor, the pope, and the king of England to expel Francis from Italy. Victory attended the arms of the allies at Pavia, where they made the king of France prisoner. The emperor finally liberated Francis,

---

* Lr., Vol. I. ch. v.–x.; Vol. II. ch. i.–iii. See Chapter XVI., after, for *Reformation*. Robertson's Charles V.

mainly on his promise to restore Burgundy and deliver his two sons as hostages. Burgundy was not restored by the king of France, nor the two children by the emperor. England and the pope united with Francis to compel Charles to return the young princes on the payment of a reasonable sum of money as a ransom. Charles was again victorious, and Rome fell into his hands. The mother of Francis and the aunt of Charles at last settled the affair by the treaty of Cambray, which provided that Francis should pay two millions of crowns for his children and resign Flanders and Artois and Italy, whilst Charles should cease to demand the restitution of Burgundy. Francis still entertained designs on Italy, yet he was not able to do more than assail the domains of the Duke of Savoy. Charles seized Milan on the death of its duke. War was again renewed. The emperor entered France at different points with a great army which was eventually compelled to withdraw for want of subsistence, as the country had been completely desolated by royal authority. The claim of the emperor to Flanders and Artois was now forfeited by the French. A furious war would have followed but for the interference of the pope. The truce only stayed hostilities; the first occasion kindled the flame. The ministers of Francis were shortly afterwards put to death by the governor of Milan. Reparation was demanded and evaded. The French were soon in arms, and the battle of Cerisoles gave them a victory over the imperialists. The rival monarchs became tired at last of contention and bloodshed. The treaty of Crespy followed, by the terms of which Charles was to give his eldest daughter, or the second daughter of his brother Ferdinand, to the Duke of Orleans with the investiture of Milan, while Francis was to cease all pretensions to Naples, Flanders, and Artois, and Charles to Burgundy, and both unite their arms against the Turks.

Francis I. dying shortly after this event, Henry II., his son, took the sceptre. An alliance with the Elector of Saxony enabled the French to master Metz, Toul, and Verdun. To arrest these movements Charles invested Metz. The French advanced on Italy, took Calais and Thionville, and checked the Spanish in Picardy. The dreadful waste of human life threatened by this state of affairs was averted by the treaty of Chateau Cambresis, which restored all conquests since the comencement of the war in 1551 made west of the Alps by either of the belligerents; provided that Savoy and all its dependencies should be returned to Emanuel Philibert, its duke, upon his marriage with Margaret of France; and directed that the French king should renounce all claim to Tuscany and Siena, receive the Genoese into favor, retaining the possession of Metz, Toul, and Verdun.

Francis II. came to the throne on the death of his father, Henry II. The power was in the hands of the Duke of Guise. Two objects distinguished this administration: the destruction of the Protestant influence by the ruin of the king of Navarre and the Prince of Condé; the union of France and Scotland in order to place the crown of England on the head of Mary, queen of the Scots, the niece of the minister and the wife of the monarch. The death of the king blasted these prospects by bringing the queen-mother, Catharine of Medicis, into power as guardian of her son, Charles IX., now ten years of age. The condition of France was exceedingly critical. Catharine increased troubles by the practice of her favorite maxim of dividing in order to govern. Endeavoring to balance the Catholics against the Protestants, the Prince of Condé against the Duke of Guise, the regent threw power into the hands of Condé and the Huguenots. An edict was issued by which the Protestants were permitted the free exercise of religion without the walls of towns, provided they taught nothing contrary to the Council of Nice, the Apostles' Creed, and the Old and New Testament. This law was one of the results of the conference of Poissy, where the two forms of faith had been discussed. Pursuant to the privilege granted, a body of Protestants, when holding their meeting in a barn at the town of Vassay, were assailed by the retinue of the Duke of Guise, who happened to pass. A tumult ensued in which sixty of the unarmed worshippers were slain. The Protestants throughout the kingdom flew to arms under Condé, Coligny, and Andelot; while the Catholics rallied under the Duke of Guise and the Constable Montmorency, who, having got possession of the king's person, obliged the queen-mother to join their party. Philip of Spain assisted the latter with six thousand men, and Elizabeth of England sent as many to the aid of the former. A portion of the British forces succeeded in throwing a small re-enforcement into Rouen, but the Catholics took it by storm. The Protestants put their army in motion to protect the British at Havre, which brought on the battle at Dreux. The field was obstinately contested. The Catholics had the credit of victory, yet a singular fact deprived them of its benefits. Montmorency was captured by the Protestants, Condé by the Catholics. The Protestants soon rallied and took some important places in Normandy. The Catholics, aiming a mortal blow at their enemies, laid siege to Orleans, where Montmorency was a prisoner. The Duke of Guise, however, falling by the hand of violence, the movement was unsuccessful. Condé and Montmorency, tired of captivity, began to think of peace. Conferences were held; a general amnesty and toleration settled; offices, civil rights, and privileges restored irrespective of religious distinctions; peace proclaimed, and the captives set at liberty. This happy adjustment of affairs was shortly disturbed. The Spanish queen and the French king met at Bayonne, where they formed the Holy League, as it is denominated, by which the destruction of the Protestants in the Low Countries, in France, and throughout Europe was resolved upon. Civil war again raged. A battle was fought at St. Denis, where Montmorency was slain, though the Protestants were defeated. Condé, undismayed, collected his forces, appeared in the field, laid siege to Chartres, and forced the court to an accommodation. The arrangement proving to be insincere on the part of the queen-mother, the war was renewed with more fury than ever. Battle was joined at Jarnac; the Catholics were again successful, Condé made prisoner and killed in cold blood. Coligny rallied the Protestants, and was defeated at Moncontour with the loss of ten thousand men. The Catholics, supposing that the means of their adversaries were exhausted, confidently believed there was an end of the war. Defeats, however, merely rouse the energies of great minds. Coligny was dauntless. The Catholics were soon surprised to hear that at the head of a great army he was on his march to the gates of Paris. The king was in no condition of defence. Negotiations ensued; all past offences pardoned; Protestants declared eligible to all offices, civil and military; the edicts of toleration renewed; and Rochelle, La Charité, Montauban, Cognac ceded to the Huguenots as places of refuge and pledges of security. A radical change appeared to have been wrought in the royal mind. The Protestant leaders were invited to Paris and treated with distinguished regard. Charles affected the greatest interest for Elizabeth of England, proposing a marriage between her and the Duke of Anjou. As if to seal the king's professions of friendship by one of the most sacred of all acts, he gave his sister in marriage to the young king of Navarre. The principal Protestants, thinking this act would allay all animosities, assembled at Paris to participate in the festivities of the occasion. A few days after the nuptials Coligny was wounded by a shot from a window. Suspicions were quieted by explanations till the eve of St. Bartholomew (A.D. 1572), when a massacre of the Protestants commenced.* The king incited the mob. Coligny and near five hundred gentlemen of rank were murdered in Paris alone, besides ten thousand persons of inferior condition. The inhuman butchery spread over the kingdom. Above sixty thousand Protestants fell a sacrifice. This deed, at the thought of which the heart sickens, was hailed in Spain and Rome as the triumph of the Church militant! England and the Protestant powers of Europe were so alarmed by these sanguinary measures as to put themselves in a condition to protect their civil and religious liberties. A similar course was pursued by the Protestants of France. Finding their numbers greatly increased, they crowded the cities and fortresses. Sancerre, though obliged to surrender after sustaining a gallant defence, obtained liberty of conscience for its inhabitants. Rochelle, which in the course of eight months repelled nine general and twenty particular assaults, compelled the Duke of Anjou, who lost twenty-four thousand men in conducting the siege, to grant an advantageous peace.

In the midst of these commotions Charles IX. died leaving no male issue, and his brother, the Duke of Anjou, succeeded under the title of Henry III. The monarch endeavored to moderate religious hatreds by acting as an arbiter between the contending parties, but he eventually lost the confidence of all. The Protestants were strength-

---

*Rev. xiii. 7. New. Dis., xxiv., v., pp. 501–2. Scott's Com. in loc. Chapter V., ante.

ened by the accession of the Duke of Alençon, the arrival of a German army under Condé, and the presence of the king of Navarre. Further action was restrained by the pacific measures of Henry. Peace was settled on the basis that the Protestants were to enjoy the public exercise of their religion, except within two leagues from court; were to have an equal representation in the parliaments; all attainders were to be reversed against them; and eight cautionary towns were put into their hands. Offended at this treaty, Guise laid the foundation of a league which again involved France in a protracted civil war. Eventually Henry, the last of the line of Valois, was supplanted by the arts of Guise; and both having been assassinated, the king of Navarre, the first of the Bourbons, assumed the crown under the title of Henry IV. The king's attachment to the Protestants induced one half the royal army to desertion. The siege of Paris was abandoned and Henry retired to Normandy. The Catholics proclaimed the Cardinal of Bourbon king, under the title of Charles X. In this extremity the queen of England assisted Henry with men and money, and his prospects brightened in consequence of securing Caen and Dieppe and repulsing the Duke of Mayenne at Arques. Marching immediately to Paris, the king would have taken it had not Mayenne entered it first; as it was, the duke was defeated at Ivry, and capital invested. But for Henry's tenderness of human life, Paris would have been carried by storm. It was relieved by the arrival of Spanish troops commanded by the Duke of Parma; which event, together with the junction of the pope's forces to those of the Duke of Savoy and the bull of the former pronouncing Henry a relapsed heretic, presented new obstacles in the way of the Protestants. A rupture among the Catholics finally brought Henry to the throne and gave peace to France. The faction of Sixteen who governed Paris, the principal members of which were pensioners of Spain, had hanged the president of the parliament for not condemning to death a man obnoxious to their displeasure. Mayenne, fearing the power of the faction, caused four of them to be executed. Parma pressed the calling of the states-general to deliberate on the election of a king. The assembly was convoked. Parma was prepared to enter France with a large army in order to enforce the interests of Spain, when his death relieved Mayenne from a rival, Henry from a foe, and France from becoming a province. The states-general met, according to the edict, at Paris (A.D. 1593). The pope's legate proposed that they should bind themselves never to support Henry, though he should abjure Protestantism. The Spanish faction supported, but the assembly rejected, the motion. After having attempted to gain the Duke of Mayenne by the offer of Burgundy and a large sum of money, the ambassador of Spain proposed that the states should choose the Infanta Eugenia queen, and Albert, the archduke, to whom she was to be married, king in her right. Serious opposition arising to such settlement, it was finally so modified as to provide that the Infanta should marry the Duke of Guise. Mayenne, unwilling to become dependent on his nephew, called in question the authority of the ambassador. The assembly refused to commit the sceptre to the hands of a female, it being contrary to the provisions of the Salic law. Meantime Henry pushed his military operations with great vigor, and the anxiety of the Catholics as to his religious views daily increased. Conferences were held between the divines of the two forms of religion. Soon afterwards Henry abjured the Protestant faith, received absolution from the archbishop of Bourges, and was crowned at Chartres (A.D. 1594). A war with Spain restored all the captures which had been made by its king during the civil contentions. The Protestants obtained free exercise of their religion, a share in the administration of justice, and the privilege of every employment of trust, profit, and honor, by the Edict of Nantes. The wretched condition to which France had been reduced by the protracted civil wars was relieved by wholesome reforms; and the national revenue was increased, though the taxes were diminished. Henry made extensive preparations to assist the Protestants of Germany, but his assassination in the streets of Paris deprived them of his presence.

Louis XIII., the son of the late monarch, succeeded under the regency of Mary, his mother. Sully, the wise minister of the former reign, was discarded. Concini and his wife, Galligai, were possessed of power. Luines ruined them, procuring the husband to be shot, the wife to be executed. The regent was imprisoned. The new favorite contracted the insolence and heired the disgrace of his fallen rivals. A civil war ensued which resulted in the confirmation of the Edict of Nantes. Cardinal Richelieu, who had risen to notice by an opposition to the Luines and an adherence to the queen-mother, becoming the king's favorite, soon governed his councils. Three objects mark this administration: the humiliation of the nobility, the ruin of the Protestants, and the reduction of the power of Austria. On the death of the king, his minor son, Louis XIV., succeeded. Cardinal Mazarin assumed the administration of government. The changes and conflicts incident to a regency succeeded. The minister and his rival, the Prince of Condé, were alternately elevated and overthrown, and France rent by contention and war. Peace was restored by the king's arrival at age, and the war with Spain was terminated by the treaty of the Pyrenees, which extended the boundaries of his kingdom in the north to Gravelines, in the southeast to Pignerol, and in the southwest to Roussillon, and brought him the Infanta as a wife. These fortunate events made Louis XIV. the most ambitious monarch of the age.

CHAPTER XIII.

THE NEUSTRIAN DIVISION OF THE EMPIRE OF THE FRANKS TO THE EXECUTION OF LOUIS XVI.

THE avarice of Louis XIV. was equal to his ambition. On the death of his father-in-law, Philip IV. of Spain, he laid claim to Brabant, and would have captured all the dominions of that kingdom in the Netherlands had not England, Holland, and Sweden arrested his progress.* Intent upon the United Provinces, the French sovereign soon afterwards managed to unite his arms with those of England in a war against them. The cupidity of Louis, however, missed the prize in consequence of peace being procured by the treaty of Aix-la-Chapelle. England being united to his interests, Louis renewed the war; yet the Dutch, aided by the emperor and Spain, were able to terminate difficulties by the treaty of Nimeguen. The terms of this instrument were that Louis should retain Franche Compte, Cambray, Aire, St. Omer, Valenciennes, Tournay, Ypres, Bouchain, Cassel, and Charlemont; that Maestricht should be returned to the states; that Spain should be put in possession of Charleroy, Oudenarde, Aeth, Ghent, and Limbourg; that the Elector of Brandenburg should return to Sweden his conquest in Pome-

---

*Lr., Vol. II., ch. iv.–ix. Russell's Mod. Europe, Vols. III.–VI. Voltaire's War of 1741.

rania; and that the treaty of Westphalia (Ch. XVI.) should remain in full force over Germany and the North. The ambition of the French king was rather increased than diminished by this settlement. A standing army was retained, arbitrary tribunals for uniting to the crown such territories as had depended on the late conquests were established, troops introduced into Strasburg, the Protestants oppressed by harsh laws as well as by the revocation of the Edict of Nantes (A.D. 1686), and the pope offended by a refusal to grant his reasonable request. Spain, Holland, Denmark, Sweden, Savoy, and England united to humble the pride of Louis. France marshalled an army of four hundred thousand men, overwhelmed the Palatinate, but sustained a defeat at Walcourt. Its ally, the Porte, shared a similar defeat at Nissa and Widin. Fortune, however, soon smiled on both. The French swept all before them in Italy; their fleet defeated the combined powers of England and Holland at Beachy Head, while the Turks made great progress in Hungary. Nothing is more fluctuating than the events of war. A subsequent campaign checked this prosperity both in Italy and on the Save. Louis nevertheless regained his glory by the victories of Steinkirk, Neerwinden, Heidelburg, Marsalgia, Roses, and the capture of four hundred merchantmen, Dutch and English, known as the Smyrna fleet. Famine produced great distress among the French populace, and death deprived their sovereign of Louvois, his minister, and Luxembourg, his general. Most parties became tired of the war, and it terminated by the treaty of Ryswick (A.D. 1697), which left the Bourbon succession to the Spanish throne in full force; provided that William of Orange should be acknowledged by Louis as the lawful sovereign of Britain and Ireland; secured the duchy of Luxemburg, Chiney, Charleroy, Mons, Aeth, Courtnay, and all places united to France by the chambers of Metz and Brisac, as well as Catalonia, to Spain; and restored Friburg, Brisgaw and Philipsburg to the emperor, Lorraine and Bar to their native prince. In order to sustain the succession of his grandson, Philip V., to the throne of Spain, Louis was soon involved in another tedious war against England, the emperor, and the United Provinces. The French and Spanish compelled the imperialists to raise the blockade of Mantua, but they were defeated at Fridlingen. The imperialists were overthrown at Passau and Hochstet. A total defeat befell Louis' forces at Blenheim, and the English wrested Gibraltar from Spain and cut off the French fleet near Malaga. The south of France was disturbed by civil commotion. The allies penetrated Spain, took Barcelona, Valencia, and Catalonia. Greater part of Spanish Flanders fell into the hands of the confederates in consequence of the victory of the Duke of Marlborough at Ramillies. In Spain and Italy Louis was equally unsuccessful, and the English fleet snatched from him Majorca and Ivica. Unfortunate in every quarter, and failing to procure aid from Sweden, the monarch of France sought peace in vain from the confederates. A last effort was made, in which the French were overcome at Oudenarde and Malplaquet. Reverses in Spain and Alsace inclined the allies to peace; but success following in Spain and Flanders, they terminated the conferences. Internal divisions effect what external foes never can accomplish. Discord entered the ranks of the allies; and although they were at the gates of Paris, Louis obtained peace (A.D. 1713). Treaties between France, England, Portugal, Prussia, Savoy, and the Provinces were signed at Utrecht. The articles provided for a distinct succession to the crown of Spain from that of the throne of France; for the cession of Sicily to the Duke of Savoy, for the cession to him of the valleys of Pragelas, Oulx, Sezanne, Bardonnêche, Chateau Dauphin, the ports of Exilles and Fenestrelle, and the restoration to him of Savoy and the county of Nice, with their dependencies; for the navigation of the river Amazon in South America to the king of Portugal; for the cession of Spanish Guelderland, Neufchatel, and Valengin to the king of Prussia, in exchange for Orange, Chalons, Chatelbelin, and Burgundy, and his regal title to be acknowledged; for the Rhine being the boundary between France and Germany; and for all the fortifications beyond claimed by France being relinquished to the emperor or destroyed; for the cession in Italy of Naples, Milan, and the Spanish possessions on the Tuscan shore to Austria, as well as the Spanish Netherlands, but that the Elector of Bavaria retain all in his possession until reinstated in his German dominions, except the Upper Palatinate, and also be put in possession of Sardinia, with the title of king; for the donation of Luxemburg, Namur, Charleroy, Mons, Menin, and Tournay to the United Provinces; for the restoration to France of Lisle, Aire, Bethune, and St. Venant; for the acknowledgment on the part of France of the title of Queen Anne and the Hanoverian succession; for the destruction of Dunkirk; for the property of England to St. Christopher's, Hudson's Bay and Straits, the town of Placentia in Newfoundland, and Nova Scotia in North America; for the possession of the British to Minorca and Gibraltar, and for their right to furnish for thirty years all the negroes to South America. The emperor persisted in hostilities, but his efforts proving hopeless, the next year the treaty of Rastadt followed, by which he lost many fortresses beyond the Rhine, and the king of France got the Electors of Bavaria and Cologne established in their dignities; the former relinquishing Sardinia to the emperor for the Upper Palatinate, and the king of France acknowledging the electoral rights of the Duke of Hanover; while Italy and the Low Countries were to remain on the footing of the treaty of Utrecht. Shortly afterwards died Louis XIV., leaving his grandson, Louis XV., a minor. The Duke of Orleans was appointed regent.

The distracted condition of the finances gave ample scope for the scheme of John Law, a Scotch adventurer. A bank was established under the patronage of government, the credit of which rested entirely upon the anticipation of inexhaustible wealth from the commerce of Mississippi, China, and Senegal. Upon the detection of the fraud the institution lost public confidence, France was compelled to redeem its notes, and Law made his escape. The attempt of the emperor to dethrone the king of Poland, the father-in-law of Louis XV., brought on a war, which was concluded by the Polish king renouncing his claims for the duchy of Lorraine; the duke of which took Tuscany and an annuity from Louis of three million five hundred thousand livres till the death of the last prince of the house of Medicis; the emperor acknowledging the king of the two Sicilies and receiving for them Parma and Placentia, and ceding to the king of Sardinia the Novarese, the Tortonese, and the fiefs of Langes, and taking in return from Louis the French conquests in Germany, and a guarantee of the pragmatic sanction or the domestic law, by which the succession of Austria was secured to the heirs female of Charles VI. if he should die without male issue. Contrary to this law, Louis resolved to support the pretensions of the Elector of Bavaria to the kingdom of Bohemia and the imperial crown, and concluded a treaty with him and the king of Prussia for this purpose, as well as a division of the Austrian dominions. The French army, commanded by Bellisle and Broglio, entered Germany, reduced Lintz, took Prague, crowned the elector king of Bohemia, and proceeded to Frankfort, where he was elected emperor under the name of Charles VII. The battle of Czaslaw might have proved fatal to the Austrians had they not detached the king of Prussia from the French interest by conferring upon him Silesia and the county of Glatz. All the posts from the Danube to the Rhine were wrested from the French, and to crown their misfortunes they were beaten at Dettingen. Austria strengthened by an English, and France by a Spanish alliance, made vast preparations for prosecuting the war. Louis and his ally, attempting to regain the sovereignty of the Mediterranean, sustained an overthrow at the bay of Hières. Though better success attended them in Italy, they were convinced of their incompetency to cope with their foes, and obtained assistance from Sweden and Prussia. Louis made great progress in Flanders, and entered Dunkirk in triumph. Charles VII. dying, his son declined the succession. Determined to cripple Austria, France, however, continued the war. Despite the successes of their enemies at Fontenoy and in Flanders, the electors met at Frankfort and chose the archduke emperor, entitled Francis I. The king of Prussia was detached from the alliance by the treaty of Dresden, which secured to him the payment of one million of German crowns upon the evacuation of his hereditary dominions, as also the confirmation of the treaty of Breslau, which gave him Silesia. This event did not dishearten the French, who made rapid progress in Flanders, and, though not as fortunate in Italy and at Cape Breton, eventually by the victory of Val secured the navigation of the Scheldt. The treaty of Aix-la-Chapelle put an end to the war by confirming all treaties from that of Westphalia, and providing for a mutual restitution of all conquests from the beginning of hostilities, and a release of prisoners without ransom (A.D. 1748).

France attempted an extension of power in America and India. Louis supposed it would be possible for him by connecting his settlements on the north in Canada and at the south in Louisiana by a line of forts to force the English colonists west of the Alleghanies, if not to subject them entirely to his sway. The scheme was checked at the outset by Washington on the Ohio, though the British commander, Braddock, through his own imprudence, was some time afterwards not as successful in the neighborhood of Pittsburg. Misfortune attended the French arms on Lake George, where Dieskau, their general, was mortally wounded and captured. Alliances having been formed with Russia, Sweden, and Austria, France commenced vigorous operations. In Europe, Hanover fell into its hands; in America the great lakes were mastered; but conquered at the battle of Rosbach, it was driven from the former, and, losing Louisburg, it was eventually deprived of the latter. An effort to regain Hanover was frustrated by the victory of Prince Ferdinand at Minden. The capture of Vandivash and the conquest of Surat ruined the cause of France in India. An attempt to invade England and Ireland destroyed the fleet of Louis. This long and bloody struggle was settled by the treaty of Paris (A.D. 1763), which stipulated that France should cede to Great Britain all her former possessions in North America except New Orleans, together with that part of Louisiana which lies on the west side of the Mississippi; that the French should be permitted to fish on the banks of Newfoundland, having the islands of St. Pierre and Miquelon for the benefit of their fisheries, not being permitted to build forts thereon; that Spain shall relinquish her right to fish on the banks of Newfoundland, permit the English logwood-cutters to build houses in the Bay of Honduras, surrender what she may have taken belonging to Portugal, and cede Florida to England, for which she was to have Havana and all Cuba conquered by the British; that Minorca shall be restored to England; Martinique, Guadalupe, Goree, and Bellisle to France; and that France shall cede to England the forts and factories lost on the river Senegal, the island Granada, and the Granadieres, giving up all claim to the neutral islands St. Vincent, Dominica, and Tobago.

France, delivered from external difficulties, fell a prey to internal discord. Louis directed the continuance of several imposts which, when created, were to be confined to the duration of the war, and also demanded new contributions. The parliament of Paris remonstrated. Many of the provincial towns joined in similar appeals to the throne. The assembly of Rouen assumed the position that the people of Normandy were not subject to any tax unless imposed by the three estates. In Languedoc the opposition to these royal exactions ran so high that some members of the parliament of Toulouse suffered severe restriction of their personal liberty from the governor of that province. This act incensed that body to such a degree that they passed a vote authorizing his imprisonment. The people sided with the remonstrant members, and Choiseul, the chief minister, secretly supported them, in order to awe his sovereign into subserviency to the house of Austria. The bankruptcy of the East India Company, the consequent private failures, the prodigality of the court, and the decay of trade reduced the kingdom to a calamitous condition. Louis, instead of making an effort to rescue the nation from impending ills, yielded himself up entirely to the pursuit of his amorous gratifications, even permitting his mistress, Madame du Barry, to influence his councils. Choiseul, either from interest or pride, would not court the favor of the lady. The chancellor Maupeou and the Duke d'Aiguillon, considering it a good opportunity to supplant their benefactor, sought her smile. The duke was shortly afterwards removed from the government of Bretagne in consequence of maladministration. Choiseul confirmed his authority by bringing about a marriage between the son of the deceased dauphin, Louis, and Marie Antoinette, daughter of the empress-dowager of Austria. After this event the king annulled the proceedings against D'Aiguillon, governor of Bretagne. The parliament of Paris suspended the duke from the peerage. The king cancelled the proceedings. Choiseul was dismissed and recalled. An edict for rendering the courts subservient to the king's will was opposed by the parliament, a bed of justice held, and the peers refusing to act while D'Aiguillon sat among them, the king commanded them to proceed. Choiseul was dismissed; the peers persisting in their refusal, the king deprived them of their employments and banished them to different parts of the country. Three edicts were promulgated: one abolished the former parliament; one suppressed the Court of Aids; one formed a new parliament, consisting of seventy members nominated and pensioned by the sovereign. Six provincial councils were created, which were to be held at Arras, Blois, Chalons, Clermont, Lyons, and Poictiers. Aiguillon was appointed secretary for the foreign department. The court was brought completely under the influence of that nobleman and the Countess du Barry, than whom none could be more exceptionable. Discontent spread over France, rebellion broke out in Sicily. The death of Louis XV. brought his grandson Louis XVI. to the throne.

The first acts of Louis XVI. were to revoke the Six Councils and recall the magistracy. But the popularity acquired by these acts was impaired by the "regulations of discipline," which gave the great chamber the exclusive power of registration, made the president despotic, checked the falsity of remonstrance, and multiplied the grounds of removal and confiscation of which a new court was to take cognizance. National disgust was somewhat allayed by the determination of the court to engage in favor of the American colonies against England, but the measures of the minister Callone counteracted this auspicious state of affairs. Insisting upon a tax on the nobles and clergy, hitherto unburdened by public expenses, he advised that the notables, a body selected from the privileged orders, should be assembled. Upon the meeting of the assembly, Callone stated to them that the revenues of the government were insufficient for its support, and suggested a mode of supplying the deficit by levying a land-tax and imposing new duties. Necker's party charged the minister with mismanagement. The notables required exact accounts; Louis banished Necker; dismissed Callone; and appointed as his successor De Brienne, archbishop of Toulouse. Endeavoring to procure the assent of the notables to the land-tax and stamp-duties, but not succeeding, the minister advised their dissolution, and his measures were proclaimed in the form of edicts. The parliament refused registration until the accounts demanded by the notables were furnished. Intimidation and the dismission of Lamoignon, who had become unpopular with the court by advocating the simplification of legal proceedings, procured assent to the collection of two twentieths of the tax.

The mode of collecting the new revenue now became a subject of dispute.* Parliament desired it to remain on the old basis, which favored the privileged orders ; the minister wished an inquiry into the exact amount of

---

* Lr., Vol. II. ch. x., xi.; Vol. III. ch. i.-xi. Mod. Eu., Vol. VI. p. 205.

property, and that the provinces should compound for the impost. The promise of the king to collect the two twentieths in the established mode quieted the controversy. Nobles, parliament, and clergy demanded a meeting of the states-general. The minister, desirous to negotiate a loan, consented to convoke the states of the realm. A royal sitting was proclaimed, which was so stormy that some of the members were imprisoned for the freedom of their remarks. Other parliaments united with that of Paris against the court. The minister attempted to strengthen his power by forming bailiwicks to diminish the authority of the parliaments, and plenary courts to consist of persons chosen by the king. The capital became a scene of commotion, and the provinces of organized opposition to the court. Brienne left the cabinet. Necker was recalled. The parliaments were restored to their authority, the laws to their accustomed operation, and financial affairs assumed a solid basis. Louis, thinking to render himself still more popular, agitated the calling of the states-general. The constitution of this assembly created controversy. Parliament insisted upon an adherence to the plan of 1614. Necker suggested a popular representation at least equal to the aggregate amount of ecclesiastical and noble deputies. The notables were again assembled, in order to settle the matter. Notwithstanding their rejection of the minister's plan, the court determined that the third estate should be equal to the nobles and clergy combined.

The states-general met at Versailles (A.D. 1789), were opened by a speech from the king, Necker, and the keeper of the seal. Louis enlarged on the propriety of settling the finances and quieting the distractions of the community. Necker agitated the question as to the manner of voting, proposing that in cases which required joint action they should so consult. The commons peremptorily insisted upon the verification of powers being joint. The nobles disregarded this requisition. Some of the clergy joined the third estate. The ascertainment of powers being completed, the commons assumed the title of the National Assembly, resolving that the absence of deputies and even classes ought not to preclude the members from exercising all their rights. Louis, disapproving this course, proclaimed a royal sitting, which was to take place in the hall of the states. Bailly, president of the commons, demanded admission; but the guard refusing to allow it, about two thirds of that body met in a tennis-court room, where they bound themselves by oath not to separate finally till they had effected political regeneration. A governmental scheme combining popular liberty with monarchical power was presented to the king. Louis insisted on the distinction of the three orders, and annulled the vote of the commons. Nothing daunted, that body adhered to their position and resolved that the persons of the deputies were inviolable. The clergy on the next day discussed the question of joining the commons. One hundred and forty-two members out of two hundred and ninety-four voted for the union, nine remaining silent. The junction was effected by bringing over the silent members. A small portion of the nobles, headed by the Duke of Orleans, joining the commons and clergy, raised the popular feeling to such a pitch as to compel the king to direct the whole order to follow their fellows. The advance of several regiments to the neighborhood of Versailles was authorized by the crown. Mirabeau called the attention of the assembly to the event. Louis was desired to cause the removal of the troops. The action of the assembly was not only disregarded, but Necker, suspected of colluding with them, was discharged. The military thus arrayed by royal authority against the populace, scenes of violence ensued, in one of which the Bastile was demolished at Paris. The king, yielding to the torrent, withdrew the troops from the capital and courted the protection of the assembly. La Fayette was appointed to the command of the Parisian militia; Necker was recalled; Louis with a train of deputies visited Paris and was presented by the new mayor with the keys of the city. The king consenting, the assembly modified the privileges of nobility and clergy, towns and provinces. Men and women presented themselves at the bar of the assembly begging bread. A riot having for its object the king's person induced his removal to Paris. The assembly followed. Talleyrand, archbishop of Autun, procured the seizure of church-lands, an allowance being secured to sufferers; provincial assemblies were suppressed; courts of justice rendered inactive; assignast substituted for money; oppressive taxes abolished; monopolies annulled; and a new form was given to municipal corporations. Popular commotions, attended by riot, bloodshed, and destruction of property, prevailed throughout the capital.

On the anniversary of the revolution, Louis bound himself by oath to sustain the new constitution, and a similar sanction united all classes in its support. Peace might now have been restored but for the intrigues of the Jacobins and the arts of the Duke of Orleans. Necker lost his influence, resigned his place, and returned to Switzerland, his native country. The clergy, disgusted at the disposal of their benefices, refused acquiescence; the assembly sought in vain to enforce compliance on the mass of them by inflicting new penalties. Mirabeau, the president of the assembly, gained over by the court, endeavored to procure a dissolution of the body; but failing in this attempt, he advised the king to remove to a more tranquil place than Paris. After the death of this adviser, Louis again fell a prey to rash counsels. Conferences were held at Mantua with the emperor. It was concluded to put in motion an army sufficiently large to intimidate the assembly. The royal family left Paris for Montmédy, but were arrested in their course. The code providing for the sovereignty of the people in the choice of their own officers and representatives, limiting the power of the crown, securing the gratuitous administration of justice, was completed by the assembly, approved by the king, and that body dissolved. On the opening of a new legislature, the monarch recommended to their consideration the state of the army, public credit, general justice, and national education. A new cabinet was formed; but on the king refusing his assent to the ordinances, inflicting transportation on ecclesiastical nonjurors, and authorizing the encampment of twenty thousand men near Paris, it fell to pieces. War was declared against Austria. The command of the army was devolved on La Fayette. Violence prevailed in the capital; the king and his family became its victims; the Jacobins reigned in triumph; royalty was abolished. After an indecisive battle the Austrians withdrew from France. The brilliant successes of the army in the Netherlands, Savoy, and Germany emboldened the convention to proceed to ulterior measures against Louis, whose execution followed within twenty-four hours (January 21, 1793) after his condemnation.

CHAPTER XIV.

THE NEUSTRIAN DIVISION OF THE EMPIRE OF THE FRANKS TO THE DOWNFALL OF LOUIS NAPOLEON BONAPARTE AS EMPEROR.

FRANCE declared war against England, Holland, and Spain. Before such a strong array the generals of the convention were worsted at Aix-la-Chapelle, Winden, Pellenberg, Vicogne, Famars and Landau. Hoche, a youth of twenty-five years of age, succeeding to the command which Dumouriez, Dampierre, and Custine had in turn held during the recent calamities, drove back the allies within the imperial boundaries. The Jacobins gained the ascendency in the convention over the Girondists, imprisoning many and threatening the infliction of capital punishments. These movements were followed by open opposition in La Vendée, Marseilles, Lyons, and Mende. The first was reduced with great slaughter. The last felt the full measure of Jacobinical vengeance. The guillotine, which was drenched with human blood at Lyons, was not idle under the eye of Robespierre at Paris. The queen was despatched upon it. Brissot and Bailly, Le Brun and the Duke of Orleans, with a host beside, suffered the same fate. The tyranny of the times was not limited to political causes. Religion was denounced, apostasy encouraged, death declared to be an eternal sleep, the wicked taught no longer to fear the judgment of another world, the good no longer to cherish hopes of a blissful immortality.

The English taking advantage of the disaffection of Toulon, seized and strongly fortified it. Dugommier, conducting the siege on the part of the convention, was assisted by Napoleon Bonaparte, a young Corsican who now first appeared in public life. Notwithstanding the success of the allies in the commencement of their movements, the French armies, under Pichegru and Jourdain, eventually took most of West Flanders and triumphed in Germany. In the midst of these operations Jacobinical sway was undermined. Robespierre fell by the same means which he had practised so successfully in the destruction of others. The pride of France was humbled by a series of decisive naval victories obtained on its western coast over its fleet by the British. Peace was concluded with Prussia, by which the French obtained a part of the duchy of Cleves. The fall of the Jacobins was followed by the accession of the Girondists to their seats in the convention. France received a new constitution. The executive power was lodged with five directors. The legislative power was reposed in two bodies, one consisting of five hundred, the other of two hundred and fifty members. Four parties existed: the friends of the new constitution and of the code of 1793; the royalists and the semi-royalists. The defeat of Jourdain and the retreat of Moreau in Germany filled the nation with gloom: the success of Bonaparte in reducing the Milanese, dispossessing the English of Corsica, and compelling the king of Sardinia to quit the confederacy inspired it with joy. During the succeeding year this illustrious hero forced the pope to cede Bologna, Romagna, Ferrara, to pay over twenty-one millions of livres; proceeded into the hereditary dominions of the emperor, took Gradisca, obtained possession of the greater part of the Tyrol, and procured articles of peace between France and Austria at Leobin. Meantime, Hoche and Moreau gained much glory and conquest on the Rhine. The treaty of Campo Formio followed the preliminaries of Leobin. This instrument extended the boundaries of France to the Rhine, giving it Corfu, the neighboring islands, the Albanian establishments below the Gulf of Lodrino and the Netherlands; secured to the emperor the Venetian capital, and to the Duke of Modena, Brisgaw. Geneva was united to France, the insurgent Swiss cantons reduced, Malta subdued. The master-spirit of these movements was Bonaparte, whose ambition now induced him to seek nobler spoils in the execution of a project to enter the British Indies through the Persian territory.* Arriving in Egypt,

---

* Th. Rev., Vol. IV. p. 356.

he effected repeated conquests, but his glory was eclipsed by the loss of his fleet in the Bay of Aboukir by the British under the command of Nelson. Encouraged by this success, the English formed an alliance with the Russians, the emperor, the king of Naples, and the Turks, which was fatal to the French at Cassano and Magnano, at Trebbia and Novi. Though France was able to retain Switzerland, it lost Germany by the battle of Stockach.

The divisions of the directory, the financial embarrassments they had created, their severe laws against the relatives and friends of the Vendéans, as well as their military miscarriages, rendered certain their downfall. Sieyès, one of their number, held conferences with Talleyrand and others, where it was concluded that a consulate should be formed, with a man of great military talents at its head. As a preliminary of the plan, Napoleon Bonaparte was proposed for the chief of the military in the capital, to which the Ancients consented. In the succeeding commotions, the directors resigned. Napoleon insisted upon an immediate change for the benefit of the republic; but being opposed in the Council of Five Hundred, he supported his demand by a display of military force and cleared the hall of the members. A provisional government was created with Napoleon at its head. A constitution was finally proclaimed, which established a consulate, a tribunate of one hundred members, a legislative body of three hundred, a senate of eighty, and a council of state consisting of five. Napoleon and Cambacérés were chosen consuls for ten years, and Le Brun for five. Overtures of peace were made to England, which being rejected, the war was continued. Successful at Montabello, Marengo, and Hohenlinden; the republic obtained the treaty of Luneville, by which the emperor made additional grants to the cessions of the former pacification and yielded the Tuscan duchy to the

Duke of Parma. The British, though deprived of an ally, pressed the war and reduced Malta, Cairo, and Alexandria. Peace, however, soon followed, and the treaty of Amiens was signed (A.D. 1802), by which, of all his conquests during the war, his Britannic majesty only retained Ceylon and Trinidad, and his ally, the queen of Portugal, lost Olivenza and a part of Guiana; Corfu and the other Venetian islands were constituted a republic, and Malta restored to its former possessors. Thus France now had the Netherlands, a portion of Germany, Geneva, Savoy, Piedmont; Spain was a degraded ally, the cisalpine state was under its yoke; Tuscany was virtually a province, and the Ligurian republic was its mere creature. The internal condition of the nation engaged the attention of the consul. A reconciliation was effected with the pope, and Catholicism established, subject to the supervision of ten prelates and fifty bishops. The acts against emigrants were relaxed; the ardor for military distinction promoted by the creation of the Legion of Honor; the cause of education advanced by the establishment of schools in every branch of science; and the jurisprudence of the kingdom promoted by the adoption of a new code of laws. A vote of the people extended the power of Napoleon to the term of his life, and a new constitutional provision rendered him in reality a monarch.*

Misunderstandings arose between France and England. Napoleon complained that England favored the Bourbons and allowed its press to treat him in an improper manner. The British denied these charges, retorting on the consul that he permitted his own press to traduce their government. Napoleon's interference in Swiss affairs became the absorbing charge against him in England while the French were loud in their declamation of the English on account

---

* Th. Con. and Em., Bk. XVI.

of not having surrendered Malta and Egypt pursuant to the convention at Amiens. An open rupture ensued. Hanover fell a prey to the French; in their turn they lost many possessions in the East and West. Preparations for the invasion of England were made upon the most extravagant scale. The threatening aspect of continental affairs prevented this occurrence. Foreign and domestic contentions, arising out of the plots of the Bourbons against the life of Napoleon and his retaliatory measure in the execution of the Duc d'Enghien, one of their blood, induced the senate to declare Napoleon hereditary emperor; upon the acceptance of which six new appointments were made: grand elector, constable, arch-chancellors, arch-treasurer, high admiral. The most distinguished generals were created marshals. An unsuccessful proposition of peace with England followed. The assumption of the kingship of Italy by Napoleon matured the ill feeling already existing into a coalition between England and the continental powers. Nelson's victory over the combined fleets of France and Spain at Trafalgar would have deeply affected the emperor had not the exploits of the army afforded abundant cause of exultation. Gaining an advantage over the advance of the Austrian army, the emperor came up to the main body under General Mack at Ulm. Mack agreed to surrender in eight days if he received no Russian re-enforcements; but loosing all hope, he only held out three. Napoleon hastened towards Vienna, and refusing the emperor Francis an armistice, soon had possession of that capital. In Italy his forces were equally as fortunate; and appearing at Austerlitz, he obtained a complete victory over the combined powers of Austria and Russia. The treaty of Presburg followed, by which Francis relinquished his interest in Venice; acknowledged the title of Napoleon as king of Italy, provided the crown should be kept separate from that of France; ceded Burgau, Eichstadt, Tirol, to the Elector of Bavaria, and resigned a part of Burgau to the Elector of Wirtemberg; the remainder, with Ortenau and the city of Constance, to the Elector of Baden. Joseph Bonaparte, brother to the emperor, took Naples and became its king. The seizure of the Ragusan territory, on the opposite side of the Adriatic, soon followed. Louis, another brother of the emperor, was crowned king of Holland. Many of the states of Germany were created into a new power, denominated the confederacy of the Rhine.* This act rent asunder the amicable relations which had existed between the king of Prussia and the emperor, while differences as to the possession of Sicily placed both England and Russia among his enemies.

Success still attended the emperor of the French in every step. Triumphant at Jena, mastering Berlin, the Hanoverian territories, the Silesian province, he repelled the Russians at Pultush and Golomyn.† At Berlin a decree was published which declared the British Islands in a state of blockade and prohibited all commerce with them (A.D. 1807). Successful at Eylau, the emperor laid siege to Dantzic, which surrendered. Battle was joined at Friedland, where the French were victorious. The surrender of Königsburg was the result of this triumph. An armistice was granted to the Russian general at Tilsit. Napoleon and Alexander held a conference on a raft in the Niemen. A treaty was signed soon after, in which Alexander agreed to the spoliation of his Prussian ally, the erection of the kingdom of Westphalia, the increase of the territories of the Elector of Saxony; acknowledged the Confederation of the Rhine, the royal titles of Joseph and Louis Bonaparte; promised to

---

* Al. Eu., ch. xlii. Th. Con. and Em., Bk. XXIV.
† Th. Con. and Em., Bk. XXVII.

withdraw his troops from Moldavia, and to accept the mediation of France to effect peace with the Grand Seignior. The Prussian monarch procured peace on the deprivation of more than one third of the provinces between the Elbe and the Rhine, which, together with Hanover, Brunswick, and Hesse-Cassel, were assigned to Jerome, the brother of Napoleon, created king of Westphalia. The Elector of Saxony got the greater part of Prussian Poland, was titled Duke of Warsaw, and the city of Dantzic was restored to nominal independence under the king of Prussia. Portugal refusing to comply with the requirements of the Berlin decree, and abandoned by its king, was seized by Junot, the French general. Napoleon, by intrigue and intimidation, procured the resignation of the king of Spain and the election of his brother Joseph to his crown. The Spaniards, indignant at the usurpation, resisted the French, succeeded in capturing their fleet at Cadiz, and in gaining some advantages over their forces. Joseph withdrew from Madrid. The Portuguese were roused to action by the success of the Spaniards, and, assisted by the English commander, Sir Arthur Wellesley, were victorious in the battle of Vimiero. Napoleon was not dispirited. Several severe conflicts ensued; his troops reduced, Madrid and Joseph returned. Saragossa still held out, but it was finally taken by the French, who pushed their advantages into Portugal.

The conduct of the French emperor towards Spain and Portugal induced the Austrian powers to invade Bavaria. Napoleon, prompt to repel the attack, seized Vienna, suffered loss at Aspern and Esling, but was triumphant at Wagram. Peace was restored by the treaty of Vienna, which ceded to Napoleon Goritz, Carinola, the city of Trieste, all the Austrian dominions on the right bank of the Save; to the Confederacy in Germany, Saltzburg, a portion of Upper Austria; to Bohemia, West Galicia; to

Russia, East Galicia; and guaranteed the acknowledgment of Joseph Bonaparte as king of Spain. Notwithstanding these successes on land, France lost meantime seven ships of the line, together with the possession of Cayenne, Martinique, and three of the Ionian Isles. Divorcing Josephine, his wife, Napoleon effected a marriage with Marie Louise, the daughter of the Austrian emperor.* This act of Napoleon before he had received a direct negative reply to his proposal to the Russian princess, connected with his refusal to comply with the wishes of that court in regard to Poland, as well as his interference in the affairs of Sweden, gave great offence to Alexander. The same result was produced in other quarters by the annexation of Holland to France. Guadalupe, Bourbon, and the Isle of France were stripped from the emperor in rapid succession, though great success crowned his arms in Spain. Avowing dissatisfaction with Alexander on account of his non-compliance with the provisions of the Berlin decree (1812), Napoleon prepared for an attack on Russia. At his first approaches the Russians retired before him, and he obtained possession of Lithuania. Their ardor being kindled, they displayed intrepidity at Smolensk, Valentia, and Borodino. Upon their retreat the French moved towards Moscow, found it deserted and solitary, seized its immense possessions, which were suddenly snatched from their grasp by the devouring flames lighted in every direction by the torches of concealed citizens and serfs. An armistice and a peace were proposed and rejected. Late in the autumn Napoleon commenced his fatal retreat, and quitting his army in disguise on the sixth of December, he arrived at midnight on the eighteenth of the same month in Paris. Signal as was this failure, it was but the precursor of

---

* Al. Eu. in loc.

greater misfortunes. Russia, Prussia, and Sweden were now united in a firm alliance against the French emperor. Notwithstanding his dreadful previous losses, Napoleon was able to bring into the field an army of three hundred and fifty thousand men. Many indecisive actions took place during the summer. Though the French emperor was weakened by the desertion of German confederates, he triumphed at Lutzen and Bautzen. Peace would have followed this success had not the failure of Joseph in Spain, at Vittoria, determined the Austrian court in favor of the allies, thus bringing a greatly augmented force into the field. A bloody struggle followed. Notwithstanding Napoleon's success at Dresden, defeats in other directions threw a deep gloom over his affairs. From the sixteenth to the eighteenth of October the decisive engagements took place at Leipzig, where the emperor was totally defeated and near falling into the hands of his enemies. This victory changed the condition of Germany and re-established the house of Orange. In such strength did the allies now appear that they refused peace on any condition but that of reducing the French Empire to the territory between the Pyrenees, the Alps, and the Rhine. On Napoleon's refusal to accede to this proposition they commenced the invasion of France. In six months the capital was captured. This decisive stroke produced the emperor's deposition, and at last his abdication, being provided with a retreat on the island of Elba, the sovereignty of which, with all his titles, he was to enjoy, as well as a revenue of two millions of francs yearly. The duchies of Parma, Placentia, and Guastalla were secured to Marie Louise (A.D. 1814).

Monarchy was re-established in France and Louis XVIII. recalled to the throne. The king subjected the press to censorship, interdicted traffic, and forbid theatrical amusements on the Sabbath. Discontent spread throughout the realm, which was fomented by the friends of the late emperor. Napoleon, taking advantage of this state of things, landed in France with a force of eleven hundred and forty men. Traversing the country unmolested, he arrived at Lyons, where he held his court. Deserted by citizens and soldiers, the cause of Louis XVIII. became hopeless and he retired to the Netherlands. Napoleon entered Paris amid the acclamations of the populace, and took possession of the palace. Freedom was given to the press, the severity of the consolidated tax was alleviated, and many popular laws were promulgated. The allied powers, however, were resolute in their purpose. Although Napoleon gained advantages at St. Amand and Ligny and appeared triumphant at Waterloo, yet the tide of fortune turned against him on the approach of the Prussians, and victory was accorded to Wellington. Resigning the imperial authority under the impression his son would succeed to it, the fallen hero retired to Rochefort. After having in vain endeavored to escape by sea to America, Napoleon formed the resolution of throwing himself upon the generosity of England. Maitland, the commander of the Bellerophon, conveyed him to Torbay. The allies exiled him to St. Helena, where he died on the 5th day of May, 1821.

Louis XVIII. resumed the throne. A general pacification took place at Paris, by which the French were compelled to support foreign troops to the number of one hundred and fifty thousand in the frontier fortresses for five years, pay seven millions of francs, and unite with the four powers in the exclusion of Bonaparte and his family from France, as well as in the suppression of revolutionary principles. Marshal Ney and General Labedoyère were tried for having united with Napoleon, convicted and shot. Scenes of blood occurred at Avignon, Marseilles, Lyons, and Paris: at the first of which places Marshal Brune was assassinated in open day, and his body thrown into the Rhone; at the last, the Duke de Berri shared a similar fate. On the death of Louis XVIII., his brother, the Count of Artois, succeeded as Charles X. The rancor of party was allayed by the successful expedition of the French against Algiers. The joy consequent upon this event had scarcely subsided when the privy council represented to the king that the government and throne were in danger from revolutionary principles. Charles, smarting under the remonstrance of the chamber of deputies against the ministers, on the receipt of which he had dissolved the parliament, hastily lent an ear to the advice of his cabinet. Two edicts were issued: one suspended the liberty of the press, the other modified the laws relating to the election of deputies. The effect produced by these measures upon the Parisians was soon displayed in unequivocal acts. The press continued in defiance of the king, and the people sustained it by their patronage. Officers were sent to seize or destroy the presses; mobs assembled; the gendarmes were commanded to disperse them; the populace assailed them; the report of firearms was heard; a sanguinary conflict ensued which raged without intermission for three days. Charles, finding the people triumphant, revoked the edicts. It was too late. Men of influence, among whom was La Fayette, had determined the government should be changed. The king offered to abdicate the throne in favor of the dauphin. The proffer was rejected, a provisional system established, and the Duke of Orleans created lieutenant-general of the kingdom. Charles was finally compelled to leave France, and took up his residence at Holyrood House in Edinburgh, Scotland.

Parliament remodelled the constitution and conferred the crown on the Duke of Orleans, cousin to the late king, who took the title of Louis Philippe I., King of the French. Proceedings were instituted against the ministers of Charles. All but three were taken and condemned to perpetual imprisonment. Prince Polignac, who had been prime minister, was pronounced out of the protection of the law. Louis was not yet firmly seated on the throne. Both the republicans and the friends of the late government were his enemies. So violent was the opposition from this source that it came well-nigh producing a revolution. Foreign transactions measurably diverted the public mind. Yet notwithstanding the brilliant achievements of the French at San Juan de Ulloa, Antwerp, and in Algeria, the spirit of reform which pervaded the masses rendered insecure the throne of Louis. The electoral law of 1831 enabled only about two hundred thousand out of thirty-five millions of people to enjoy the right of suffrage. An extension of this privilege had from time to time been promised by the ministry. The reform party, impatient at the delays of government, organized a central committee at Paris. Sub-committees were created in every part of the kingdom. Lamartine, Barrot, Arago, and other deputies favored the movement. The ministry attempted to counteract the measure. An address to the king denounced the leaders as hostile to the national interests. A violent contest ensued in the chambers, but the ministry triumphed. The government prepared to prevent the banquet of the clubs (Feb. 22, 1848). The populace attacked the hotel of the minister, Guizot, as well as the palace. The royal guards interfered; a scene of violence followed; the soldiery joined the people; the ministry was dissolved; the king abandoned France. The deputies rejecting the Count of Paris, next heir to the crown, a provisional government was established. In the succeeding May the national assembly proclaimed a republican constitution, the first executive office under which was devolved by popular vote upon Louis Napoleon, the nephew of the deceased emperor. Before the expiration of his official term the president destroyed the existing order of things, proclaimed a new legislature, consisting of two houses, and was eventually created hereditary emperor of France, and from his accession to power was prominent in the important events of the times: the war with China, which opened that kingdom to commerce, Christianity, and civilization; the war with Russia, by which the designs of that nation on the Ottomans were frustrated; and the war with Austria, by which the sovereignty of Italy was secured.

The prominence of the Prince of Hohenzollern, a relative of King William of Prusia, as a candidate for the vacant throne of Spain gave offence to Louis. As the assumption of that crown by the prince would surround the French by German influences on the North and South, most of the other sovereigns of Europe sustained the emperor in his protest against the German movement. William, feeling the pressure of public sentiment, caused the prince to decline the proffered crown (A.D. 1870). Had Napoleon stopped here he would have come out of this controversy with triumph. No sooner, however, was the emperor master of events than he demanded of William a guarantee that none of the German princes should in the future aspire to the Spanish honors. The Prussian shrewdly dallied until he was able to put his forces in motion and then, bidding defiance to the Frenchman, commenced a war which he had long contemplated in order to obtain possession of Alsace and Lorraine. The first blow, at Metz, divided the army of France; the second, at Sedan, was followed by the surrender of the emperor and his army. After this, although the French fought with their accustomed bravery, the vast numbers of the Germans overpowered them. France was in a few months overrun, and Paris would have surrendered had not a peace ensued, by which the Germans gained Alsace and Lorraine and four milliards of francs as indemnity for the expenses of the war.

France was doomed to suffer more by the hands of her citizens than by the arms of foreign foes. Scarcely had the national assembly at Versailles effected the peace with Germany than a monstrous insurrection arose at Paris, which was not terminated until near one hundred thousand lives were lost and one third of that city destroyed by fire (A.D. 1871). A republic was declared with Thiers at its head; who soon becoming unpopular, General McMahon succeeded as president; he being in turn followed by Grévy, the present (1884) chief executive.

CHAPTER XV.

THE AUSTRASIAN DIVISION OF THE EMPIRE OF THE FRANKS FROM THE ELECTION OF CONRAD OF FRANCONIA TO THE DEATH OF MAXIMILIAN I.

The Germanic states conferred their sovereignty upon Conrad Count of Franconia (A.D. 911).* This confederation embraced Franconia, Bamberg, Suabia, Constans, Basle, Berne, Lausanne, Bergundy, Besançon, Lorraine, Metz, Liege, Cambray, Arras, Flanders, Holland, Zealand, Utrecht, Cologne, Treves, Mentz, Worms, Spire, Strasburg, Friesland, Saxony, Hesse, Westphalia, Thuringia, Watteravia, Messin, Brandenburg, Pomerania, Rugen,

---

* Kohlrausch's Ger., ch. vi. p. 15. Aug. His., Vol. V. p. 223; Vol. VII. p. 66. Rev. xiii.–xx.

Stettin, Holstein, Austria, Carinthia, Styria, the Tyrolese, Bavaria, the Grisons, and all their dependencies. Notwithstanding this powerful array of strength, the emperor was compelled to purchase an ignominious peace from the Huns. Henry, surnamed the Fowler, was elected emperor by the states. The empire was fortified by walling the principal towns and placing the frontiers under marquises, who were furnished with soldiers and subsistence. Lorraine was subdued, and the Huns were defeated at Merseburgh. Previous to the emperor's death, the states settled the succession on his son Otho. The Huns made another incursion upon the empire. Otho overthrew them at Dortmund. Shortly afterwards Bohemia revolted. The emperor reduced it to a tributary condition, compelling its inhabitants, then pagans, to receive the Roman Catholic religion. A triumph equally signal was obtained over Everhard Duke of Bavaria, who refused to do homage on the pretence that he was not the vassal but the ally of the emperor. The dominions of the defeated duke were given to his uncle Bartolf, and one of his brothers was created count palatine, or supreme judge, of Bavaria; the other of the Rhine. In order to reduce the power of the nobles, Otho conferred duchies and counties on the clergy. The Danes were forced to receive baptism and pay tribute. Italy was successfully invaded; the emperor crowned by the pope and dignified by the title of Augustus; the pope swearing allegiance to the emperor on the tomb of St. Peter, and receiving a renewal of the donations of Pepin and Charlemagne. No sooner, however, had Otho withdrawn than the pope renounced his allegiance. Otho returned to Rome. The pope was deposed, Leo VIII. elected, who, with the clergy and citizens, renewed the oath lately taken, binding themselves neither to elect nor consecrate a pope without the consent of the emperor. The attention of Otho was directed to Spoleto in consequence of some disturbances there. John XII., the late pope, was restored; Leo VIII. dethroned. Shortly afterwards John was assassinated, but his party refused to acknowledge Leo and proceeded to elect Benedict V. Informed of these proceedings, the emperor returned to Rome, reduced it, and restored Leo to his honors. The pope, clergy, and people agreed that Otho and his successors in the kingdom of Italy should always have the power of naming a pope and of giving investiture to bishops. Notwithstanding this agreement the Romans again rebelled, on the election of John XIII. Otho entered Rome, banished the consuls, hanged the tribunes, caused the præfect to be whipped through the streets, and, having restored John XIII., retired to Capua, where he received ambassadors from the Greek emperor. Otho II. became emperor on the death of his father, Otho I. Reducing Bavaria, Denmark, Bohemia, and settling the difficulties in Lorraine, the emperor marched into Italy, took possession of Rome, chastised the rebels, who had again agitated the difficulties of the papacy; but, in attempting to wrest Calabria from the Greeks, he was cut to pieces by the Saracens, their allies. Not long after, the emperor dying, Otho III., a minor, came to the sceptre. A troublesome regency ensued. The emperor arriving at age, gave clear evidence of talent. Rome, still refractory, was subdued on the appearance of Otho; as soon as he withdrew, the flame of discord kindled in all its fury. Returning, however, with a strong army, the emperor took the city by assault, inflicting the most sanguinary punishments upon the heads of faction. After the death of Otho III. a sharp contest arose about a successor. Henry Duke of Bavaria was finally elected emperor. The disturbances in Germany and Poland were quelled, Italy subdued, and Henry crowned at Rome by Benedict VIII. Conrad of Franconia, his successor, was equally successful in Germany and Italy. His son, Henry III., came to the possession of power on the death of Conrad. The triumphs of this were not behind those of a former reign, both in Hungary and Italy.

Henry IV., afterwards surnamed the Great, was only six years old at the death of his father, Henry III. Upon his arrival at age he assumed the reigns of government. Troubles arose in Saxony in consequence of the emperor's conduct to Otho of Nordheim. A war followed in which Henry was victorious; the bitterest feeling, however, was entertained against him by the Saxons. Gregory VII., by appearing to side with the emperor, procured the confirmation of his election.* This end accomplished, the pope threw off the mask; excommunicated every clergyman who received a benefice from a layman, every layman who conferred one; attempted to free the clergy from the civil power, and subjected all temporal princes to the see of Rome. Henry, enraged at being summoned before the pope for continuing to bestow investitures, sent an ambassador to Rome with a formal deprivation of Gregory. In turn the emperor was deposed and excommunicated, and was so depressed by ecclesiastical revenge that he humbled himself at the feet of his holiness. Supported by the Germans, Gregory procured Rudolph of Suabia to be elected to the sceptre. All thus at stake, Henry was driven to arms; met his enemies; defeated them in several engagements in Germany; marched to Italy, where, his cause being favored, he degraded the pope, procured the election of another, and made himself master of Rome after a siege of two years. A similar success

---

* Kol. Ger., pp. 143–153. Rev. xiii.–xv. Chapter V., ante.

attended the imperial arms in Germany, where the Saxons had set up a king of the Romans. New troubles arose in Italy. Conrad, the emperor's eldest son, rebelled. The Italian cities and nobles supporting the usurpation, the emperor found it impossible to succeed and retired to Germany, where Conrad was denounced and his brother Henry declared king of the Romans. Meantime Conrad died, and young Henry was incited to action by the pope. Both father and son prepared to decide the contest by the sword. The latter, dreading the military superiority of the former, implored his forgiveness, imputing his folly to the advice of evil counsellors. The father, taking him into favor, immediately dismissed his forces. The credulous Henry was seized by his perfidious son, who assembled a diet, deposed the emperor, and was himself proclaimed as Henry V. Degraded and a prisoner, Henry IV. suffered every species of outrage, and as his affairs were about taking a more favorable turn he suddenly died at Liege.

Henry V. was no sooner seated on the throne than he asserted the right of investiture, and marched into Italy an army of thirty thousand men.[*] A battle ensued; the emperor was victorious; Pope Pascal II. was taken prisoner, and the affair was settled by a confirmation of Henry's right of investiture. New scenes of violence, however, soon occurred upon the old subject of investitures. A general council was convoked. The whole matter was eventually arranged by the emperor yielding the free choice of bishops and the right of investiture by the ring and staff; in return for which the election was to take place in his presence or that of his plenipotentiary, with reserved power on his part to decide doubtful cases or those in which the electors could not agree, and to make investi-

---

[*] Kol. Ger., 154.

tures of temporal possessions with the sceptre and spiritual ones in Germany in the same manner. On the death of Henry V. without issue, Lothario, Duke of Saxe-Supplenbourg was chosen emperor. Enlisting in his favor Conrad of Franconia and Frederick of Suabia, and subduing the Bohemians, Lothario was involved in the contest between the rival popes Innocent and Anacletus. The former was finally restored, and the allies of the latter the Norman princes of Apulia and Calabria, compelled to surrender their possessions. Conrad of Franconia succeeded to the sceptre. His throne was disputed by Henry Duke of Bavaria, whose family name was Guelph, from which his partisans were called Guelphs. The Imperialists, from the paternal castle of Conrad,—Viebling,—were styled Ghibellines. Henry, though able to conduct the war for some time, was eventually overpowered. Conrad used his good fortune with tenderness, and the matter was accommodated. An unfortunate crusade to the Holy Land terminated the events of this reign. Frederick surnamed Barbarossa, nephew of Conrad, succeeded to the sceptre. After receiving the congratulations of nearly all the kingdoms of Europe and the oath of allegiance from his vassal, the king of Denmark, the emperor settled the affairs of Germany and proceeded to quiet the disturbances in Italy. At his coronation Frederick was offended with the ceremony of holding the stirrups and bridle of the pope; but his scruples were finally overcome, and he went through all the formalities of prostrating himself before his holiness, kissing his foot, and leading his white palfrey by the bridle nine Roman spaces. New difficulties arose in Bohemia and Poland. The activity and valor of the emperor succeeded in humbling the former and in conquering the latter, which was erected into a tributary kingdom. The Italian states asserted their independence. After alternate defeat and success a reconciliation was effected by granting a general pardon to the Roman cities, with liberty to use their own laws and forms of government. Meanwhile Germany was disturbed by the encroachments of Henry Duke of Saxony, who was subdued and received into favor. Resolving on a crusade to the Holy Land, the emperor set out with a large army; crossed the Hellespont; defeated the Turks in several battles; took Iconium; but was accidentally drowned in the river Cydnus. Henry VI., his son, succeeded to the throne. A bloody effort to recover Sicily from the possession of Tancred, the natural brother of his wife, occupied the life and reign of this emperor. Three persons were proclaimed by as many separate diets: Philip of Suabia, Otho of Brunswick, and Frederick son of Henry VI. After a desolating civil war, Frederick, being successful over his rivals, was crowned at Aix-la-Chapelle. Two large armies furnished to the crusaders were forced to conclude a dishonorable treaty with the soldan of Egypt and Syria. Some years afterwards, Frederick having married the daughter of De Brienne, the titular king of Jerusalem, and goaded into the expedition by the pope, set out for the recovery of the Holy Land, and procured the cession of Jerusalem and its territories with less trouble and in a shorter time than any who had preceded in the enterprise. The pope illy repaid these services, filling up the remainder of the life of Frederick with feuds, rebellions, and wars. An interregnum of twenty-three years followed. The empire fell a prey to factions. Denmark, Holland, Hungary, and Poland became independent. Lubeck, Cologne, Brunswick, and Dantzic created the Hanseatic League. Italy assumed a new form of government. The cities of Lombardy purchased their freedom. Sicily changed its prince and constitution.

Rudolph Count of Hapsburg was at last raised to the

vacant throne. Some princes protested against the election; among them was the king of Bohemia, who was finally slain in battle and his Austrian possessions transferred to Albert, the eldest son of the emperor. Rudolph spent the last years of his life in establishing the grandeur of his own family. Disappointed in the death of the son who bore his name and chagrined in not being able to procure his son Albert to be elected king of the Romans, the emperor died after a reign of eighteen years. Adolphus of Nassau succeeded to power. A scene of turmoil terminated in his deposition and in the elevation of Albert of Austria. Civil war ensued, and Adolphus was slain in the battle of Worms by the hand of Albert. The diet of Frankfort confirmed the title of Albert, and his coronation followed at Aix-la-Chapelle. The first years of the emperor were consumed in a quarrel with the pope, which was terminated by the admission of Albert that emperors and kings derive their power from his holiness.* Albert lost his life in an attempt to subdue the Swiss, who had shaken off the Austrian yoke. The Count of Luxemburg was elected emperor under the name of Henry VII. With a view to crush the independent feeling which displayed itself in Italy, the emperor marched thither a large army. Some places submitted; others resisted; eventually all were subdued. An interregnum of fourteen months occurred after the death of Henry VII. The intrigues of Louis of Bavaria and Frederick of Austria distracted the empire. The former was elected; the latter was supported by a strong faction. The battle of Muhldorf placed Louis firmly on the throne. Pope John XXII. denounced the title of the emperor. Negotiation proving ineffectual, an assembly of princes, civil and ecclesiastical, was convoked

---

*Chapter V. New. Dis., xxvi. pp. 605, 606; Rev. xiii. 16, 17.

at Frankfort, which decreed that the plurality of the suffrages of the electoral college confers the empire without the consent of the holy see, and that during a vacancy the government devolves on the count palatine of the Rhine. The war, however, was continued until the death of Louis, when the Margrave of Moravia became possessed of the imperial power under the name of Charles IV. In this reign the university of Prague was founded and the famous golden bull promulgated by the diet of Nuremberg. An electoral college was constituted by this instrument, consisting of the archbishops of Mentz, Cologne, and Treves, the king of Bohemia, the count palatine, the Duke of Saxony, and the Margrave of Brandenburg. Wenceslaus, the son of Charles IV., succeeded to his dignities. The welfare of his people occupied his attention for some years, but eventually falling into all sorts of debaucheries, the emperor neglected public concerns and was deposed by a diet held at the castle of Lænstein. Rupert of the Palatinate was elected to his place. An unsuccessful invasion of Italy and attempts on the Hussites in Bohemia were the prominent acts of this emperor. Sigismund, brother of Wenceslaus, came to the sceptre. Desirous to heal the wounds of the Roman Catholic Church, the Council of Constance (A.D. 1411) was convoked by the emperor. The renunciation of all the pretenders to the popedom was recommended. Two complied; the third, Peter de Luna, persisted in his claim to the last, and was deposed. Martin V. was elected. John Huss, who opposed the infallibility and supremacy of the Roman hierarchy, was burnt. Jerome of Prague shared a similar fate for like conduct. The religious opinions of these evangelical men, however, were too well established to be destroyed by the decree of a council or the fury of persecution. The opposition to the hierarchy of Rome set in with fearful power from this period. John emphatically describes the times when he exclaims, "I heard a voice from heaven, as the voice of many waters and as the voice of a great thunder" (Rev. xiv. 2).* Albert II. of Austria succeeded to the sceptre, but soon died in an ineffectual war against the Turks. Frederick, his cousin, was chosen emperor. Procuring a settlement of the conflicting claims for the popedom in the Council of Basle, he proceeded to Italy, where he was crowned. Though his arms were unavailing in Hungary and Lower Austria, the victory of John Hunniades Corvinus forever stayed the progress of the Turks in Europe. Maximilian I., his son, took the sceptre. Possessed of the Low Counties by marriage with the heiress of Burgundy, the emperor was able to form those powerful alliances which made him so terrific to Louis VIII. of France.

CHAPTER XVI.

THE AUSTRASIAN DIVISION OF THE EMPIRE OF THE FRANKS TO THE PRESENT TIMES.

THE grandson of Maximilian I., Charles, king of Spain, was elected emperor.† The first object which Charles V. desired to accomplish was the suppression of the reformed religion. Martin Luther, professor of theology in the university of Wittenberg, had been cited before the diet of Augsburg in the last reign; but denied a fair hearing, he appealed to Rome. Notwithstanding

---

*New. Proph. Dis., xxiv., xxv. p. 523.
† Kol. Ger., ch. xvii., xl. Robertson's Charles V. Cox's Austria. Rev. xiii., xx. New. Dis., xxiv. pp. 537-585. Scott in loc.

the condemnation of the reformer's opinions by the Pope, Charles summoned another diet at Worms. Luther attended under the safe-conduct of the emperor. His firmness was remarkable. Admitting the acrimony of his controversial writings, he refused, though threatened with death, to renounce his opinions until convinced of their error. He finally departed to Saxony, where he flourished under his old patron the elector, notwithstanding the diet condemned his tenets and outlawed his person.

After the peace of Cambray the Italian states were in the power of Charles. As well from a fear of the Ottomans as from political considerations, he was induced to pursue a mild course of conduct. Nearly one half the Germanic states now adopted the sentiments of the reformers. In order to stay the rapid progress of the Reformation the emperor convoked a diet at Spire. This body issued a decree confirming the edict of Worms. Many of the princes and free cities protested against it and were hence called Protestants. The diet of Augsburg followed the next year, where the Protestants presented their opinions in a written form, which is denominated the Confession of Augsburg. Neither party was now disposed to yield. Charles turned to the patron princes of the reformers, who refused to forsake them or their doctrines. A decree was issued condemning the Protestant tenets and prohibiting the toleration of those who taught them. The Protestant princes entered into a league at Smalcald for mutual defence. Charles, dreading an invasion of the Ottomans and the loss of Protestant influence in that event, granted to that party by the treaty of Nuremberg liberty of conscience until the meeting of a general council. Charles took the field against the Ottomans. Solyman II., fearful of his powerful foe, retired without striking a blow. The effort of the Hungarians against the Porte was not equally happy, though the emperor had occasion for joy in consequence of the success of his African expedition, the suppression of the mutiny among his troops, and the reduction of Castile and Ghent, both of which had been in open rebellion.

The Protestants, having repeatedly demanded a general council, now pressed the appointment of a conference where the points in dispute might be examined. This opportunity was afforded in the diet of Ratisbon. Only a few points were settled. An edict of recess decreed these matters concluded, and reserved the other points of controversy for the adjudication of a general council or a national synod. Meantime no innovations were to be made or means employed to gain proselytes. This edict was offensive to both pope and Protestants. Charles, to obtain the favor of the latter, granted them a private declaration of exemption from whatever they deemed oppressive in the edict. After the unfortunate expedition of the emperor against Algiers his conduct towards the Protestants underwent a radical change. Concluding the disadvantageous peace of Crespy with France, and procuring a truce with Solyman II. by confirming his right to one half of Hungary, as well as that of his brother to the remaining portion of that country on the payment of tribute, Charles, in connection with Pope Paul III., commenced vigorous measures for the extirpation of the Reformed religion. Meanwhile a general council sat at Trent. The Protestants, considering it a body assembled to condemn rather than to examine their opinions, resolved not to admit its authority. Charles, concluding to compel them, concealed his purpose by various pretexts, so as to raise sufficient force to effect his purpose. The leaders of the Protestants did not suffer themselves to be deceived, though they were greatly dejected by the death of Luther.

Collecting an army of over seventy thousand men, they would have carried their point had they not by imprudently spending their time in negotiation afforded their adversaries opportunity for action. Maurice of Thuringia, a neutral prince, was induced by the emperor to invade the electorate of Saxony. Ulm, a city of Suabia, was subdued. In a short time the Elector of Saxony and the landgrave were the only supporters of the league of Smalcald. Its destruction would have been inevitable but for assistance from France. The elector was defeated and taken prisoner near Muhlberg. The landgrave, left without a hope, yielded to the emperor, who carried both his conquered foes about with him in triumph.

A diet was summoned to meet at Augsburg, finally to compose the controversies in regard to religion. The Council of Trent having been meantime transferred by the pope to Bologna, the emperor sent two ambassadors there to protest against the removal. A system of doctrine denominated the Interim was published, conformity to which was required until the meeting of a general council. Both parties were dissatisfied. The pope dying, his successor, Julius III., ordered the general council to reassemble at Trent. The council at last (A.D. 1551) met at Trent, though the Gallican deputies were not present, having been prevented from coming, as was alleged by the French ambassador, by the war of Parma, on which ground he protested against the proceedings at the outset of the session. The pope's legate treated the protest with contempt. The council went into the consideration of the topics for the settlement of which it had been assembled. Its decrees completely established the Roman Catholic tenets. The Protestants, refusing compliance, were exposed to much persecution. Maurice, Elector of Saxony, resolved to oppose the civil and religious despotism of the emperor. In the execution of the plan he conducted himself with such adroitness that Charles never suspected him, while the Protestants were all brought to repose full confidence in his sincerity. Effecting an alliance with Henry II. of France, Maurice struck the first blow at Innspruck, where the emperor would have fallen into the hands of his foes had he not escaped over the Alps. Peace was concluded at Passau (A.D. 1552) on the following terms: The confederates were to lay down their arms by the twelfth of August; the landgrave was to be released; a diet was to be assembled in six months to settle religious disputes; meantime both parties were to enjoy full religious liberty; the imperial chamber was to administer justice to both parties impartially, where both were to sit indiscriminately as judges; all encroachments of constitutional liberty alleged to have been committed were to be submitted to the diet, and in case that body could not terminate the religious difficulties all the rights secured to the Protestants by this treaty were to be continued to them forever. The contest still continued in Germany by the Margrave of Brandenburg was decided at Sieverhausen, where Maurice gained a victory, but died in consequence of a wound received in the battle.

The diet sat conformably to the peace of Passau, but its deliberations were prevented by the troubles created by Albert of Brandenburg. Its decrees eventually settled that the cities and princes adhering to the Confession of Augsburg should enjoy their worship and faith without molestation; that the Catholic clergy within their limits should claim no jurisdiction, but should enjoy it within those cities adhering to the pope without Protestant interference; that no means except those of persuasion should be used to settle religious differences; that the civil power of every state shall determine the form of faith and worship, permitting dissenters to withdraw with their effects; and that the benefices of the church shall remain as at the peace of Passau, unless in case of an ecclesiastic renouncing Catholicism, which should work a forfeiture of his benefice. Charles V. shortly afterwards resigned the imperial sceptre and dominions to his brother Ferdinand and retired to private life.

The pope attempted to reassemble the Council of Trent. The Protestants persisted in denying its authority. The body was eventually dissolved without effecting anything but an effort to exalt the ecclesiastical over the civil power. Maximilian II. was the son and successor of Ferdinand I. Soon after his elevation he was engaged in a war with the Ottomans, who entered Hungary and subdued Sigeth after a gallant defence. On the death of the sultan a peace of ten years was concluded with his successor. Rudolph II. succeeded to power on the death of his father, Maximilian II. The Ottoman invasion of Hungary was renewed and thwarted by Mathias, the brother of the emperor. The grateful Hungarians placed their crown on the head of their deliverer. The Protestant states, deprived of their privileges by new imperial impositions, formed a confederacy called the Evangelical Union, which was opposed two years afterwards by another denominated the Catholic League. A controversy arose as to the succession of the duchies of Cleves, Juliers, and Berg. The emperor ordered the possessions to be sequestered, and Leopold his brother was sent as governor over them until the difficulty should be settled. These acts gave offence to two of the competitors, the Elector of Brandenburg and the Duke of Neuburg, with whom the Evangelical Union took sides. Preparations were made for war by securing the alliance of the French king. Henry IV. being killed, these hostile bodies seemed to be dissolved, though the claimants still continued their pretensions and expelled the sequestrator. Meantime Rudolph II. died and his brother Mathias came to the throne. Having no lineal issue, the emperor's cousin, the Duke of Stiria, a violent Catholic, was elected king of Bohemia and acknowledged in Hungary. King Ferdinand, considering himself the champion of papacy, soon assailed the Protestants. Hungary and Bohemia revolted. The former was appeased; but the latter, joined by Silesia, Moravia, and Upper Austria and headed by Count de la Tour, who was supported by a body of German Protestants under Count Mansfeldt, held out, and a furious civil war arose. Amidst this commotion the Duke of Stiria succeeded as emperor under the title of Ferdinand II. Bohemia deposed the emperor from its throne and chose for its king Frederick V., elector palatine. The elector was utterly ruined by his defeat at Prague. The other claimant to the crown resigned his pretensions. The house of Austria was consequently completely established in Germany, and sought by a close alliance with Spain to become more than a match for its continental neighbors. The king of Denmark and the league in Lower Saxony could not withstand Ferdinand, who, imagining that he had rendered Catholicism triumphant forever, went so far as to issue an edict ordering the German Protestants to restore the church-lands held by them since the peace of Passau. The Protestants remonstrated against the edict of restitution; which proving ineffectual, they formed an alliance with Gustavus Adolphus, king of Sweden. After fortifying himself by treaties with England and France, the king entered Germany, defeated the imperialists at Leipsic, and made himself master of the country from the Elbe to the Rhine. Repulsed at Naumburg, Gustavus retreated without material loss; but joining battle at Lutzen, he was killed, though his forces were ultimately victorious. The alliance, however, was continued, and nothing could have prevented its successful termination had not the members of the Evangelical Union been thrown into consternation by the victory of the imperialists at Nordlingen. The peace of Prague followed (A.D. 1635). Its terms were that the Protestants or Lutherans should retain forever the mediate ecclesiastical benefices which did not depend immediately upon the emperor and were seized before the peace of Passau, and retain for forty years the immediate ones, though seized since that peace, if actually engaged before the twelfth day of November, 1627; that the Protestant religion shall be permitted to exist throughout the empire, except in Bohemia and Austria; that the Duke of Bavaria shall possess the Palatinate on condition of paying the jointure of Frederick's widow and giving a fit subsistence to his son on his return to duty; and that there shall be a mutual restitution of property taken since the irruption of Gustavus.

This settlement left the burden of the war to be borne by the Swedes and French. Their operations at the outset were extensive but unsuccessful. The imperialists took Kaiserslautern, mastered Vandervange, possessed themselves of Italy, triumphed in the Low Countries, and came within three days' march of Paris. The scene, however, changed. The Swedes, re-enforced by the French, triumphed at Wittstoch. Soon after this misfortune Ferdinand II. died and his son, Ferdinand III., came to the possession of the sceptre. A succession of calamities occurred. The imperialists were defeated near Rheinfels by the French. In Pomerania and Bohemia they shared a similar fate at the hands of the Swedes. Though repulsed at Saltzburg, the allies triumphed at Wolfenbuttel, Breitenfeld, Leipsic, Holstein, Friburg, Tabor, and Zusmarshausen. The emperor, overpowered by his adversaries, concluded the peace of Westphalia, at Munster (A.D. 1648). By this treaty France was to possess the three archbishoprics Metz, Toul, Verdun; Pignerol, Brisaw, Suntgaco, upper and lower Alsace, and the right to keep a garrison in Philipsburg: Sweden, besides five millions of dollars, had the archbishopric of Bremen, the bishopric Verdun secularized, Pomerania, Stettin, the isle of Rugen, the city of Wismar, in Mecklenburg, to be held as fiefs of the emperor, with three votes in the diet: the Elector of Brandenburg took, in the place of Upper Pomerania, the bishopric of Magdeburg secularized, and those of Minden, Camin, and Halberstadt, with four votes in the diet: the Duke of Mecklenburg received the bishoprics of Schwerin and Ratzeburg erected into secular principalities, in the place of Wismar: the electoral dignity with the Upper Palatinate remained with the Duke of Bavaria and his descendants of the male line: the Lower Palatinate was given to Charles Louis, son of the deposed elector, in whose favor a ninth electorate was created, which was to remain until the extinction of the house of Bavaria. All the other princes were re-established as they were before the year 1619. Switzerland was secured in its independence. The peace of Passau was confirmed. The disputed succession of Cleves and Juliers was referred to arbitration. The same privileges were extended to the Calvinists as the Lutherans enjoyed. The imperial chamber consisted of twenty-four Protestants and twenty-six Catholics; six Protestants placed in the Aulic Council; and the diet composed of an equal number of Catholic and Protestant deputies, except when convoked on concerns of either religion, when the deputies were to be elected according to the form of religion in question.

This terrific struggle broke the tie of Roman supremacy as it had existed in Europe for centuries. Since this time the hierarchy has been retrograding, until it is now the lamentation of its head that even in the countries where its ritual is maintained his power is not respected nor his mandates obeyed. " Babylon is fallen, is fallen, that great city, because she made all nations drink of the wine of the wrath of her fornication." (Rev. xiv. 8.)

Recent movements of the papacy avow a determination to re-establish its antiquated infallibility and temporal power, even though the struggle should deluge the world in blood.* If his holiness is able to produce the battle he threatens, he will be liable to two destructive fires; the one from the confederated powers outside of his church, and the other from that large and influential party inside of it which, while it adheres to the creed and ritual of Catholicity, regards the infallibility and temporal power of the hierarchy as dangerous to civil liberty and subversive of national sovereignty. Amidst such overwhelming numbers popery may finally perish. †

But in regard to all unfulfilled prophecy the observation of Sir Isaac Newton should be heeded, "that the folly of interpreters has been to foretell times and things by prophecy as if God designed to make them prophets ;‡" and it may be added that it is the folly of most papists of this day to deny all history which does not suit their purposes, and dovetail fabricated facts into the text of prophecy.

After the death of Ferdinand III. his son Leopold was elected emperor. The Ottoman irruption was repelled and Hungary reduced. Rallying from their defeat, the Ottomans fell with dreadful fury on Vienna. It would have become a prey to them if the Poles had not arrived for its relief. Occupied by the Ottoman war, the emperor procured peace from Louis XIV. by surrendering his claims

---

* Archbp. Manning's Address, 1874. † New. Dis., 25.
‡ Scott's Introd. to Rev.

to Luxemburg, Strasburg, and the fortress of Reihl for Courtnay and Dixmunde. The imperial arms were eventually successful against the Porte, and Hungary compelled to receive Joseph, the emperor's son, as its king. The treaty with the sultan ceded to Austria all Hungary next the Save, Transylvania and Sclavonia; to Russia, Azoph; to the Poles, Caminice; and to the Venetians the Morea, together with several places in Dalmatia. In the midst of the war about the Spanish succession Leopold died and his son Joseph took the sceptre. Before the conclusion of that contest Joseph departed this life and his brother Charles became emperor. A war soon followed with the sultan which, after the victory of Prince Eugene at Peterwaraden, was concluded by the treaty of Passarowitz, by which the emperor gained Belgrade and the bannet of Temeswar, the Porte got the Morea. A subsequent rupture placed Belgrade, Sabatz, Orsovia, Servia, and Austrian Wallachia in the hands of the Ottomans; fixed the Danube and the Save as the boundaries of the empires; left Azoph with Russia on condition of demolishing its fortifications; and re-established the ancient lines between Russia and Turkey.

The bloody war which placed Maria Theresa, the female issue of Charles VI., in power, while Francis her husband was nominally emperor, was scarcely over before hostilities ensued with Frederick, king of Prussia. On the death of Francis I. his son Joseph obtained the imperial dignity, and after his mother's demise he heired all her dominions. Notwithstanding this prosperity, an unsuccessful war against the sultan, the revolt of the Netherlands, and the discontent of the Hungarians broke the emperor's heart, and he died at an early age. Leopold, the brother of Joseph, succeeded to the sceptre. The Ottomans were propitiated, the Netherlands recovered, Poland crushed.

Francis, the son and the successor of Leopold, was soon involved in the commotions of France. The settlement of the congress of Vienna extended to the affairs of Germany. The empire was dissolved; a diet composed of the plenipotentiaries of the sovereign princes and free cities, in which a delegate of the house of Austria was to preside, was provided; freedom of foreign alliance secured to every member of the union, with a proviso that he should make no treaty inconsistent with the general safety or any particular branch of the confederacy; and provisions enacted for a common effort to repel hostilities, and a general guarantee to each prince of his possessions, an accommodation of all differences by the diet, and the establishment of representative bodies in each state. This pacification was disturbed by the acts of the Belgians (A.D. 1830), which so disaffected the German states that they raised the arm of resistance against the Duke of Brunswick. The Poles were emboldened to a similar effort. Both were unsuccessful. On the death of Francis II. his son Ferdinand succeeded to the throne of Austria. Seconded by Prussia and Russia, Austria destroyed in the germ the effort for independence made by the Poles in Posen, Cracow, Galicia, and as far as Moldavia; disposing of many of those unfortunate people by the most cruel and ignominious punishments (A.D. 1846). The guiding spirit in these acts was Prince Metternich, a statesman of great learning and abilities. A revolution (A.D. 1848) compelled the sovereign to abdicate and brought his nephew to the throne, under the name of Francis Joseph I. Constitutional liberty would have been procured at this period had not the excesses of the insurgents produced a reaction in favor of the monarch. Taking advantage of this circumstance, the court of Vienna established its authority at home, destroyed the confederacy in Italy, and subdued the Hungarians by means of

Russian aid; but the event of the war of 1866 between it and Prussia has destroyed its power over Germany.

CHAPTER XVII.

POWERS OF EUROPE CONNECTED WITH THE EMPIRE OF THE FRANKS.

No single power of Europe had much weight in the affairs of its empires before the latter part of the fourteenth century. Many of them were of little importance until a much later period. At the former time Margaret Waldemar, daughter of the king of Denmark and widow of the last king of Norway, succeeded to the Danish throne. Shortly afterwards she was elected queen of Norway. The Swedes, oppressed by Albert of Mecklenburg, offered their sovereignty to her, and she marched to their aid, repelled Albert, and assumed the government. Resolved to render this union perpetual, Margaret assembled the states of the three kingdoms at Calmar (A.D. 1397), where they decreed that Denmark, Sweden, and Norway should have but one and the same sovereign, who should be elected successively by each of the kingdoms, each nation retaining its own laws and the natives of one kingdom being ineligible to office or honor in another. The union did not long survive the reign of Margaret. Eric, her successor, alienated the hearts of the Swedes by his partiality for the Danes. The former revolted under Charles Canuteson, their king; returned to their allegiance under Christian I. of Denmark; again revolted, and again renewed the union of Calmar under John, his successor. Revolting a third time, they committed the administration to Stene Sture. The archbishop of Upsal, Gustavus Trolle, refused to acknowledge him. Obliged to surrender in his castle of Stecka, the bishop was degraded and deprived of all his benefices by the diet. The pope excommunicated Sture and committed the execution of the bull to Christian II. of Denmark, the Nero of the North.* Worsted in battle, Christian offered to go in person to Stockholm to treat with Sture if the Swedes would give six hostages for his safety. Securing among the hostages Gustavus Vasa, grand-nephew of King Canuteson, Christian immediately departed with the hostages to Denmark. The Dane invaded West Gothland with a more powerful army. Sture in his advance thither received a mortal wound; the Swedes dispersed. Christian wasted the country with fire and sword, took the capital, and was crowned king.

The coronation was succeeded by a bloody tragedy. After Christian had sworn at the cathedral that he would govern Sweden not as a conqueror, but as if elected by the people, he invited the senators and nobility to a sumptuous feast which lasted three days. On the last day Trolle, reminding the king that, though he had pardoned all past offences, no satisfaction had been given to the pope, demanded satisfaction in the name of his holiness. The hall was instantly filled with armed men, the guests secured, proceeded against as heretics, a scaffold erected, and ninety-four persons of rank, among whom was Eric Vasa, the father of the celebrated Gustavus, publicly executed. Meantime Gustavus Vasa escaped from Denmark in very destitute circumstances and concealed himself among the mountains of Dalecarlia. To supply himself with bread, he entered among the miners and performed their daily toil. Making himself known at an annual feast, he roused

---

* Geÿer's His. of Sweden, ch. v. Rev. xiii. New Dis. xxv. p. 537.

them to action. The governor's castle was taken, a severe retribution visited on the Danish garrison, and Gustavus proclaimed king of Sweden. Christian became unpopular with the Danes. Frederick Duke of Holstein, his uncle, was chosen in his place. Finding Gustavus firmly seated on the throne, the Danish sovereign abandoned all designs against Sweden. Frederick was succeeded by his son, Christian III., who, following the example of Gustavus, established the Protestant religion in his dominions. Upon the death of Gustavus Vasa his son Eric succeeded to the crown, from which he was deposed and his brother John elected king. An ineffectual effort to re-establish Catholicism marks the reign of this prince and that of his son, Sigismund. Charles IX., who headed the Lutheran party, was elected king and held the sceptre until his death. Gustavus Adolphus, his son, was declared his successor, though only eighteen years of age. He immediately signalized himself by heroic exploits against the Danes. In a war with Russia he subdued nearly all Finland. The king of Poland refusing to acknowledge his title to the crown, he overran Livonia, Prussia, and Lithuania. Meantime Gustavus did not neglect the domestic concerns of Sweden. A truce of six years with Poland afforded the king time to turn his attention to the affairs of Germany. In addition to his attachment for the persecuted cause of Protestantism, Gustavus was induced to take up arms against the emperor on account of his indignity to the Swedish ambassador, his assistance to the king of Poland, and his project of extending the imperial dominions over the Baltic. On the death of Gustavus Adolphus his daughter Christiana became queen, under a regency of guardians. In ten years she resigned the crown. Charles Gustavus Duke of Deux-Ponts was elected to the royal dignity. Poland was conquered, Denmark invaded; but death removed the king in the midst of the war, and the crown fell into the hands of his minor son. Charles XI. proved to be, like his father, a warrior. On his death his son, the twelfth of the same name, took the throne. Charles XII. had scarcely obtained the sceptre when he was assailed by an alliance between Poland, Denmark, and Russia.* Losing no time, the king laid siege to Copenhagen. The Danes, unsuccessful in Holstein and assailed in their capital, were compelled to execute the treaty of Travendal. With eight thousand men Charles defeated eighty thousand Russians at Narva; triumphed over the Poles and Saxons at Riga; took Courland; subdued Lithuania; and elevated his favorite, Stanislaus Leczinzki, to the throne of Poland. Elated by successes, the Swede replied to the request of the Russian sovereign for peace, "I will treat at Moscow." The summit of power is often very near the depth of ruin. Shortly afterwards Charles was defeated by the Russians at Pultowa and was cast a fugitive among the Ottomans. After a vain attempt to involve the sultan and the Russians in hostilities, the Swedish monarch returned home, invaded Norway, and accidentally loss his life.

Ulrica Elenora, sister of Charles XII., was chosen queen, but relinquished the crown to her husband, the Prince of Hesse. Peace was restored by a treaty with the king of England as elector of Saxony, by which Bremen and Verdun were ceded to him for one million of rix-dollars; by another treaty with the king of Prussia, who gave Strausland and the isle of Rugen and retained Stelin with the isles of Usdom and Wollin; and by a third treaty with the king of Denmark, who kept that part of the duchy of Sleswick conquered from the Duke of Holstein and sur-

---

* Sinding's His. of Sweden, p. 320. Kol. Ger., ch. xxx. pp. 418, 419.

rendered Wismar on condition that the fortifications should not be rebuilt. On the death of Frederick, his son Gustavus III. took the throne. The kingdom was shaken by two parties, the Hats and the Caps. The former desired to abridge, the latter to enlarge, royal power. By turns the king courted the favor of each party, until, by gaining popularity with the military, he was able to enslave both and to establish a constitution conformable to his own interests. On his death, his son Gustavus IV. took the throne. After his deposition the Duke of Sudermania, Charles XIII., was elected. Charles XIII. dying, Bernardotte was elected to the crown through French influence. Oscar, the son of this monarch, succeeded to the sceptre on the death of his father: his son Charles is the present sovereign of Sweden and Norway.

Notwithstanding the regal title of the sovereign of Prussia had been secured by the treaty of Utrecht, this kingdom did not acquire a commanding character until the reign of Frederick III., who is styled the Great. Maria Theresa determined to be repossessed of Lower Silesia, and, sustained by Russia, Sweden, and France, declared war against the Prussian monarch. Frederick, strengthened by an alliance with England, overpowered the Austrians at Lowositz and Reichenburg; but he was in turn defeated at Kollin and Grossjagerndorf. The victories of Rossbach and Leuthen placed the Prussians in possession of Breslaw, the principal city of Silesia. The triumph of Zorndorff saved Brandenburg from the Russians, and, though worsted at Hochkirch, Frederick entered Dresden in triumph. The enemy secured the possession of Silesia by the battle of Künersdorf, reduced Glatz, and threatened Brandenburg. Enraged by these calamities, Frederick fought and gained the battle of Liegnitz, thus preventing the junction of the Austrians and Russians. Notwithstanding this success, the enemy mastered Berlin, the capital of Prussia. The affairs of Frederick were desperate. The gloom, however, was quickly dispelled by the victory of Torgau, which placed in the hands of the sovereign of Prussia Saxony, Colberg, and Pomerania. Terms of peace were settled by the treaty of Hubertsburg (A.D. 1763), giving Silesia to Frederick and providing for a mutual restitution of conquests. Frederick William II., the successor of Frederick the Great, though at first attentive to public concerns, proved to be the opposite of his uncle. His successor, the third of the same name, through his energy of character preserved his crown from the arms of Napoleon. The reign of Frederick William IV., his successor, was distinguished for the occurrence of those intrigues and agitations for German supremacy which culminated in the victory of Sadowa (1866) during the sway of his son William I. and gave the prize to Prussia. The brilliant success of that monarch shortly afterwards (1870) in the war with France was followed by the reconstruction of the empire of Germany and the elevation of William to imperial power.

Russia had long been tributary to the Tartars. John Basilowitz, Grand Duke of Moscovy, threw off that yoke, expelled the Tartar officers from Moscow, invaded their territories, made himself master of Novogorod and Casan, where he was crowned (A.D. 1470), assuming the title Czar, which signifies king or emperor. The grandson of John added to these conquests Astrachan and Siberia, and concluded a treaty of commerce with Queen Elizabeth of England. Boris, the minister of King Theodore, induced him to kill his brother Demetrius. Theodore is supposed to have been destroyed by Boris, who usurped the throne. A man appeared in Lithuania alleging that he was Prince Demetrius, and being assisted by a Polish army, entered Moscow and was proclaimed czar. Zuski, a nobleman, turned the current of popular feeling; Demetrius was slain, and the factionist seated on the throne. Very soon a second and a third Demetrius appeared. Poland and Sweden took part in the contention; Zuski was delivered to the former, Demetrius massacred by the Tartars. Russia was convulsed by the parties of a fourth and a fifth Demetrius, until Michael Romanow, son of the bishop of Rowtow, of the line of czars, being raised to the throne, concluded peace with Sweden and Poland and restored tranquillity to Russia. Four reigns transpired, when appeared upon the throne Peter the Great, one of the most distinguished princes of ancient or modern times. For the purpose of improving the condition of his people the czar left his dominions in disguise, and during an absence of two years visited Germany, England, and Holland, where he was seen as a pupil in various departments of art and science.* After the conclusion of the war with Charles XII. of Sweden Peter assumed the title of emperor, which was acknowledged by the powers of Europe. Marching into Persia, the emperor restored Shah Thamas to his throne; receiving in return for his services the provinces on the Caspian Sea which anciently constituted a portion of the Median kingdom. Manufactures of every description were encouraged by introducing into the empire artists and men of science from France, England, and the Low Countries. On the death of Peter, Catharine, his widow, took the sceptre. A war with the Porte was concluded in two years without any material alteration in the state of affairs. On the death of Catharine, the sceptre fell successively into the hands of Peter II., Anne, John, Elizabeth, and Peter III., none of whom possessed the talents of their ancestor Peter the Great, and the last of whom was deposed by the chief estates of the

---

*Mod. Europe, Vols. V., VI. Lar. Out., pp. 319–326.

empire and his wife Catharine was entrusted with supreme power. Catharine II. reversed the policy of her husband, restored to the clergy their revenues, and pursued such a course as secured the affections of her subjects. The conduct of Catharine in relation to Poland, though it extended the limits of her empire, did not enhance her honor. Upon the death of Augustus II. the empress caused Stanislaus Poniatowski to be elected king of that country. Religious disputes at this time ran high in Poland between the Roman Catholics and the Christians of the Greek Church. The latter invoked the aid of Catharine, by whose intrigues a civil war was fomented. The Russians participated in this broil, and in the pursuit of a Polish party trespassed on Ottoman territory, burned Balta, and committed such outrages as produced a declaration of war by the sultan. During the first year of this contest the Ottomans were twice defeated. The Russians took Bender, were victorious in Moldavia, and in conjunction with the British despoiled the Ottoman fleet at Scio. Poland was dismembered. Frederick took Polish Prussia; Catharine, Lithuania; Maria Theresa, such portion as only left the natives Warsaw, Cracow, and the country extending from Silesia in the west to the river Berezina in the east, from Samogita in the north to the palatine of Chelm in the south and to the Black Forest in the southeast. Peace was concluded with the Porte by the treaty of Kainargi. Russia obtained the navigation of the Euxine and other seas claimed by them, with a proviso of being allowed only one armed vessel at a time in the Constantinopolitan seas, as also Azoph, Taganroh, Kerch, Jenickala, Kinburn, and the territory between the Bog and Nieper, with four millions and a half of roubles for the expenses of the war and a cessation of the dependence of the Crimea on the Ottoman Empire.

The empress turned her attention to the formation of a

new code of laws and the amelioration of the condition of her subjects. Another war, however, occurred with the Ottomans, which was soon concluded by the treaty of Yassi. The Niester was determined as the boundary between the two empires; the privileges of Wallachia and Moldavia were confirmed; their inhabitants freed from taxes for two years; the government of Georgia guaranteed by the Porte; and the sultan agreed to check the piratical outrages of Barbary. Meantime Poland had adopted a new constitution by which the crown was confined to the house of Saxony, the king's power extended, the nobles circumscribed, the middle classes rendered more respectable, and the peasantry brought under the protection of the laws. The diet resolved to augment the army to sixty thousand men. Catharine declared war against the Poles (A.D. 1792). Thaddeus Kosciusko and Joseph Poniatowski made a bold stand against their enemies, but were eventually overpowered. Catharine and Frederick ordered the seizure of all the territory between the Dwina and Niester. The Russian troops commenced the execution of the command by compelling the Poles to take an oath of allegiance to the empress or to leave the country. The Prussians conducted a similar spoliation in several provinces, as well as in Dantzic and Thorn. Four Poles, at the head of whom was Kosciusko, entered into an agreement to make a last effort for their downtrodden country. It was unsuccessful; Warsaw was reduced and Poland divided between Russia, Prussia, and Austria. The share of the empress extended to the centre of Poland; that of Prussia embraced Warsaw and other considerable towns; that of Austria, Cracow, Chelm, Lublin, and other territories. The estates of many patriots were confiscated; Kosciusko was imprisoned, and Stanislaus was deprived of his crown. Not long after these events Catharine was found dead in her room without any appearance of violence or poison about her person. Paul, her son, succeeded to the throne. Kosciusko and some Polish patriots were released. The reign, though begun well, was soon terminated by the murder of the emperor. Alexander, his son, promising to administer the government according to the policy of his grandmother, Catharine II., came to the throne. Many wise domestic regulations were established. England was appeased by yielding to it the right of search. A disposition not equally submissive to the policy of France involved the emperor in the contests of Napoleon. Nicholas, the brother of Alexander, though not the legal heir, succeeded him on the throne. A Turkish war resulted in the loss of Adrianople and the humiliation of the sultan. The Poles were crushed in every effort for liberty.* The Caucasians, more successful for years, were equally unfortunate in the subsequent reign of Alexander the son of Nicholas. Demanding additional privileges for the Greek Christian subjects of the sultan,† the emperor seized on Wallachia and Moldavia (A.D. 1853). War followed between the empires. Though successful in the naval engagement at Sinope, the emperor's forces were repulsed by those of the sultan at Tortukai, Citali, Bessarabia, Kalifat, Hirsova, and Silistria. England and France, regarding the conduct of Nicholas as an aggression on the rights of the Porte, soon became parties to the contest. Their forces penetrated the Baltic without much effect, but entering the Euxine laid siege to Sebastopol, which, after a bloody struggle of about fourteen months, was taken and peace restored. The heroic conflict which had been waged for centuries in Spain and Portugal against the Mahometans gradually diminished the power of the infidels. The total overthrow of the

---

* Sterling's Nich. † Proclamations of Nich. I.

enemy was not effected until the reign of Ferdinand and Isabella. Free from intestine commotions, the sovereigns established the prompt administration of justice throughout their dominions. The bold enterprise of Christopher Columbus found its first patrons at the court of Spain. It is a melancholy fact that in the same place was created the most destructive instrument to religious liberty, the Inquisition. Joan, the daughter of Ferdinand and Isabella, was married to Philip Archduke of Austria and sovereign of the Netherlands. Charles, the issue of this union, took the sceptre on the death of his grand-parents. When elected emperor he resigned it to his son Philip II.* The king's devotion to Catholicism was so great that he spent twenty years in building a church, a monastery, and a palace near Madrid called the Escurial. The crown of Portugal was won by the arms of Philip II. A wholesale destruction of Protestants took place wherever he had power to effect it. His principal agent in this work in the Netherlands was the Duke of Alva. This course of conduct gave rise, in 1580, to the union of Holland, Zealand, Urecht, Friesland, Groningen, Overyssel, and Guelderland. William Prince of Orange was the chief instrument in its formation. These states made an offer of their sovereignty to Elizabeth Queen of England. The queen declining, it was conferred on the Duke of Anjou. The duke was soon forced to retire, which left the contest for freedom to be managed by the Prince of Orange against the Duke of Parma, charged with the Spanish interests. The prince fell by the hand of an assassin. Maurice, his son, was elected stadtholder by Holland and Zealand. Parma overpowered Antwerp. This dreadful blow would have ruined the union had not

---

* Prescott's Fer. and Is. Robertson's Chas. V. Watson's Phil. Rus. Mod. Eu., Vol. III. Let., 69. Rev. xiii.

Elizabeth assisted it with men and money. Maurice took Breda, Gertrudenburg, and Groningen. On the death of Philip II. the crown of Spain devolved on his son, Philip III., and the sovereignty of the states on Albert of Austria, husband to Isabella, the Spanish princess. Refusing to acknowledge the authority of Albert, the states suffered the utter extinction of their trade wherever Spain held power. Great as was this loss, it was amply compensated by the success of the states in the East Indies, and at home they were finally prosperous, defeating the Spanish at Newport and mastering Rimbach, Grave, and Sluys. A truce was concluded with the states for twelve years (1609) which secured to them all their acquisitions, the freedom of commerce, and the enjoyment of religious liberty.

The states became a scene of religious contention. The parties of Gomar and Arminius were respectively headed by Maurice and the pensionary Barneveldt. The latter fell under public censure and was executed. On the conclusion of the truce Spinola laid siege to Bergenopzoom, but was compelled to relinquish it by Maurice. Breda, however, yielded to his arms. Prince Maurice died at this period. Large supplies were received from France and England. Frederick Henry Prince of Orange succeeded as stadtholder. The general war which pervaded Europe merged the conflict between Spain and the provinces. The independence of the states was eventually established. From the death of William II. the government remained in the hands of the republican party, the soul of which was De Witt. A furious naval war took place with England. It was settled by the treaty of Breda, which secured to the Dutch many English settlements on the African coast, Surinam, and Pelerone. During forty-five years the house of Orange was out of power; when, alarmed by the progress of France, the states appointed William IV., Prince of

Orange, stadtholder, captain-general, and admiral-in-chief of all the United Provinces. The dreaded evils, however, were obviated by the treaty of Aix-la-Chapelle. Prince William V. was declared stadtholder on arriving at eighteen years of age. William married the niece of the king of Prussia. This reign was prosperous and happy for many years. After the disturbances with England popular disaffection gradually pervaded the provinces. William retired from power, but through the intrigues of England and the arms of Prussia he was restored. A second abdication was not attended with similar success. A new constitution was adopted. The supreme power was vested in a pensionary and an assembly of nineteen members nominated by the administrating authorities of the eight departments; the term of the pensionary fixed at five years; declarations of war and treaties subjected to a vote of the deputies, whose meetings were to be semi-annual or oftener upon special convocation of the pensionary. French influence effected its object in the provinces. The deputies requested Napoleon to create his brother king; the pensionary resigned; and Louis assumed the royal functions. After the fall of Bonaparte, William Prince of Orange was recalled and proclaimed sovereign of the United Netherlands. The congress of Vienna not only confirmed to William his former power, but attached to his kingdom the provinces which had been subject to the house of Burgundy. This union, designed as a barrier to French ambition, became a source of bitter contention in consequence of the difference in religion, manners, and language between the two kingdoms. A dread of foreign interference prevented the Belgians from throwing off the Dutch yoke. The French revolution relieving them from fear, they proclaimed their independence and conferred their sovereignty upon Leopold, who married the daughter of Louis Philippe. The interference of France decided the contest between Belgium and William as to the ownership of Luxemburg in favor of the former.

The great objects of the reign of Philip III. were the extinction of the descendants of the Moors, the support of the Catholic League, and the establishment of the Spanish branch of the house of Austria. On the king's death, his son, Philip IV., was crowned. Olivarez, his minister, made him take the title of Great and was determined that the reign should justify the assumption. His success was not equal to his expectations. Portugal became independent and elevated the Duke of Braganza to the throne under the title of John IV. Charles II. was the heir of Philip IV. Being a minor, his mother assumed the regency. Spain was reduced to a wretched condition by the wars of Louis XIV. The Portuguese adhered to the Grand Alliance throughout the contests. Philip V. was scarcely possessed of regal dignity before his minister, Alberoni, persuaded him that his renunciation of the French crown was not binding. The Quadruple Alliance, however, soon ended this doctrine. Philip V. was succeeded on the throne by his son, Ferdinand VI., who managed during his short reign to avoid interference in the wars which distracted Europe. His successor and brother, Charles III., was not equally fortunate. The affairs of Spain were thrown into commotion by the Marquis de Squillac, the minister of Charles, who in his war on flapped hats and long cloaks created a serious riot which was only quelled by his dismission, the repeal of the monopoly of provisions, and finally the exile of the Jesuits. The minister of Portugal in like manner incurred public censure by his exertions to free the kingdom from its dependence on England. The death of the king, Joseph, and the succession of his daughter Maria produced the dismissal of the minister, and with it a peace. Charles persevered in his efforts to improve the condition of Spain notwithstanding the attempts of the pope to impede his progress. The queen of Portugal pursued a similar policy in her dominions. Ferdinand III., son of Charles III., being restored after the fall of Napoleon, stigmatized the existing cortes, restrained the press, imprisoned many individuals of high rank upon groundless charges, and was guilty of other oppressive acts which disaffected the nation. The royal tyranny induced the troops raised to subdue the revolted American colonies to refuse to perform that task A new constitution was conceded. Similar reform movements occurred in Portugal, Naples, and Piedmont, which were crushed in the last two places by Austrian influence.

The determination on the part of the sovereigns of Europe to check the progress of liberal views induced them to form the congress of Verona (A.D. 1824), where it was resolved to establish Ferdinand in Spain. In pursuance of this determination, French forces under the Duke of Angoulême, marching into that country, compelled the constitutionalists to submit. The king, thus restored to despotic power, revived in their most appalling forms those institutions which had long disgraced the government of Spain. On the death of John VI., king of Portugal, the succession to the crown devolved upon Dom Pedro, who resided in Brazil. Satisfied with his condition, he declined in favor of his daughter Donna Maria, the betrothed of his brother Don Miguel. A strong party desired the elevation of Don Miguel. England interfering, he was created regent; but he soon abrogated the constitution and usurped the crown. The young queen fled to England, and thence to her father's court at Rio Janeiro. Her cause was eventually triumphant. At her death Lewis, her son, came to the throne. Dom Pedro now reigns. Similar troubles occurred in Spain on the death of Ferdinand VII.; the succession of his daughter Isabella being contested by his brother Don Carlos. The result was the same as in Portugal; but the queen eventually became unpopular and was expelled from the throne (1868). She was succeeded by Amadeus, son of Victor Emanuel (1871), who shortly afterwards resigned, and a republic was created with Castelar at its head; but falling into disrepute in consequence of the way of managing affairs with the United States in regard to the Virginius, he gave place to Serrano.* Alfonso XII., son of ex-Queen Isabella, came to the throne, and proving successful in the struggle with his kinsman Don Carlos, was firmly established in power (1876).

The kingdom of Denmark, besides its possessions in St. Croix and St. John, St. Thomas and Guinea, Tranquebar and Serampore, Iceland, the Faroe Isles and Greenland, consists of Zealand and Funen on the Baltic, the peninsula of Jutland, and the duchies Sleswick, Holstein, and Lauenburg. The last countries being German have a member in the diet of that confederacy. The new constitution, by establishing the unity of the kingdom, interfered with the prospects of the Lauenburg house for the crown. The duchies being sustained in their opposition to this change in affairs by the Germans, the Danes by Nicholas the Russian emperor, father-in-law to the head of the Lauenburg house, a troublesome war would have succeeded had not the interference of other powers procured a settlement.†

Switzerland contains twenty-two cantons or states. Each canton manages its own domestic concerns. A congress composed of members from each canton is entrusted with the direction of foreign relations, making war and peace, raising armies, forming treaties, contracting alliances, and regulating commerce. The sessions of this body are suc-

---

* Public Des., Dec. 31, 1874. † Sterling's Life of Nicholas.

cessively held in Berne, Zurich, and Lucerne. A deadly blow was aimed at the privileged orders by the reform party. The aristocracy, thinking in the course of time to produce a change in their favor, procured the settlement of Jesuitical instructors at Lucerne. The reformers, however, gaining a majority in the national council, directed Lucerne to expel the Jesuits. The Catholic cantons leagued together against this measure. A dissolution of the union being demanded by the diet and refused by the cantons, war ensued (A.D. 1848). The army of the union was defeated and peace restored.*

Italy south of the papal dominions, with Sicily, formed the kingdom of the Two Sicilies. After the restoration of the monarch Ferdinand I. by the allied powers, his subjects were offended by the rejection of a constitution (1818). A political organization at Naples called the Carbonari ensued, the object of which was the formation of a popular legislature to control the powers of the king. A constitution was formed two years afterwards which continued to exist some months, when it was overthrown by an Austrian army and the king reinstated in absolute power. A constitutional monarchy (1848) was created after a bloody struggle by the populace. Upon the death of Ferdinand his son Francis II. came to the throne (1859), but his power being subverted by his own cruelties and the bravery of Garibaldi, his dominions form a portion of the Italian kingdom.†

The papal dominions, which stretch across Italy immediately to the north of the Sicilian kingdom, are governed by the pope and cardinals. Popular power was triumphant over this territory in 1848. A constitution was adopted. Two councils for the formation of laws were created, the

---

* Gazette eo die. † Dwight's Life of Garibaldi.

one styled the high council, the other the council of deputies; the judiciary rendered independent; extraordinary courts interdicted; the national guards placed under the sole direction of the state. Pius IX. acquiesced for a short time, but escaping to Gaeta he procured aid of France, by which the republic was crushed.*

The Austrian dominions north of the Papal States, formerly governed by two congregations, one held at Venice, the other at Milan, and by provincial congregations in each department, after the victory of Solferino became a portion of the Sardinian monarch's dominions (1859).

Sardinia, Piedmont, and Savoy are the principal states which constitute the kingdom of Sardinia. A constitution was proclaimed (A.D. 1848). The cause of free institutions appeared to be triumphant. Pope, princes, people were united in its promotion. But the Austrians set themselves in motion. Intimidation and bribery divided the confederacy. Charles Albert, the king of Sardinia, was left alone to bear the weight of the contest; overwhelmed in battle; forced to abdicate, and his son Victor Emanuel placed on the throne. The son was more fortunate than his father. Through French intervention he succeeded in repelling (1859) the Austrian powers, and accomplished the liberation of all the northern Italian states, except those of Venetia, from the dominion of their old oppressor. After the war between Austria and Prussia, Venetia fell into his hands.† Finally he made the Papal States a portion of his kingdom, and Rome became his capital (1871).‡

And thus has papal, persecuting Rome, with garments dyed in the blood of countless martyrs in Spain, France, Italy, Piedmont, Bohemia, the Low Countries, Germany, Sweden, England, Scotland, and America, been shorn of

---

* Gazette. † Prussia, ante. ‡ Procl. of king.

its power over the rack and fagot as instruments in extending its authority, and compelled to confine itself in that work to the means used by other religious sects in promoting their interests*—a fact predicted eighteen centuries ago by the prophet of Patmos.

CHAPTER XVIII.

THE EMPIRE OF THE ANGLO-SAXONS TO THE FALL OF RICHARD II.

As the power of the Romans was extinguished in Britain, the natives were scourged by the invasions of the Picts and Scots.† Obtaining the assistance of the Saxons, the Britons defeated their enemies at Stamford. Disappointed in the demand on their allies for provisions, the Saxons joined the Picts and Scots. Years of war ensued. The Britons commanded by Arthur, prince of Silures, were at last triumphant at Badon Hill. Though beaten in battle, the Saxons so augmented their numbers in the course of time, by the arrival of Angles and other German tribes, that the Britons were compelled to retire to Cornwall and Wales. In the southern portion of the island seven separate kingdoms were formed, denominated Kent, Sussex, Wessex, Essex, Mercia, East Anglia, and Northumberland. Eventually the heptarchy was united under one king—Egbert of Wessex. The kingdom was now denominated England. Danish invasions occupied the reign of the king. Defeated at Charmouth, the Danes made

---

* Chap. V., ante. Rev. xiv. 6–8.
† Hume, Vol. I. ch. xvii. Rus., Vol. I.

good their retreat. Forming an alliance with the Britons of Cornwall, they soon returned to England in greater numbers. The battle of Hengesdown followed, where Egbert was triumphant. The king did not long survive his victory. Ethelwolf, the son of the deceased monarch, came to the throne. Though overcome in repeated engagements, the Danes continued to spread havoc over the land during the time of this king and that of his sons Ethelbald, Ethelbert, and Ethelred.

Alfred, the fourth son of Ethelwolf, came to the throne at twenty years of age. Kind to a fault, the king, though he had his foes at his feet, stipulated for their safe retreat. The treacherous Danes deceived their benefactors, rallied in vast numbers, and commenced the work of destruction. Alfred again defeated them in successive battles, and again allowed them the privilege they had abused. Once more the king was deceived. The enemy became so powerful that the disheartened English refused to listen to Alfred; some submitting to the invaders, others leaving the country. Deserted by his countrymen, Alfred retired from public life, and was supposed dead by the Danes. In the space of a few months the king was so much encouraged by the success of his friends, as well as by the presumptuous confidence of the Danes, that he assailed the foe at Eddington, gained a complete victory; allowing none to remain in the country who did not submit to his authority, embrace Catholicity, and settle in Northumberland or East Anglia. The founder of the Anglo-Saxon power being firmly seated on the throne, turned his attention toward the civil and military institutions of the realm. Ruined cities were rebuilt; regular forces established in every district; fortresses erected at convenient points; a fleet of one hundred and twenty ships stationed on the coast; the kingdom divided into counties, the counties into hundreds, the hundreds into tythings. Every householder was made responsible for the conduct of his family, his slaves, and his guests who had been with him three days. All persons were bound to register themselves in a tything. A change of habitation was not allowed without warrant and certificate. Although the trial by jury had been practised among the Saxons before their settlement in Britain, yet to Alfred is to be attributed that remarkable feature in it, a unanimity among the jurors. A code of laws was enacted; schools of learning were founded; the University of Oxford largely endowed; men of science invited from all parts of Europe to settle in England; commerce and the arts encouraged by generous rewards. This illustrious hero died at the vigorous age of fifty-three. Edward, his son, took the throne. What the father had established the son maintained, though assailed by his contentious brother and oppressed by the Danes all his life. Athelstan, his natural son, succeeded to the sceptre. In order to quell the disturbances in Northumberland, the king conferred on Sithric, a Danish nobleman, the title of king, and married him to his sister Editha. After their father's death, his two sons claimed the sovereignty. Overcome by the king, one fled to Ireland, the other to Scotland. Pretending he would surrender the fugitive, the Scottish king induced him to escape. Athelstan, in revenge, invaded Scotland and severely punished its monarch. The English sovereign afterwards defeated at Brunsbury the combined army of Scots, Welsh, and Danes. The short reign of Edmund was terminated by the hand of an assassin. Edred was created sovereign. The Northumbrians were curbed by the establishment of garrisons in their county. Contentions between the new order of monks created by Dunstan, abbot of Glastenbury, and the secular clergy distracted the kingdom. Edwy, the son of Edmund, succeeded to the throne. Incurring the displeasure of the rigid Dunstan, the king was eventually deposed. Edgar, his brother, was raised to his throne at the age of thirteen. The reign of Edgar was remarkably fortunate. The fractious Northumbrians were awed, England preserved from the incursions of the Danes by the creation of a powerful navy, the submission of Wales, Scotland, and Ireland effected. On the death of the king, his son Edward came to power; but being soon murdered by the connivance of his stepmother, her son Ethelred was advanced to the sovereignty. Bribing the Danes to leave the kingdom, Ethelred, on their return, caused a general massacre. Sweyn, king of Denmark, whose sister had been murdered, breathing vengeance for the outrage, landed at the head of a powerful army, and desolated the kingdom with fire and sword. The king of England, betrayed by the governor of Mercia, fled to Normandy. On the death of Sweyn, soon afterwards, he returned. Canute, the son and successor of Sweyn, was as terrific to the English as his father. Ethelred assembled an army: the revolt of his commanders left his cause hopeless, and he died in the midst of the war. Edmond, the son of the last king, succeeded to the throne. Losing the battle of Assington, the king was compelled by his subjects to sign a treaty by which the kingdom was divided between him and Canute; the former taking the southern portion, and the latter the northern part, composed of Mercia, East Anglia, and Northumberland. Edmond was murdered soon after this settlement. Canute became sole sovereign of England; fortified his title by purchasing the favor of the nobles; rewarded his Danish favorites, and removed the young princes from the realm. The dread of Ethelred's sons succeeding to the throne was removed by the marriage of their mother to Canute. Sweden was invaded, Norway mastered. The king from this period looked on the rewards of ambition with contempt, employing his time in rearing churches, endowing monasteries, causing prayers to be said for those who had been killed in battle against him, and in what, according to the spirit of that age, was more meritorious than all beside, in performing a pilgrimage to Rome. Soon after his return he reduced Malcolm, king of Scotland. Harold, a son of Canute by his first wife, took the sceptre of his father. Death removing the king in a short time, as well as his successor and brother Hardicanute, Edward, surnamed the Confessor, son of Ethelred, was recalled, and the Danish yoke forever broken. Notwithstanding the commotions of Earl Godwin, who wished to raise his son Harold to the throne, and the death of the Duke of Northumberland, the great prop of the king, Edward matured and gave to his kingdom a body of laws which has perpetuated his fame. On the death of the Confessor, Harold assumed the crown, and defeated the Danes at Stamford.

William Duke of Normandy laid claim to the throne of England. The title of the duke rested on the pretended bequest of Edward the Confessor, as well as the oath of Harold to support his rival. Harold denied the bequest; declared the oath was extorted by dread of violence, and proclaimed that the same moment should put a period to his life and his sway. William was triumphant at Hastings; marched immediately towards London; was acknowledged by the nobility and clergy; and crowned at Westminster Abbey, taking the usual oath administered to the Saxon kings. The estates and honors of the nobility were confirmed; the franchises and liberties of London and other cities secured; but all real power was placed in the hands of the Normans, among whom were portioned the possessions of the deceased Harold and his active adherents. The king, either for the purpose of display or to provoke the English to resistance by subjecting them to the outrages of the army, left the country on a visit to Normandy. Insurrectionary movements occurred which were suppressed by the monarch. A full measure of vengeance was poured out upon the humbled natives. The country between the Humber and Tees for sixty miles was laid waste. Upwards of one hundred thousand English subjects are calculated to have perished. The estates of the principal landholders were confiscated and bestowed on Norman favorites. The kingdom, except the royal domain, was divided into baronies, reserving stated services and payments to the king. The barons parcelled their allotments to knights or vassals, who owed the same kind of duty to their lord in peace and war as he was under to the king. None but Normans were admitted to the first rank. The church underwent a revolution which placed William at its head; but so dutiful was he to the pope that he would not permit any man in his power "to buy or sell" anything whom he found disobedient to the Apostolic See.* English nationality was assailed by introducing the French language into judicial proceedings and fashionable society. Robert, the son of the king, created trouble by aspiring to the sovereignty of Main and Normandy. An English army reduced him to submission. A joke of the French king at the corpulence of William involved both countries in war. The English monarch invaded the Isle of France, and in the midst of successful military operations accidentally lost his life. William II. succeeded to the throne of England; Robert took Normandy; and Henry obtained his mother's possessions. Endeavors by Robert to disturb this division produced the invasion of Normandy and the duke's submission. The

---

* Rev. xiii., xvii. New. Dis., xxv. p. 547.

Scots and Welsh were humbled; a conspiracy to elevate to the throne Stephen Count of Aumale, nephew of the Conqueror, was crushed. The king took no part in the crusades, but he advanced money to his brother Robert for that purpose. William II. while hunting was accidentally killed by Walter Tyrrel, a French gentleman. Henry seized the crown in fraud of Robert's rights; confirmed the laws of Edward the Confessor, and did many other popular acts. Notwithstanding, a war would have arisen but for the intervention of Anselm, archbishop of Canterbury. A settlement followed by which Robert resigned his pretensions to England on the payment of an annual pension of three thousand marks; it being further stipulated that on the death of either of the princes without issue the survivor should succeed to his dominions, that the adherents of each should be pardoned and restored to all their possessions, and that neither should thenceforth countenance the enemies of the other. Henry soon violated these terms by persecuting the friends of Robert. The duke appeared as their avenger, but was compelled to purchase peace by the surrender of his pension. Normandy was finally subdued by Henry, and Robert made a prisoner in England during life.

Stephen Count of Boulogne, the grandson of the Conqueror, took the crown on the death of Henry, in defiance of the claim of Matilda, his daughter and heiress. Civil war followed, which, though bloody, did not terminate the sway of the usurper. Henry, the son of Matilda by Geoffrey Plantagenet, secured the succession to the crown on the death of Stephen. Courts of justice were reformed; crimes suppressed; the charter of Henry I. confirmed; a war with France about Toulouse successfully terminated; foreign improvements in art and science, laws and literature, introduced. The great curse of England was the exorbitant revenues of the ecclesiastics. A civil officer was appointed to preside at the courts of the clergy. The churchmen denied their responsibility to the civil power, thus affording a screen to the most notorious offenders. In order to effect a thorough reformation of abuses Henry II. appointed his chancellor, Thomas à Becket, to the see of Canterbury. No sooner was he elevated to power, than Thomas avowed himself the champion of the church. Determined to subject ecclesiastics to the civil power, the king finally procured from a convocation of bishops the constitutions of Clarendon. The pope rejected the constitutions and Becket was triumphant. To humble the prelate, the king required him to account for his administration when chancellor. Becket, appealing to Rome, fled to France. Dreading the vengeance of the pope, "who could speak great things," Henry permitted the fugitive to return to England.* Again triumphant, the prelate excommunicated the bishops of London and Salisbury because they had assisted at the coronation of Prince Henry in his absence. When this act was made known to the king in Normandy he exclaimed against his servants, whose want of zeal had so long exposed him to the insolence of the imperious priest. Four gentlemen immediately repaired to Canterbury, and on his refusal to restore the bishops to their functions they despatched Becket while at evening service. Upon the king's disavowal of any agency in the act, allowance of appeals to Rome, and promise of personal service for three years in Spain or Palestine against the infidels, the pope was appeased. The favor of the English clergy was not so easily obtained. Nothing short of Henry's pilgrimage barefoot to the tomb of Becket and the scourging of his bare back by the lashes of the priests could secure

---

* Rev. xiii. 5.

their smile. Though Ireland was annexed to England, Poitou, Guienne, Anjou, and Normandy were severed from it by the sons of the monarch.

Richard, whose heroism in the holy wars had won golden opinions, succeeded his father, Henry II. Detained a prisoner by the emperor, his liberation was purchased by the payment of one hundred and fifty thousand marks of pure silver. Shortly after his return home the king was killed in the war which was about terminating between his kingdom and France. John took the throne. The murder of Arthur Duke of Britanny, the son of his elder brother, justly launched on him the wrath of France. The pope's indignation was roused by the conduct of the king in the election of the archbishop of Canterbury. Interdict and excommunication soon followed.* The fury of Rome was allayed by the agreement of John to hold his kingdom as a fief of Rome. Disgusted and oppressed, the barons armed against the monarch and wrung from him at Runnymede the great charter of rights. John soon broke his oath, appealed to arms and ravaged the country from Dover to Berwick. The crown was offered to the eldest son of the king of France, who enjoyed but a short popularity in consequence of his attachment to his countrymen. After the death of John, his son, Henry III., was acknowledged sovereign under the protectorship of the Earl of Pembroke. The moderation of the protector restored peace to the nation. Such was the prodigality of Henry on attaining full age, that he involved his realm in the expenses of a war with France and Sicily without any prospect of public advantage. A train of disasters ensued which resulted in the provisions of Oxford, by which twenty-four barons were authorized to reform the kingdom. The Earl of Lei-

---

* Hu. Eng., Vol. I. pp. 455, 456. Rev. xiii. 16, 17.

cester was placed at the head of the commission. Knights were appointed in each county to make report of grievances to parliament. Leicester and his associates sought to perpetuate their power. The pope absolved Henry from his oath to observe the provisions, and he assumed the royal functions. The earl appealed to arms, triumphed at Lewes, took Henry and his son prisoners, and convoked a parliament in which the representatives of boroughs were admitted to seats: thus did political craft prove the origin of the choicest feature in the British constitution. Leicester again ruined his cause by severity to the Earl of Derby. Prince Edward escaped from imprisonment, rallied his friends, triumphed at Evesham (where Leicester was slain), and restored his father to power. Edward succeeded his father on the throne. The provisions of the great charter were strictly enforced. Wales submitted, and, under pretence of arbitrating between the aspirants to the crown, Robert Bruce and John Baliol, Scotland was invaded. William Wallace, the Scottish general, overpowered the forces of Edward near Stirling. Wallace was basely betrayed by Sir John Monteith, and executed as a rebel. The fate of this distinguished patriot fired the spirit of Robert Bruce, who raised the drooping hearts of his countrymen to resist the tyranny of Edward.

Edward II. relinquished the attack on Scotland, recalled Piers Gaveston, his Gascon favorite, and resigned himself to the pleasures of the palace. The Earl of Lancaster at the head of the barons, procured the banishment and finally the death of Piers. An invasion of Scotland was projected by the king with a view to win back his lost popularity. Notwithstanding the immense preparations, the Scots met the enemy at Bannockburn, totally defeated them, procured their independence, and placed Bruce on the throne. This defeat, together with the excesses of his two favorites, the Le Despensers, sunk Edward so low in public opinion, that when his queen refused to return from France unless the minions were banished, she was sustained by the nation, and her young son Edward proclaimed king under the regency of his mother. Edward III. having restored quiet in England, defeated the Scots at Halidown Hill and placed Baliol on the throne. Pretending to the crown of France, as nephew by his mother's side to Charles IV., Edward commenced war with that kingdom.* Bruce, instigated by the French, invaded England, but was defeated by the queen at Durham. The death of Edward III. and his eldest son brought the son of the latter, Richard II., to the throne. A tax of three groats a head was imposed on every person over fifteen years of age. The improper conduct of a collector arrayed one hundred thousand men in rebellion under a leader by the name of Wat Tyler. Richard met the mob; their commander being struck dead by the mayor of London, and their demands granted by the king, they dispersed. A force sixty thousand strong invaded Scotland, but effected nothing of importance. The king falling under the influence of a dissipated favorite, Robert de Vere, was compelled to resign his crown. Governmental powers were confided in a council of fourteen persons selected by parliament. The uncles of Richard becoming reconciled to him, he was restored to the throne. Misfortune is not always the parent of wisdom. Richard, notwithstanding the lessons his calamities had suggested, continued to be a lover of pleasure and a companion of worthless favorites. The Duke of Gloucester endeavored to raise himself to the throne of his incorrigible nephew. The scheme was detected, the duke sent a prisoner to Calais and there murdered. The dukes of Norfolk

---

* See Chap. XI., before.

and Hereford, who had effected the fall of Gloucester, did not long enjoy the royal smile. Lancaster, the father of Hereford, stung by the wrongs of the king to his family and supported in all quarters, flew to arms. Richard II., deserted by his army, was seized by his enemies, deposed, and murdered.

CHAPTER XIX.

THE EMPIRE OF THE ANGLO-SAXONS TO THE DEATH OF JAMES I.

THE Duke of Lancaster was proclaimed king under the name of Henry IV.* Scottish incursions on England were repelled and the Welsh reduced. Brilliant as was the military success of Henry IV., he marred his reputation by severities against the followers of Wickliffe, the reformer. Henry V., his son, took the crown on the death of his father. Excessively dissipated before, the king became a model of virtue after his accession. The complicated relations with France were managed with distinguished ability. In this reign, as in the last, the reformed opinions were bitterly proscribed, and those who held them put to death. The will of the king committed the person of the young Prince Henry to the Earl of Warwick, the regency to the Duke of Gloucester. On attaining age Henry discarded Gloucester, falling entirely under the influence of his wife and the Earl of Suffolk. The earl and his successor, the Duke of Somerset, lost favor; the former in consequence of his connection with the murder of Gloucester, the lat-

---

* Hume, Vol. I. pp. 18-49. Rev. xiii.

ter because of the reverses in France under his administration. The Duke of York finally became protector. Descended from the Duke of Clarence, the second son of Edward III., the protector considered his title to the throne better than that of Henry VI., who was descended from the third son of that monarch. Civil war with all its ferocities followed. At the battle near St. Albans the royalists were defeated, the king made prisoner, and Somerset and Northumberland were slain. The Duke of York was now virtually king, and tranquillity was restored.

A petty quarrel between the servants of the houses of York and Lancaster again threw the kingdom into a flame. The Lancastrians were defeated at Blore Heath. The treachery of Sir Andrew Trollop, however, shortly afterwards, reversed events near Ludlow. The Duke of York fled to Ireland. The Earl of Warwick rallied his forces and defeated the royalists at Northampton. Queen Margaret having defeated and slain the Duke of York near Wakefield, marched toward London; was victorious at St. Albans, and threatened to blast the hopes of Warwick. The appearance of Edward, the son of the late Duke of York, who had routed the Lancastrians near Hereford, compelled the queen to withdraw. Edward was proclaimed king, his followers assuming the badge of a white rose, his enemies that of a red rose. The queen was defeated at Towton. Henry and Margaret escaped to Scotland, where they raised another army, invaded England, and were beaten at Hexham. The queen made good her retreat to Flanders; the king was thrown into the Tower. Though triumphant and in possession of the throne, Edward soon felt the curse of him who puts his trust in princes. Warwick, offended at the king, tumbled him from the throne and replaced Henry VI. in power. The scene again shifted: Warwick became unpopular; Henry was defeated at Barnet and Tewksbury; the king-maker was killed, and Edward repossessed of the sceptre. A war with France gave Edward indemnity against expenses: fifty thousand crowns a year during the joint lives of the sovereigns of the two realms, and the same sum as a ransom for Queen Margaret. Edward IV. left two sons, and his brother Richard Duke of Gloucester regent. The object of Richard being the throne, acts of the foulest outrage were committed to attain it. The Duke of Buckingham, the minion by whom Richard rose to power, eventually accomplished his destruction. Henry Earl of Richmond, the grandson of Owen Tudor by Catherine, relict of Henry V., descended from John of Gaunt, Duke of Lancaster, son of Edward III., was selected for the throne. In order to harmonize all interests a marriage was concluded between the earl and Elizabeth, the daughter of Edward IV. The rivals met at Bosworth, where Richard was defeated and killed. Henry VII. was not free from prejudice against the house of York. Commotions followed: one, headed by Viscount Lovel, was soon suppressed; another, under the pretence of avenging the rights of the fugitive Earl of Warwick, the son of the Duke of Clarence, was not terminated with as little trouble. The battle in Nottingham blasted the hopes of the insurgents by placing the objects of their concern, Simon and Simnel, the first in prison, the last in the king's kitchen. Perkin, a similar impostor, with many of his adherents were brought to the block. Matrimony and money occupied the remainder of the reign. A match was effected between Arthur, the eldest son of the king, and Catharine, the daughter of Ferdinand, the Spanish monarch; but that prince dying, his brother Henry was substituted in his stead. Margaret, the king's daughter, was married to James IV. of Scotland. Empson and Dudley, two lawyers, were used as the tools for royal extortion, performing their work so well as to fill the coffers of the king and bring themselves to the block.

Henry VIII., the son of the last king, succeeded to the throne. This reign affords the most remarkable instances of domestic causes producing national changes of any one on record. Unable to obtain a divorce from Catharine of Arragon, his wife, through the pope, Henry procured himself to be declared the protector and supreme head of the church and clergy of England. The archbishop of Canterbury then pronounced the divorce, and the king was soon afterwards married to Anne Boleyn. Dreading excommunication, Henry detached himself from Rome, and was declared by parliament the only supreme head of the church of England on earth. Sir Thomas More and Fisher, the late bishop of Rochester, refusing to acquiesce in this ecclesiastical change, suffered on the block. Those nurseries of vice and superstition, the monasteries, were all eventually abolished. Jane Seymour attracting the heart of Henry, Anne was condemned and executed. The king enforced the belief and practice of the six doctrines—the real presence, the communion with bread only, the utility of private masses, the celibacy of the clergy, the perpetual obligation of vows of chastity, and the necessity of auricular confession—with quite as much severity as Rome ever displayed on matters of religion. Jane Seymour died a natural death. Anne of Cleves was married by the monarch, but was soon exchanged for Catharine Howard, who was eventually put to death. James V. of Scotland, who married a daughter of the Duke of Guise, remained attached to the Roman see, which produced a collision with the king of England, his uncle. Overpowered by Henry, James died. Previous to his death Mary Stuart, his daughter, was born. For the purpose of securing a union of the two kingdoms, Henry effected a treaty with

Scotland for the marriage of his son Edward with that princess. On the restoration of peace the king married Catharine Parr, relict of Lord Latimer.

Edward VI., son of Henry VIII., was a minor at his father's death. The administration was committed to sixteen persons, by whom the Duke of Somerset was created protector. Ecclesiastical affairs were settled upon the basis on which they now stand. Somerset was not equally fortunate in regulating the church of Scotland, though victorious at Pinckney. A council of regency, with the Earl of Warwick at its head, rose on the ruined fortunes of Somerset. The object of Warwick was to elevate to the throne Lady Jane Grey, wife of Guilford Dudley, his fourth son. Procuring from Edward a settlement disinheriting his sisters, Mary and Elizabeth, and from the Duchess of Suffolk, the next heiress to the crown, a declination of her rights, the earl supposed his object accomplished. The scheme, nevertheless, failed. Mary took the throne after the death of her brother, Edward VI. The short reign of Mary was a scene of bigotry and blood. Uniting herself with Philip II., king of Spain, in marriage, and her kingdom with the see of Rome in ecclesiastical communion, a dreadful persecution of the Protestants was commenced, in which Rodgers, Hooper, Ferrar, Ridley, Latimer, Cranmer, and a host of learned and pious persons were sacrificed at the stake "because they would not worship as the pope commanded." The accession of Elizabeth re-established the reformed religion. Rome could not tolerate the attack of the queen on its power. A Bull declared her illegitimate. Mary Queen of Scots and her husband, Francis II., king of France, assumed the arms of England, under the direction of the Duke of Guise.* To effect the pur-

---

* Robertson's His. of Scotland, in loc. Rev. xiii.–xv.

pose indicated by this act, the regent of Scotland, the mother of Mary, commenced an attack on the Protestants of that realm. Treating with indignity the petition for a reformation of the church, the regent cited some eminent Protestant teachers to appear before the privy council at Stirling. The preparation of parishioners to attend the trial of their pastors so alarmed the regent that she promised to desist from further proceedings. Relying on this assurance, the pastors did not appear at Stirling. The regent, faithless to her word, pronounced them outlaws in consequence of their default. An act so perfidious roused the indignation of the public to the highest pitch. Both parties prepared for war, but the intervention of the Earl of Argyle and the prior of St. Andrew's averted the catastrophe by an agreement that indemnity should be granted to all concerned in the late insurrection, and that a parliament should be immediately assembled to compose religious differences. The regent again broke her engagement in both its obligations. The Protestants appealed to arms; churches were despoiled and monasteries laid in ruins. New treaties were formed and broken, and new ravages were committed. Meanwhile the Earl of Argyle, the prior of St. Andrew's, the Duke of Chatelherault, and his son, the Earl of Arran, presumptive heir to the crown, joined the Protestants, and the capital fell into their hands. The redress of civil and religious grievances, as well as the immediate expulsion of the French forces, was demanded. The regent, after many insincere promises, being re-enforced from France, denied the requests of the reformers and directed them to disband. Instead of complying with the order, the reformers called together the whole body of the peers and representatives of boroughs adhering to their party and deposed the regent. Betaking herself to the town of Leith, she foiled her adversaries by means of

French arms. Shortly afterwards the regent died, an English army made its appearance, and the treaty of Edinburgh, was signed by Francis and Mary with Elizabeth. This instrument stipulated that the French troops should be immediately withdrawn from Scotland; that the French sovereign should thenceforth abstain from wearing the arms or assuming the title of king and queen of England; that past offences should be forgiven; that none but natives should hold office among the Scots; that no foreign troops should be introduced into the kingdom without consent of parliament; that out of twenty-four persons nominated by parliament the queen should choose seven and that body five, in whom should be vested the entire administration during the queen's absence; that the queen should neither make peace nor declare war without the consent of parliament; and that parliament should take into consideration at its first meeting religious differences, representing its sense of them to the king and queen. The foreign forces immediately left the kingdom. Parliament ratified the principal articles of the treaty; gave its sanction to a Confession of Faith; prohibited the exercise of the Romish rights, and established the Presbyterian worship. Francis and Mary refused to ratify these proceedings. Parliament immediately put their statutes into execution.

After the death of Francis, Mary returned to Scotland, where she was received with expressions of regard by her subjects. Bestowing her confidence on the Protestants, the queen's government was for some time popular. So radical, however, was the difference between the Catholic Mary and her Protestant subjects that mutual jealousies were engendered. Mary's marriage with Lord Darnley, being opposed by Elizabeth, became objectionable. Rizzio, the queen's favorite, was killed in her presence by the king's command. James Hepburn, Earl of Bothwell, who succeeded to Mary's smile, avenged the insult to his mistress by procuring the death of her husband. The widowed queen became the earl's wife. The nation could no longer tolerate the enormities of Mary. An appeal to arms secured the persons of the queen, young James, her son by Lord Darnley, as well as the flight of Bothwell. A prisoner in the castle Lochleven, the queen was compelled to resign the crown. James was proclaimed king, and the Earl of Murray created regent. Jealousy of Murray, on the part of the friends of the Duke of Chatelherault, raised a party in favor of Mary, whose escape from prison was effected. A battle was fought at Langside which blasted her prospects. An outcast at home, the dethroned queen fled to England, where Elizabeth refused her an asylum until she was exonerated from the murder of Lord Darnley. Mary offered to submit her cause to the arbitrament of her kinswoman, but commissioners were eventually appointed whose investigations resulted in the close confinement of the Scottish fugitive. Various combinations were formed in process of time, under French and Spanish influence or connivance, to relieve Mary. The last involving an attack on the life of Elizabeth, all parties, the Scottish queen not excepted, suffered death. Notwithstanding the assaults on the throne and the life of the queen, and the failure of her favorite, the Earl of Essex, to reduce O'Neill in Ireland, the Spanish Armada, which was designed to crush the Reformation in Europe, met with defeat, and England attained an unprecedented prosperity throughout this reign.

James I., the son of Mary Queen of Scots and the great-grandson of Margaret, eldest daughter of Henry VII., succeeded Elizabeth on the English throne. The king was unpopular from the commencement of his reign. The selection of an able ministry formed the principal hold that James possessed on public confidence. The Puritans, who in the last reign were the opponents of royal prerogative, at a conference held at Hampton Court demanded a greater purification of the English church.* The king being present, displayed his eloquence and learning. On a motion to revive the bodies formerly in existence, called prophesyings, James declaimed against them vehemently, as nurseries of rebellion and faction. Indeed the whole tenor of his course was utterly opposed to what the conference expected from a Scotch Protestant, especially from the author of a dissertation proving "modern Rome to be the whore of Babylon" and "the pope antichrist." After the desolating plague had subsided a parliament assembled. James pressed the union of Scotland and England; but the measure failed. The prerogative rights of purveyance and wardship, by which the monarchs had been entitled to seize provisions for their household wherever they travelled, and to hold the estate of heirs during minorship, or compel their female wards to marry whom they pleased, were abolished. Parliament assumed the power to issue writs to supply the places of those members who did not take their seats. The Catholics, plotting the destruction of both king and parliament, attempted to execute their purpose by exploding the house where they were to assemble, with gunpowder. The leaders of the conspiracy, Wright, Catesby, and Percy, were executed. A temporary prosperity was now enjoyed by the sovereign. During the continuance of this auspicious season James introduced the English laws into Ireland; the county of Ulster in that country was settled by colonies from England; and great commercial advantages were secured to the kingdom. These favorable events might have won for the king the affections of his subjects. But the frivolity of his character,

---

* O'Neall's His. of Puritans.

together with the extravagance of his favorites, Robert Carr and George Villiers, involved him in new troubles. A rapid succession of unpopular acts followed. The execution of Sir Walter Raleigh was deemed as unnecessary as it was unjust. Thinking to stem the torrent, James projected a match between his son Charles and the Infanta Maria, daughter of Philip IV., king of Spain. Elated with the prospect of this match, the cause of the monarch's son-in-law, the elector palatine, was treated with contempt. The Protestants were stung to the quick by this act. The house of commons entreated the king to espouse the cause of the elector, to abandon the Spanish match, and to commence war against Spain. James informed their speaker in reply that they ought not to presume to meddle with anything that regarded his government or with deep matters of state. The house maintained its right to interpose its counsel in all governmental affairs, as well as its entire freedom of speech in all debates on public business. Thus commenced the controversy concerning the prerogatives of the crown and the privileges of the commons which long engaged the most gifted minds, then deluged the nation in blood, and at last renovated the English constitution.

CHAPTER XX.

THE EMPIRE OF THE ANGLO-SAXONS TO THE ESTABLISHMENT OF WILLIAM PRINCE OF ORANGE IN POWER.

CHARLES I. took the throne on the death of his father, James I.* Loaded with the debts of the last administration and those incurred by the war about the Palatinate, the king sought of parliament a large appropriation of money. That body, however, determined to reduce the prerogatives of the crown, only granted a portion of the sum requested by the king. Applications of the same nature from Charles met with a similar fate in subsequent parliaments. Levies for money were made by royal authority on subjects, many of whom were cast into prison for non-compliance with the king's demand. Sir Thomas Darnel and others made an effort to obtain their release by law; but the court of king's bench deciding that Charles possessed the power to impose taxes, the petitioners failed in accomplishing their object. The king was not equally fortunate in his expeditions against Cadiz and Rochelle. Pleased with the release of persons in confinement in consequence of the non-payment of royal assessments, and the passage of the Petition of Right, the new parliament granted an appropriation of money which was satisfactory to the king. Quiet appeared to be restored by these measures. Parliament, however, declaring against the tax of tonnage and poundage, all things were thrown into commotion and its session suspended by royal authority. A succeeding parliament pursuing the same course being dissolved,

---

* Hume. D'Aubigné's Protect. Carlyle's Crom. Papers. Macaulay's Hist. of Eng.

Charles determined to dispense with these bodies, and to rule the nation by his own arbitrary counsels. John Hampden refused to pay the tax of ship-money. The twelve judges decided against him, sustaining the position that necessity justified the king in imposing such a tax, and that he was the sole judge of that necessity.

Charles introduced episcopacy into Scotland. A popular tumult ensued at Edinburgh. The Marquis of Hamilton was deputed to treat with the Scots. After repeated fruitless negotiations the Scots agreed to submit the disputed points to the general assembly and parliament. Not heeding the refusal of the bishops to sit in the assembly, and its dissolution by the royal commissioner, that body continued its session, abolishing episcopacy with all the religious innovations introduced from the accession of James I. to the throne of England. A military force was enlisted by the Scots, which was entrusted to the command of Lesley, Earl of Leven. Charles put himself at the head of an army of more than twenty thousand men. A reconciliation was effected, by which it was stipulated that the sovereign should withdraw his forces, that the Scots should dismiss their army, that the royal authority should be acknowledged, and that the general assembly and parliament should compose differences. These bodies soon sat, but the latter was prorogued in order to prevent it from ratifying some acts of the assembly which did not suit the royal pleasure. War was renewed; the Scots were triumphant; a cessation of hostilities was agreed upon. Parliament, regaining its authority, assailed the measures and ministers used by the king for the last few years. The Earl of Strafford, Archbishop Laud, Lord Keeper Finch, and Secretary Windebank were impeached: Strafford was condemned and executed. The courts of star-chamber and high commission were abolished. Ship-money was declared illegal. The sentence of Hampden was reversed. Compositions for knighthood were stigmatized. The extension of forest laws was condemned. Patents for monopolies were annulled. The tenure of all judges was altered from that of pleasure to that of good behavior. The influence of Charles was completely subverted in Scotland. Taking advantage of the troublesome state of affairs, the Catholics of Ireland committed dreadful massacres of the Protestants, particularly in Ulster. Proceeding to charge thirteen bishops, the commons demanded the surrender of their persons by the peers. The demand was refused, but a portion of the peers took part with the house. Scenes of violence ensued between the populace, denominated roundheads, and the adherents of the king, styled cavaliers. The bishops, asserting their dread of being attacked by the former, withdrew from the house of peers, protesting against all votes which might be passed in their absence. A conference took place between the two houses, at which the impeachment of the thirteen bishops was sanctioned, and they were committed to custody. Charles ordered an accusation for treason to be preferred against Lord Kimbolton, Sir Arthur Hazelrig, Hollis, Hampden, Pym, and Stroud. Failing to obtain the persons of the accused, the king offered to drop the proceedings and make concessions to the commons for the breach of their privileges. The apology was resolved to be insufficient, unless the advisers of the measure were discovered. Thus victorious, parliament placed their own governors in all seaport towns and assumed the exclusive command of the militia of the kingdom. Charles removed to York; the queen fled to Holland. A warfare of the pen ensued. At last parliament levied an army, under the command of the Earl of Essex. The king raised forces and erected his headquarters at Nottingham. A bloody but indecisive battle was fought at Edgehill. Essex was unsuccessful at Oxford, and a portion of his main body was defeated at Carlsgrave Field by Prince Rupert, where John Hampden was killed. At Stamford and Lansdown Hill the parliamentary forces fared no better, and were totally defeated at Roundway Down. Bristol was taken by Rupert, and Gloucester invested. Charles published a manifesto in which he professed a desire for peace. Edmund Waller, a member of parliament, together with Tompkins and Challoner, endeavored to effect it. Parliament, though thus far unsuccessful in arms, resisted all attempts at compromise and condemned Tompkins and Challoner to death. A reverse occurred in the king's affairs in consequence of the victory of Sir Thomas Fairfax at Wakefield and that of Oliver Cromwell at Gainsborough. A union was formed with the Scots. Their army under the Earl of Leven, and the English forces commanded by Fairfax and Cromwell, were triumphant at Marston Moor. York and New Castle fell into the hands of the parliamentary leaders.

The independents becoming dominant in parliament, resolved that no member of that body should be in command of the army. Essex resigned; Fairfax took his place; Cromwell, though a member of the house, was permitted to hold his position in the military. Archbishop Laud was brought to the block. Strengthened in Scotland by the exertions of the Marquis of Montrose, Charles rallied his forces, relieved Chester, took Leicester, and in marching to raise the siege of Oxford joined battle with the parliamentary army at Naseby, where he was utterly ruined. Every place of importance was soon captured by the generals of the parliament. Charles having taken refuge in the camp of the Scots, was surrendered by them to parliament. The army and parliament now disagreed. The former seized the person of Charles. The city of London insisting on the removal of the officers of the independents, the army approached the capital. At Hounslow Heath the speakers of both houses, eight peers, and sixty commoners, imploring their protection, were reinstated in power by the military. Charles was brought to Hampton Court, from whence, in dread of attacks on his life, he fled to the Isle of Wight, where he was made a prisoner. A council of officers determined to bring the king to an account for his conduct. Parliament still indulged the hope of a settlement, and proposed as its basis that Charles should allow it all military power, ratify its acts, annul all patents of peerage from the time of Lord Littleton, and permit the two houses to adjourn as they pleased. As negotiations were on the eve of a favorable termination, the army, which had been absent in suppressing outbreaks in the kingdom, approached London and drove all the members from both houses but its own adherents. This body, styled the rump parliament, formed a high court of justice for the trial of the king, by which he was condemned and executed (A.D. 1649). Kingly power and the house of peers were abolished; a new seal ordered, with the inscription, "In the first year of freedom, by God's blessing restored"; the powers of government vested in a body of persons called "the conservators of the liberties of England"; the statue of the king cast down, and on its pedestal engraven the words, "The tyrant, the last of kings, is gone."

Young Charles was proclaimed king in Scotland, and was supported in Ireland. Cromwell soon blasted his prospects by subduing both countries. Every portion of the empire in England, Ireland, Scotland, America, and India was submissive to the commonwealth. Failing to obtain its terms with the Dutch, parliament passed the Navigation Act, by which all goods from Asia, Afria, and America were excluded from England unless brought in its own ships. War ensued with the Dutch, who were at first triumphant, but were finally reduced by Dean and Monk. The army petitioned for their arrears of pay and demanded a new representative body. Commons determined to fill the vacancies in their number by an election. Enraged at this measure, Cromwell with a band of three hundred soldiers cleared the house. A new parliament was convened, which resigned their powers to the military and dispersed. A council of officers proclaimed the instrument of government, and declared Oliver Cromwell protector or supreme magistrate of the commonwealth. The Dutch war was renewed. Monk and Dean were eventually triumphant. The Dutch were glad to purchase peace by yielding to England the honor of the flag. The war with Spain also added greatly to the glory of the English navy, as well as to the fame of Blake and Penn. Tunis was bombarded; reparation for wrongs obtained from the Duke of Tuscany; Jamaica was captured; the piratical hordes in the Mediterranean were crushed; the Spanish fleet destroyed in the Bay of Santa Cruz. After the successful termination of this war, the protector convoked a parliament which presented to him a form of government differing little from that contained in the instrument. Having declined the title and office of a king, the protector was inaugurated under the new constitution at Westminster Hall (A.D. 1658). On the death of Cromwell, his son Richard became protector. Cabals which Richard had not the talents to control soon forced him to resign. The military officers again seized the reins of government. The Rump parliament was assembled. A council was appointed by this body for the management of public affairs. Offended at not holding the power in the council, the military officers created a committee of safety consisting of twenty-three persons. Monk, protesting against this arbitrary act, declared for the parliament. A reaction occurred in public sentiment which placed Charles II. on the throne of his ancestors. All judicial decrees from the time of Charles I. were confirmed; an act of indemnity was passed; six of the regicides, with four of their abettors, were executed; the bodies of Cromwell and his son-in-law Ireton were taken from their coffins at Westminster, drawn on hurdles to Tyburn, hanged by the neck for some hours, their heads chopped off and placed upon Westminster Hall, their bodies thrown into a hole beneath the gallows. Similar barbarities were perpetrated in Scotland. The Marquis of Argyle and Guthrie were among the victims. The royalists had a decided majority in the new parliament. An act of uniformity was passed which required that a clergyman should possess episcopal ordination to hold a benefice; should declare his assent to every dogma in the Book of Common Prayer; take the oath of canonical obedience to abjure the League and Covenant; and renounce the right of taking arms against the king. The marriage of Charles with Catharine of Portugal, together with his subserviency to Louis XIV., and his cruelties to the Presbyterians of Scotland, confirmed the nation in a dread of arbitrary power and popery. Titus Oates, aided by Dr. Tongue, a London clergyman, pretended that there was a plot to murder the king, to subvert the government, and to destroy the Protestant religion. Trifling as the evidence was at first in support of this declaration, it so accumulated in time that parliament eventually believed it; executed Viscount Stafford as one of the conspirators; and pressed the exclusion of James, the brother of the king, from the succession to the crown, inasmuch as he was a Catholic. Overpowered by the opposition, Charles made a written appeal to the nation which he caused to be read in all the pulpits of the established church throughout the kingdom. This shrewd movement had a tendency in a great measure to relieve the king from the odium which his unpopular acts had brought upon him. Taking advantage of this good fortune, government caused the charter of London and other cities to be forfeited in order to increase its power by restoring them upon its own terms. Oppression seldom fails to create resistance among freemen. A combination was formed for the re-establishment of the constitution which was denominated, from the place where its supporters usually held their meetings, the Rye House Plot. Before the measures of the conspirators were ripe for execution the crown detected and executed their principal members, Lord Russell and Algernon Sidney. Death cut short the career of Charles II. His brother, the Duke of York, succeeded to the crown under the name of James II. The rebellion headed by the Dukes of Monmouth and Argyle was suppressed. The leaders were executed. Persons concerned in this rebellion were brought to the block by the wholesale, through the agency of Chief-Justice Jeffreys. Emboldened by his recent successes, James dispensed with the test act in favor of some Catholics. The house of commons protested against this arbitrary conduct of the king; the judges nevertheless sustained it. The Earl of Powis with other zealous Catholics were placed at the council-board; Talbot, of the same faith, created Earl of Tyrconnel, was appointed lieutenant of Ireland; Earl Castlemain was despatched to Rome in order to reconcile the pope; public audience given in England to the nuncio of his holiness; papists introduced into the universities of Oxford and Cambridge. Attempting to form a coalition between Catholics and other dissenters, James commanded his Declaration of General Indulgence to be read in all the pulpits of the state establishment throughout the kingdom. Sancroft, archbishop of Canterbury, with six bishops, presented a petition to the crown in opposition to this order. The petitioners were committed to the Tower, but being acquitted by a jury were set at liberty. Whigs and Tories united in resisting the oppression of the crown. The aid of William Prince of Orange, the son-in-law of James II., was invoked. William landed in England without opposition. James made his escape to France. Tranquillity was restored by the passage of the Act of Settlement (A.D. 1669). By the terms of this instrument the Prince and Princess of Orange were declared king and queen of England during their joint lives and the life of the survivor, the sole administration being in the prince; after the death of both, the heirs of the body of the princess were to succeed to the throne; and in default of such issue Anne of Denmark and the heirs of her body to succeed before the heirs of William by any other wife. Provision was also made against the encroachments of the crown, reducing its authority within such limits as would preserve popular rights from those invasions to which they had long been liable.

CHAPTER XXI.

THE EMPIRE OF THE ANGLO-SAXONS TO THE PRESENT TIMES.

WILLIAM proclaimed a toleration of all forms of Protestant worship in England and re-established Presbyterianism in Scotland.* The Irish who adhered to the cause of James II. were defeated at the battle of the Boyne. The Scots who supported the dethroned monarch were scat-

---

* Rus., Vol. IV. Let. 17, p. 180. Smollett, Vol. I. ch. ii. §§ 25–28.

tered after their success at Killiecrankie. Cruelties by the king's friends at Glencoe, in Scotland, induced a conspiracy to restore James II., which was aided by France. It was crushed by a naval victory over the French fleet at La Hogue. On the death of the queen, William was exposed to the intrigues of his enemies. Sir George Barclay headed a plot to destroy the king, which was frustrated by the execution of its principal supporters. The desperate character of this combination in aiming at the life of the sovereign, together with the brilliant successes against France, ended the hopes of James II. and seated William firmly on the throne. No alteration in the conduct of the continental affairs occurred upon the accession of Anne of Denmark to the English sceptre. Lord Godolphin and the Duke of Marlborough still controlled the national movements. Scottish troubles were terminated by a union between Scotland and England (A.D. 1706). The terms of the arrangement provided for the unity of the two kingdoms; the succession of the Princess Sophia, duchess dowager of Hanover, and her heirs being Protestants; the representation of Scotland in parliament by sixteen peers and forty-five commoners; the freedom of trade; the permanency of the courts and laws of Scotland; and the rights of royal boroughs in that kingdom. A grant of near four hundred thousand pounds of money was made by the English parliament to be paid in Scotland for preserving an equality of trade throughout the united kingdoms. The strife for power between Mr. Harley, Godolphin, and Marlborough, the hero of the French war,* preyed upon the spirits of the queen to such an extent as to impair her health. Her death brought to the throne George, son to Ernest Augustus, Elector of Brunswick, by the Princess Sophia, great-

---

* Chap. XIII.

granddaughter to James I., who was proclaimed king under the title of George I. The change in the administration threw some of the officers of the last reign into disgrace. One of the number became the leader of the Jacobites, who advocated the right of the son of James II. to the throne. A large force was raised in Scotland and the north of England in support of this cause. The defeat of the insurgents at Sheriffmuir put an end to their operations. Sir John Blount, under pretence of lowering the interest on the national debt by making the South-Sea Company the sole public creditor, threw the kingdom into commotion by the failure of his scheme. The panic was allayed by the punishment of defaulters and the indemnity of sufferers. Splendid results attended the war with Spain.*

George II., the son of the last monarch, took the throne. Sir Robert Walpole's excise measures and the iniquitous act of the Charitable Corporation, formed for lending money on pledges, agitated the reign. War was declared against Spain. Admiral Vernon, in charge of the English fleet, took Porto Bello, in South America. In a subsequent expedition against Carthagena that admiral and his colleague Wentworth lost twenty thousand men. Nor was Anson less unfortunate, though he eventually captured the Manilla galleon. Taking advantage of the enormous expenses of the war about the succession of Maria Theresa, the Jacobites made an effort to restore the Stuarts. The young pretender landed in Scotland, where, joined by Lochiel, Cameron, and Highland chiefs, he took possession of Dundee, Dunkeld, Perth, Edinburgh, and was victorious at Prestonpans and Falkirk. The forces of George destroyed the prospects of the invader at Culloden. Scotland was reduced by depriving its Highland chiefs of their exclusive

---

* Chap. XVII., Spain.

jurisdiction. Lords Balmerino and Lovat and the Earl of Kilmarnock were executed. Scenes of riot and frustrated attempts at invading France spread abroad dissatisfaction, which might have been detrimental to the king but for the success of his arms in America, in the East Indies, and under his ally, Frederick of Prussia.*

George III., the grandson of the last monarch, succeeded to the sceptre.† The war with Spain not only sustained the king of Portugal, but placed England in possession of Havana and the whole range of the Philippine Islands. The unpopularity of the treaty of Paris forced its author, the Earl of Bute, from power. Grenville, his successor, was equally objectionable. John Wilkes, the editor of the *North Briton*, in an attack on the minister, brought on his head the vengeance of government. Weak as was the minister at home, he ventured upon the perilous policy of taxing the American colonies.‡ Rash conduct in his successors on the same subject created a rupture between the two countries. Measures of national reform, though ably advocated, were but imperfectly applied. Efforts to remove Catholic disabilities being warmly opposed, occasioned disturbances in the capital. In regulating the concerns of the East India Company parliament became the scene of bitter contention. Warren Hastings, the late governor-general of British India, was impeached for improprieties alleged to have been committed by him during his administration. The indisposition of the king resulting in mental derangement, his son George became regent. The father, however, was afterwards restored to health and resumed the management of public affairs. Reparation was procured from Spain for wrongs on English shipping. Liberty was also

---

* See Chap. XIII. Orme's His. India. † Bisset.
‡ See Chap. XXII.

obtained from that kingdom for English settlements north of the Spanish colonies on the western coast of North America. Parliament exempted the Catholics from many disabilities on abjuring the doctrines that excommunicated princes might be deposed, that no faith was to be kept with heretics, and that the church could dispense with moral duties or pardon sins. A constitution was provided for Canada which secured to that country a representative assembly and the right of internal taxation. Efforts for parliamentary reforms involved some of their advocates in prosecutions, which were abandoned after the acquittal of Tooke and Hardy. A stoppage of specie payment by the national bank, together with a mutiny among the seamen in the fleet, produced great popular excitement. The panic nevertheless subsided on explanations in regard to the solvency of the bank and the execution of the ringleaders in the mutiny. An outbreak in Ireland was suppressed by the battle of Ballinahinch. England and that country were united by an act which confirmed the Protestant succession; consolidated the legislative bodies; united the churches of the two countries; secured to the subjects of both realms the same commercial privileges, leaving the public debt of each on a separate basis; guaranteed the maintenance of the laws and courts then in existence, subject to legislative revision; and ordained that four prelates should sit alternately in parliament, twenty-eight lay-peers should be chosen for life, while two members for each of the Irish counties and thirty-six citizens and burgesses were to represent the Hibernian commons (A.D. 1801).*

Nelson's naval victory off Draco Point established the supremacy of England in the northern seas. Emmet and Russell, deeming the troublesome negotiations with France

---

* Al. Eu. Bisset, Vol. IV. ch. lxvi.

to afford a fit time for action, made a bold effort for the liberation of Ireland. The movement failing, the leaders were executed. Sir Arthur Wellesley and General Lake were triumphant in the East Indies. The Cape of Good Hope was reduced. Great but temporary advantage was obtained at Buenos Ayres, in South America. Brilliant success attended the English arms in the southern peninsula. Another fit of derangement in the king brought his son to the regency. Java and Batavia fell into the possession of the English. Outbreaks arising from a general want of employment agitated the kingdom. The success of Lord Exmouth's expedition in humbling Algiers, liberating an immense number of Christian captives, extorting from the dey the total abolition of slavery in his dominions, and procuring reparation for all the powers which had sustained injury from the barbarous acts of these people tended greatly to allay popular commotions. The same result was promoted by the marriages solemnized between Charlotte Princess of Wales and Leopold Prince of Saxe-Coburg; between the Duke of Gloucester and his cousin, the Princess Mary; and between the Dukes of Kent, Clarence, Cambridge, and different princely families of Germany. Conflicting views on parliamentary reforms gave rise in Manchester to bloodshed. Hunt and other leaders suffered imprisonment. Sir Francis Burdett, reflecting in a letter to his constituents on the action of government in the recent disturbances, was convicted of libel. Parliamentary acts followed to prevent seditious meetings, to prohibit training and arming, to check blasphemous and seditious writings, and to tax cheap publications.

On the death of George III., his son George IV. succeeded to the crown.* The Cato-Street Conspiracy, hav-

---

* Croly's Geo. IV.

ing for its object the assassination of the ministers, was detected. Thistlewood, its prime mover, was executed. Proceedings in parliament by the king to obtain a divorce from Queen Caroline delayed the coronation. Ireland, Scotland, and Hanover were visited by George IV. English power was greatly strengthened in India by the defeat of the Burmese. Ottoman atrocities on the Greeks fired the indignation of Europe. A treaty for the protection of Greece was signed at London between England, Russia, and France. The fleet of the allies, commanded by Sir Edward Codrington, destroyed that of the Ottomans at Navarino. Greece was created a kingdom under Otho of Bavaria. William Duke of Clarence succeeded to the throne on the death of his brother, George IV. Reform measures in regard to Catholic emancipation, Jewish disabilities, and the education funds constituted the absorbing objects of this reign. William's popularity waxed or waned as he advanced or retarded these movements.

Alexandrina Victoria, daughter of the Duke of Kent, fourth son of George III., came to the throne after the death of William IV. Two years after the accession of the queen she was married to Albert Prince of Saxe-Coburg. Difficulties arose in Canada.* The reform party, thinking to expedite certain favorite measures, refused to pass supplies for public expenses. In revenge, the governor declined to sanction the act for the encouragement of education, as well as other acts. Popular indignation was excited, under the influence of rival clubs. Government officers arrested two citizens for the part they had taken in the contest. The prisoners were rescued by the populace. Having overstepped the law by this act, the reformers flew to arms, as the most likely expedient

---

* Thellier's His. of the Outbreak.

for their own security. Government suppressed the outbreak by severe actions at St. Denis and St. Charles, at St. Eustache and Navy Island. Breadstuff monopoly was destroyed in England by the repeal of the corn-laws. China having interdicted the opium trade, created a breach which was only healed by the grant of enlarged commercial privileges to English subjects. Timely interference on the part of England and the great powers of Europe prevented a dismemberment of the Ottoman Empire, by restraining Mehemet Ali to his Egyptian dominions. Dread on the part of the East India Company that the friendly feelings existing between the natives and the Russians might enable the latter to penetrate from the Cabul to the ocean on the south, and thus establish a commercial rival, produced extensive preparations by the English to restore Shah Soojah, the exiled prince, to the throne of his ancestors.* This project was seconded by Runjeet Singh, the head of the Punjab nation, through whose territory north of the Sutledge River the company's forces were compelled to pass. Two decided victories by the English were followed by a settlement which surrendered to England in full sovereignty the territory, hill and plain, lying between the rivers Sutledge and Beas; secured to the victors indemnity for the expenses of the war, and committed to them the entire regulation and control of both banks of the river Sutledge, as well as the future boundaries of the Sikh state, together with the administration of its public affairs. The revolutionary spirit which swept the continent of Europe in 1848 with such dreadful havoc created disturbances in Ireland and England. Prompt measures on the part of government

---

* A Narrative of the Afghan War, by Steele. Dub. Un. Mag., Vol. II. No. 3, Sept. 1842. Orme's His. of India.

suppressed them in both countries. The rebellion in India was not as easily terminated. After having progressed to a fearful extent of blood and outrage, it was only crushed by the greatest severities inflicted upon the natives.* The war with China (1858), in which England, France, Russia, and the United States were engaged, resulted so far in the humiliation of the eastern power that it was only able to procure peace upon a treaty which contained promises of indemnity for public and private losses to the western nations and their citizens, the allowance to them of resident ambassadors, unrestricted trade and travel, and the free exercise of the Christian religion.† The invasion of Abyssinia humbled that kingdom and liberated the English whom it held in captivity (1868). The discontents in Ireland it was supposed would be allayed by the measures of parliament in abrogating its church establishment, which has heretofore existed in that nation (1869).

CHAPTER XXII.

THE UNITED STATES OF AMERICA TO THE ADMINISTRATION OF THE YEAR 1872.

The thirteen English colonies in North America carried on a considerable trade with the French and Spanish residents of the new world previous to the treaty of Paris.‡ Gold and silver had been procured from this commerce in sufficient quantities to make purchases in England on ad-

---

* Walsh's Memorial.
† Huc's China. Taylor's Manual, China. Gazette.
‡ Ramsay's His. Am. Rev. Pitkin's Pol. His. U. S. Marshall's and Irving's War. Bancroft's His. U. S. Holmes' Anns.

vantageous terms. Parliament interfered with this traffic by loading it with enormous duties. Unwise as was this policy, the complaints of the colonists would have subsided had they not been followed by the Stamp Act. This law required instruments of writing in daily use among the people to be on stamped paper or parchment, which was charged with duty. Such an attempt to raise a revenue from the new world to pay in part the debt of one hundred and forty-eight million of the parent-portion of the old world kindled a flame of indignation throughout the colonies. Virginia led the way. The house of burgesses passed resolutions denying the right of parliament to tax the colonies. Five months subsequent a continental congress assembled at New York which confirmed this doctrine (A.D. 1766). The objectionable law was repealed by parliament. In about one year, however, that body passed another law imposing duties on glass, paper, painter's colors, and tea. Although this measure was presented by the ministry merely as a means of regulating commerce, it was assailed by most of the colonial writers, particularly by Mr. Dickinson of Pennsylvania, as one directly enacting the odious principle of parliamentary taxation. Viewed in this light by the country, it produced, as the only means which could be adopted as a remedy, a non-importation agreement among the residents. Notwithstanding the unpopularity of the law, the ministry directed a board of commissioners to be established. Sustained by the common sentiment of the colonists, the assembly of Massachusetts demanded a repeal of the law. In order to counteract this step, the home minister addressed communications to all the assemblies imploring them to recede from their position. This imprudent act, connected with the seizure of the sloop Liberty by the crown officers, gave the strongest impulse to the colonial cause (A.D. 1768).

Supercilious subordinates often involve their governments in the worst complications. The haughty bearing of the royal tax-collectors increased the already embittered state of feeling. Two regiments and armed vessels were sent to Boston for the protection of the crown officers in exacting the duties. Both houses of parliament approving of the course of the king in regard to the colonies, suggested the appointment of a commission to prosecute all persons charged with treason or misprision thereof within the realm of Great Britain. The burgesses of Virgina promptly declared their exclusive right of taxation, as well as of petition for redress of grievances; the lawfulness of procuring the concurrence of the other colonies in measures of common interest to all; and the sole right of colonial courts to try offences within their jurisdiction. Other assemblies sanctioned these principles and, like that of Virginia, were dissolved for the act by gubernatorial authority. Conduct so arbitrary excited opposition. The people anew formed non-importation conventions. Governor Hutchinson attempted to counteract these movements in Boston by creating associations of an opposite character; which induced the Bostonians to determine on a reshipment of the merchandise sent from England. Unable to enforce the law, parliament repealed all its provisions except that which imposed a tax of threepence per pound upon tea (A.D. 1770). An assurance was at the same time given by the ministry that this impost would eventually be abandoned. Quiet might have been restored at this period had not an affray in Boston between the military and the populace, coupled with the arrogance of crown officers, continued the bad state of feeling. The discovery of Governor Hutchinson's letters in England concerning the colonists, made by Dr. Franklin, also tended to exasperate the public mind.

A crisis was created in events by the cupidity of the

East India Company. In consequence of the non-importation resolution of the colonists, the tea of this establishment had been stored in England to the amount of seventeen millions of pounds. Procuring a law to authorize its exportation free of duty, preparations were immediately made to throw it into the American market. In view of this act, an expression of public opinion was made at Philadelphia and throughout the country. Despite this the company persisted in their project. The cargoes were returned from New York and Philadelphia, landed and stored at Charlestown; but in Boston seventeen individuals disguised as Indians entered the ships, broke open three hundred and forty-two chests, the contents of which were thrown into the sea. Upon the announcement of this act in England, parliament passed two bills: the first directed the closing of the port of Boston, transferring its rights as a place of entry to Salem; the second stripped the colony of its charter, vesting in the crown or governor the appointment of all the important officers. Acts so fatal to the rights of all the colonies excited among them a sympathy for Boston. The people were rent into two parties: that which advocated the rights of the Bostonians was denominated Whig; that which adhered to the mother-country was styled Tory. After sharp discussions it was resolved to convoke a congress to consult upon the state of affairs. At Boston the assemblies were dissolved, the courts closed; troops arrived from the northern possessions, and General Gage, who was in command, commenced operations by fortifying his post. The colonists were not idle: covenants were formed to suspend commercial relations with England until grievances were redressed; strength tested by military arrangements; and the causes of complaint placed before the world in their true light (A.D. 1774).

Congress assembled at Philadelphia. Twelve colonies, containing a population of three millions, were represented. The position taken from the commencement of the controversy on the subject of taxation was confirmed; the right of trial by jury of the vicinage demanded; the various charter privileges which had been assailed asserted; and the acts concerning Boston condemned. Desirous only of a redress of grievances, no measures were adopted but a non-consumption, non-importation, and non-exportation agreement, together with addresses to the people of England, to the inhabitants of British America, and to the king. Conciliatory as were these movements, the ministerial party in parliament rejected them, persisting in the terms they had for years dictated. Chatham's compromise failed and the fishery bill succeeded. At this critical period of affairs (1775) General Gage resolved to destroy the stores and arms which the colonists had secured at Concord, a town but a short distance from Boston. A force of considerable strength was sent by him to that place, which effected his object after a brave resistance by an undisciplined militia. This contest and that of Lexington demonstrated to the colonists the necessity of making vigorous efforts to place themselves in an attitude of defence. Shortly afterwards a re-enforcement of British troops arrived, under the command of Burgoyne, Howe, and Clinton. Gage issued a proclamation which, by offering peace on submission to all but Samuel Adams and John Hancock, was a signal for war. At the entrance of the peninsula of Charlestown was a height called Bunker Hill, the possession of which was of the utmost importance in case of hostilities. The colonial commander directed this to be secured. A thousand men were ordered to entrench it. By mistake they seized on a hill nearer Boston, known as Breed's Hill. The British brought all their forces to bear on their antagonists (June 17); but with such desperate courage did they resist that the post was maintained until the ammunition failed. Notwithstanding their success, the royal commanders were convinced that their enemies were their equals except in the munitions of war.

The first object of congress was to repel the injuries inflicted on their constituents by the fishery act. Exportations to the British possessions in the north, sales to British fishermen, supplies to the British army, were interdicted. Means of defence were provided, and the command of the continental forces was committed to the hands of George Washington, of Virginia. Still the representatives, feeling it to be their duty to place their position as well as the causes which had led to it fairly before the world, voted addresses to the neighboring powers and the home department. The commander-in-chief, regarding the northern frontiers as of the utmost importance, made arrangements for securing Ticonderoga and Canada. The former point was carried under the direction of Arnold and Allen. The latter failed, though Montgomery fell in attempting its accomplishment. Hard pressed by Washington, the British abandoned Boston. Convinced of the impossibility of effecting a redress of grievances, congress proclaimed the Declaration of Independence (July 4, 1776). The resolutions of parliament had been formed with a view to a speedy termination of hostilities. Near one hundred thousand men, many of them German mercenaries, had been drafted; a forfeiture of American shipping, as well as the impressment of American sailors, directed. Although unsuccessful in their assaults at the South, the British mastered the city of New York. Washington was forced into Jersey and thence into Pennsylvania. These misfortunes reduced the cause of the Americans to the brink of destruction. A change, however, suddenly occurred. The American commander in the dead of night recrossed the Delaware, and by signal advantages at Trenton and Princeton restored the confidence of his countrymen (Dec. 24, 1777). The British, foiled in their attempts on New Jersey and Pennsylvania, retired to Amboy and betook themselves to their fleet. Intending to approach Philadelphia by the Delaware River, but fearing its navigation, the royal commander landed his forces in Maryland and proceeded with them over the country. They were met at the fords of the Brandywine by Washington's army, where a bloody struggle ensued in which the English were victorious. Amongst the wounded was General La Fayette a young French nobleman who in support of the American cause had sacrificed the ease of his native court for the toils of a foreign camp. The possession of Philadelphia by the British, the massacre of the Americans at Paoli, and their defeat at Germantown again cast a deep gloom over their concerns. From the North, however, where the English were defeated at Saratoga by General Gates, sprang sources of encouragement.

All prospect of settlement with the mother-country being extinguished, France formed an alliance with America. Washington in conjunction with the French fleet prevented any depredations of the enemy, except those at Norwalk and Fairfield. Dreading that the foreign fleet might block up their squadron in the Delaware, the British left Philadelphia, notwithstanding the loss sustained at Red Bank in securing it. In the progress of their land forces through Jersey to New York they were severely handled by their adversaries at Monmouth. Savannah was snatched from the Americans. The invaders incited the Indians to butcher a considerable number of the settlers of Wyoming. Charleston was captured by the English. Gates, the congressional commander, was defeated. Arnold turned traitor. A sudden reverse in events restored the South, placed Cornwallis in the hands of Washington at Yorktown, and utterly ruined the British cause. A pacification was finally signed at Paris (1783). The treaty declared the thirteen colonies free, sovereign, and independent states. Their limits were marked by a line drawn from the northwest angle of Nova Scotia, passing toward one of the heads of the Connecticut River, thence to Lake Ontario, through the middle of that lake and of Lakes Erie and Huron, to the Lake of the Woods, thence to the Mississippi River, which formed a boundary as far south as Fort Mobile and the borders of Florida. That river was left open to both nations. The right of taking fish in the Gulf of St. Lawrence and on the banks of Newfoundland was given to the Americans. Restitution of property to the Tories was recommended to the states. Pondicherry and the settlements in the East Indies, in St. Lucia, and in Gorce were restored to the French, who agreed to return all their conquests in the West Indies on the return of Tobago. The Spanish retained Minorca and Florida, the English Gibraltar, and the Dutch were protected in all their territories except Negapatam.

The revolutionary struggle left the states in a condition which soon proved the insufficiency of the confederation by which they were united. Congress had no exclusive fund from which the arrears due the soldiery could be paid. Commerce was independent of its control. The only appeal was to the state legislatures, which were rendered totally inoperative by their divisions, as well as by the poverty of the people. The latter cause operated strongly in Massachusetts, where a large body of the citizens, choosing Daniel Shays as their leader, demanded a suspension of the laws in relation to the collection of debts and the emission of paper money. Prompt government measures put an end to this outbreak. A remedy for the prostrate condition to which the conflicting state regulations had subjected the commerce of the country was first suggested in a scheme by which the citizens of Virginia and Maryland proposed to regulate the navigation of the Potomac River and Chesapeake Bay. Commissioners appointed by these states met at Alexandria. It was proposed that a board with enlarged powers should be created. To this suggestion Delaware, Pennsylvania, and New York responded. The commissioners of these states assembled soon afterwards at Annapolis and recommended the selection of delegates by the state legislatures. The delegates thus chosen commenced their sessions (1787) by appointing General Washington president. A form of government was published which secured to each state a constitution with limited powers, created a national establishment with a distinctly defined jurisdiction, the executive functions of which were lodged in a president, who, together with the vice-president, was to be chosen every four years by electors assigned for that purpose by popular vote; the legislative functions of which were to be exercised by a congress consisting of a senate composed of two members elected by each state legislature for six years, of which body the vice-president was made speaker, and a house of representatives, elected every two years by the people of the states; the judicial functions of which were reposed in a bench of judges appointed by the president and confirmed by the senate, who were to hold their commissions during good behavior. Eleven states adopted the constitution; General Washington was elected the first president; and the two remaining states acceded in the course of a year. The state liabilities incurred by the late war were assumed by the general government; the principal to be paid by the sales of public lands, the interest to be met by a tax on articles of luxury and liquors distilled in the country. A national bank was established; the war with the southern and northwestern Indians terminated; an outbreak in western Pennsylvania in consequence of the tax on domestic liquors suppressed; and a treaty effected with England by which that kingdom agreed to surrender the posts claimed by the republic and make compensation for illegal seizures, while the United States were obligated to pay a sum of money to Britain in trust for debts due by American citizens to her subjects. The free navigation of the Mississippi, together with commercial privileges at New Orleans, was obtained from Spain. French republicans expected assistance from the states in their struggle with England. Having recalled the minister appointed by the dethroned monarch, Genet was deputed. Received at Charleston in a highly flattering manner both by the governor and citizens, he was emboldened to vigorous exertions in behalf of his government. The president issued orders to defeat the ambassador's projects, on a remonstrance against them by the British minister. The successors of Genet were less violent, but equally determined to involve the states in the quarrel of their government. Disappointed in this design, France assailed the shipping of the states. The president, however, determined to avoid a rupture with the republic, recalled Mr. Monroe and sent Mr. Pinckney minister to Paris. At this juncture of affairs John Adams was elected president, Thomas Jefferson vice-president. Mr. Pinckney's rejection was soon announced; a special meeting of congress called; and Mr. Marshall and Mr. Gerry united to the French embassage. The directory refused to accredit the new ministers. Immediate preparation was made for war; the army increased, Washington placed in command; the navy strengthened; enlarged powers given to the president in reference to foreign residents and seditious movements. Actions took place between the American frigate Constellation and the French frigates L'Insurgent and La Vengeance, in which the first was victorious. The universal sorrow consequent on this melancholy breach between the two nations was increased by the death of the illustrious Washington (Dec. 14, 1799). A treaty of peace was concluded with Napoleon in the following September, which congress confirmed at its first session in Washington.

Thomas Jefferson was chosen president and Aaron Burr vice-president after thirty-five ballots in the house of representatives. A war with Tripoli humbled the pride and diminished the power of the bashaw. Louisiana was purchased from France for fifteen millions of dollars. Unexampled prosperity had attended the citizens of the United States in maritime operations. From small beginnings they advanced from one state of improvement to another, until the recent wars of Europe threw into their possession its entire carrying trade. Sudden events involved them in disaster. The Berlin and Milan decrees of Napoleon deprived them of British trade; the retaliatory orders of the English council produced equally calamitous consequences upon their commercial dealings with France. England increased these embarrassments by insisting on her right to search American vessels and impress British seamen found on board of them. The reparation for the exercise of the latter authority on board of the Chesapeake was counterbalanced by the excessive increase of contraband articles, as well as by a refined system of blockade. No alternative was left for the states but an embargo. Popular complaint soon compelled congress to substitute for this policy an interdiction of commercial intercourse with France and England. Mr. Madison, who was elected president at the expiration of Mr. Jefferson's terms, finally proposed to these powers that the last measure should be repealed if they would abandon the acts which had given rise to international difficulties. Napoleon acceded, but the British continued their offensive orders. War with England was the result (A.D. 1812). The first attack of the republic was on Canada, under the direction of General Hull. The improper conduct of the commander rendered it a failure. This advantage of the British was counterbalanced by their naval losses in the capture of the Guerriere and Frolic, the Macedonian and the Java. Another attempt was made on Canada by General Winchester, who was defeated at Frenchtown. General Pike was more successful at York. Notwithstanding the triumph of British arms at the head of the Miami, at Fort George, and in some naval engagements, their glory became at least questionable by the victory of Chauncey on Lake Ontario, of Perry on Lake Erie, the consequent defeat of Proctor, the repossession of Michigan by Harrison, and the success of Scott and Brown at Niagara. Through the meditation of Russia conferences were opened at Ghent between the contending powers. Hostilities were, however, continued. The British defeated the Americans at Bladensburg, making an inroad on Washington; were unsuccessful at Baltimore; sustained an overthrow on Lake Champlain and at Plattsburg; and were routed by Jackson at New Orleans. Previous to the last event peace had been settled by the treaty of Ghent, which stipulated that all conquests should be mutually restored; that disputes on boundaries should be referred to persons chosen by the two nations; that the savages should be placed in the condition they held before the war; and that both parties should use their endeavors to abolish the slave-trade.

The peace of Europe, by rendering each power the conductor of its own commerce, together with the excessive speculations of local institutions during the war at home, produced embarrassments in the condition of the United States. Resolved to sustain the country against all emergencies, congress revoked the policy by which it was induced some years before to refuse charter privileges to a national bank. An institution of that description was created to continue for twenty-one years, with a capital of thirty-five millions of dollars. Domestic manufactures were protected, whilst the navy was increased. During the succeeding administrations of Mr. Monroe and Mr. Adams the national fortifications were increased; the number of the states was augmented; internal improvements advanced; treaties of commerce formed; popular gratitude evinced to La Fayette; sympathy aroused for the suffering Greeks; the slave-trade suppressed; and the Mexican gulf rendered a safe thoroughfare for the traffic of the world by the destruction of the hordes of pirates which had long infested its waters. The overthrow of the national bank; the bold measures of the Nullifiers; the establishment of the sub-treasury system; the northern and southern Indian wars, marked the terms of General Jackson and Mr. Van Buren. The death of General Harrison prevented a radical change in the measures of the two preceding administrations. The protective system was re-established; the northeastern boundary determined; and the bank-bill vetoed while Mr. Tyler had charge of national affairs. Oregon and Texas difficulties occupied the term of Mr. Polk. The northwestern or Oregon boundary had been a subject of discussion for nearly half a century.* This protracted controversy was at last terminated by a convention with England (1846). The boundary between the two nations was fixed at the forty-ninth parallel of latitude to

---

* Greenhough's Memoirs.

the middle of the channel which separates the continent from Vancouver's Island and thence southwardly to the Pacific, said channel and straits to remain free and open to both nations; the navigation of the Columbia River is reserved to the Hudson Bay Company and British subjects trading with it, and their rights of property are to be respected, while the Americans have the privilege of purchasing the lands held by the Puget Sound Agricultural Company, at such price as may be agreed upon between the parties.

Mexico, being desirous to populate its northeastern territory, after the adoption of the free constitution offered extensive grants of land to settlers. Inducements thus alluring drew to the soil of Texas an enterprising population from the United States.* Application was made to the congress of Mexico for admission as a department in the confederacy. Shortly after the rejection of this application the federal union was succeeded by the central government. The people of Texas protested against the change; declared their independence; and hostilities commenced. The battle of San Jacinto terminated the contest in favor of the republic, which was acknowledged both in Europe and America. Conscious of its own weakness, Texas soon sought to be admitted into the confederation of the United States. It was, however, deemed advisable that the republic should make trial of its own strength before it became a portion of that establishment. A constitution was adopted; officers chosen; laws enacted; an army and navy established; and government administered. Affairs having thus progressed for some years, Mexico offered to acknowledge the independence of Texas provided it would not attach itself to any other government. This offer being

---

* Slidell's Letter.

declined, the republic was received into the Union. Mexico prepared to assert its sovereignty over the new state. After some ineffectual attempts at negotiation hostilities commenced. In the course of a few months Matamoras, Santa Fé, Tampico, Tobasco, and Monterey fell into the hands of the Union, the forces of which, commanded by General Taylor, defeated the whole Mexican army under Santa Anna at Buena Vista. General Scott, the commander-in-chief of the United States army, was no less fortunate in the east, carrying St. Juan d'Ulloa, capturing Vera Cruz, overpowering Santa Anna at Cerro Gordo, and mastering Mexico, the capital. Peace was restored by the treaty of Guadalupe Hidalgo (A.D. 1848), which fixed the line between the two nations at a point in the Gulf of Mexico three leagues from shore opposite the mouth of the Rio Grande; from thence up the deepest channel of that river till it strikes the southern boundary of New Mexico; thence westward along the southern boundary of New Mexico to its westward termination; thence northward along the western line of New Mexico until it intersects the first branch of the river Gila, down the middle of that river until it empties into the Rio Colorado, and thence following the division-line between Upper and Lower California to the Pacific. The accession of California, by opening the gold regions to the enterprise of all the citizens of the republic, presented to congress the determination of momentous interests. Slave-states claimed an equal right to the common acquisition with those in which slavery had no existence. Sharp contentions ensued, which congress determined by leaving the question of slavery to the citizens of California, and by securing the South in their right to arrest their fugitive slaves wherever found on free territory. The administration of Mr. Fillmore, which was for the greater part of the term of the lamented General Taylor, was succeeded by that of Franklin Pierce, elected by the votes of all the states save four. In an early period of this administration its supporters procured the passage of the act constituting Nebraska and Kansas into territories, which repealed as to these portions of the republic the provisions of the Missouri Compromise passed by congress in 1820, by which slavery is interdicted north of latitude 36° 30'. A violent contest at once arose all over the states which not only distracted the term of President Pierce, but supplied the material by which the subsequent presidential canvass was conducted, in which James Buchanan was successful.

The agitation which resulted in the elevation of Mr. Buchanan to power continued throughout his administration. It was much embittered by the judgment of the supreme court in the Dred Scott case, virtually determining that slaves could be transported to any of the territories of the republic at the will of their owners. The efforts of the South to plant slavery in Kansas under executive patronage also added fuel to the flame. Popular excitement at this period became intense. The Democratic party favored, the Republican party opposed, these measures. At the succeeding election in the fall of 1860 the Democratic candidates of the two branches of their several conventions—Messrs. Douglas and Breckinridge—had jointly the majority of the popular vote; but Mr. Lincoln, the Republican candidate, receiving a greater number of the electoral votes than either of the other candidates, was declared duly elected president. Before his inauguration in the following March (1861) the states of Virginia, North and South Carolina, Georgia, Mississippi, Alabama, Florida, Louisiana, Texas, Arkansas, and Missouri withdrew their representatives from both branches of congress; seceded from the national union; formed a constitution providing in the strongest terms for the protection of slavery; elected their own officers, of which the chief executive was Jefferson Davis; and proclaimed themselves to the world as the "Confederate States of America." Failing to obtain a recognition of their independence from the United States government, they levied a large military force and prepared for war. Succeeding in the capture of Fort Sumter in the harbor of Charleston, the Confederates were emboldened to vigorous exertions in the North. Mr. Lincoln, not fully appreciating the powers of the rebellious adversary, placed in the field an army of only seventy-five thousand men for three months' service. But, determined to make the best possible use of this small body, he at once prudently covered Washington and pressed forward upon Richmond, the capital of the Confederates. A disastrous panic in the Union army, after a fairly won battle at Bull Run, gave the Southern power the credit of victory.

Impressed now with the importance of the contest, the United States government made the amplest preparations for deciding it. An army of over half a million of men was placed in service; General McClellan entrusted with the chief command; every munition of war provided; and a proper disposition of the forces made from the Atlantic to the utmost exposed western border of the republic. The policy of the Union at this period became not only the extinction of rebellion, but also of slavery. Early in the year 1862 General McClellan made an advance upon the rebel capital. For some weeks its doom appeared certain; but a reverse occurring in consequence of the able movements of Generals Lee and Jackson in the rebel service, the Union forces were only saved from utter destruction by the superior talents of their commander. Still the danger was imminent, and the administration was induced to withdraw General McClellan from the command and commit the direction of the army to General Pope. In falling back on Washington another disaster occurred at Bull Run. Flushed with his success, General Lee made rapid advances northward, intending, if possible, to seize Philadelphia, Baltimore, and Washington, and at once to end the war. The hopes of the rebel chief, however, were blasted by a crushing repulse which he received at Antietam from the Union army, now for the second time under General McClellan. The lateness of the season, together with the crippled condition of his forces in consequence of the recent fight, were alleged by General McClellan as reasons for not pursuing the adversary with a promptness which, in the opinion of the administration, might have turned his repulse into a capture. In consequence of this difference between the commander and the president General McClellan was superseded, and the victor of Newbern, General Burnside, appointed in his place. A vigorous pursuit of the retreating enemy was enjoined upon the new commander by the government and expected by the people. As soon as the season and circumstances would allow, an advance was made upon the retiring foe. The catastrophe to the Union army at Fredericksburg, and that which occurred a few months later at Chancellorsville, when General Hooker was in command, again reversed the condition of the belligerents. General Lee now made a more serious inroad upon the North than formerly, and, sweeping everything before him, actually penetrated as far as Gettysburg, in the State of Pennsylvania. At this point he encountered the army of the Potomac (July 2, 1863), under the command of General Meade, where he was utterly defeated and compelled to make a hasty retreat to his own borders.

While the army in the East protected the capital and

prevented inroads on the North, the navy and the army of the West regained the dominions of the republic and dealt death-blows to its enemies. The navy, placed in the best condition for service, destroyed that wondrous arm of rebel power, the Merrimac; established a strict blockade along the eastern seaboard and the gulf-coast; captured many points of importance in these quarters; took New Orleans, and cleared the Mississippi River, under the command of Foote and Porter.

The army in the West was not behind the navy in the importance of its advances. In Missouri and Arkansas the rebellion was crushed, after a series of bloody conflicts directed by the talents of Generals Lyon, Fremont, Sigel, Pope, Curtis, and other illustrious leaders, which terminated in the decided victory at Pea Ridge. The entire territory from the Ohio River to Vicksburg and Atlanta was in less than three years rid of the rebel forces by the armies of Generals Grant, Buell, Rosecrans, Hooker, Halleck, Thomas, and Sherman. In the progress of these grand achievements occurred the battles at Somerset, Forts Henry and Donelson, Shiloh, Knoxville, Murfreesborough, Corinth, Jackson, Chattanooga, Vicksburg, Atlanta. After the surrender of Vicksburg, General Grant, the leading chieftain in this stupendous work, was created lieutenant-general of the whole Union army, and took command of the department in the East. An advance on Richmond was at once commenced. Lee being driven back by the bloody battle of the Wilderness, Richmond was soon closely environed by the Union forces. Its wily defender again tried to relieve himself by diverting the foe to the North, in order to suppress an inroad on its borders by General Early; but the scheme was effectually checked by General Sheridan, who, in several brilliant engagements, overpowered the adversary.

Shortly subsequent to the fall of Atlanta commenced General Sherman's expedition through the heart of the rebel states to Savannah, in the state of Georgia, and thence to Goldsborough, in the state of North Carolina—a military exploit not surpassed in any period of the world, and in reflecting on which the mind is at a loss whether to admire most the completeness of the execution or the grandeur of the conception. The immediate results of this bold work were the capture of Savannah, the surrender of Charleston, which had resisted all assaults for over two years, as well as the downfall of intermediate strongholds and the destruction of invaluable rebel stores. These Union successes, together with the conquest of Fort Fisher by Commodore Porter and General Terry, rendered the cause of the Confederates hopeless, and Richmond was shortly afterwards evacuated and all the rebel armies surrendered.

The joy which abounded throughout the republic at the fortunate termination of the war was suddenly checked by the melancholy tidings of President Lincoln's assassination. But for the liberal conditions accorded to the Southern leaders at Fortress Monroe by Mr. Lincoln, now over a month in his second term (April 14, 1865), it might be supposed that chagrin at their fate led them to instigate and arm the vile assassin to destroy the leader of the North; but, inasmuch as they were the most interested of all persons in preserving the life of the president, they can hardly be suspected of complicity in the nefarious act by which it was destroyed.

Five hours after Mr. Lincoln expired, the vice-president, Andrew Johnson, was sworn into office by the chief-justice, and entered upon the discharge of the duties of the chief executive of the government.

After the trial and execution of the assassins of Mr. Lincoln, the first matter which claimed the attention of the president was the settlement of the states of the South. The policy pursued was of a pacific character, requiring only the extinction of slavery from the states and restoring their citizens to all their political rights upon taking the oath of allegiance, with few exceptions: in which cases liberal terms of pardon were extended to them. At a subsequent congress this scheme of settlement was repudiated, and it was determined by that body not to admit representation from the seceding states until they not only agreed to abolish slavery, but to amend their constitutions so as to declare the Union perpetual; disavow the war-debt of the south, as well as guarantee that of the North; extend equal protection to all the citizens of the United States in all the states; and apportion representation according to the number of inhabitants in each state without reference to color, but excluding Indians. These terms being rejected by the South, congress, at its next session, declared the seceding states under military law until they should conform their constitutions and elections to the principles contained in the rejected amendments, and directed the president to appoint in each of the ten districts military officers possessed of supreme civil powers and who should at once proceed to form registries of voters, procure the election of representatives who could be received in congress, and provide for the perfect restoration of the states in the Union. On these terms a settlement was finally effected between the North and the South, but not until after the election of General Grant to the presidency (1868). The rights of citizenship were extended to colored persons in all the states early in this administration.

CHAPTER XXIII.

AMERICAN NATIONS CONNECTED WITH BRANCHES OF THE EMPIRE OF THE FRANKS.

Mexico was governed by the Spaniards from the conquest of Cortes (1521) to the commencement of the nineteenth century. At the latter period, the viceroy Don José Iturrigaray, having received contradictory orders from Spain, called a junta composed of representatives from each province. Offended at this act, because it raised the creoles to a level with the European population, the Spaniards transported the viceroy. In revenge the creoles resolved to overthrow the power of Venegas, the succeeding viceroy. Hidalgo and Rayon, who successively headed the revolutionary movements, were defeated by the Spaniards. Morelos, though for a time more fortunate than his predecessors, was eventually overpowered, captured, and shot. Teran and Mina made the last feeble effort in the expiring cause of the creoles.

The revolution in Spain induced the clergy of Mexico to favor a plan of separation from the parent-power.* Don Augustin Iturbide became the leader of the movement, and eventually emperor of Mexico. The harsh conduct of Iturbide offended Santa Anna, Governor of Vera Cruz, who, possessing himself of the military influence, expelled the emperor. A federal constitution, similar to that of the United States, was adopted (1824). Victoria was

---

* Modern Traveller, Vol. VI. Folsom's Mexico. Gregory's His. of Mexico, America, and West Indies (Long, Porter & Co.; Lond. ed., 1845).

chosen president. The Spanish power was totally subverted. Pedraza came to the helm; Guerrero snatched it from him, but was soon compelled to give place to Bustamente. Pedraza again enjoyed a temporary power upon the revolt of Santa Anna, who, as soon as he had obtained sufficient strength, abolished the federal constitution and established a central government, of which he was the chief. During the imprisonment of the dictator after the battle of San Jacinto, Bustamente held the reigns; but on the release of Santa Anna, he again took the direction of affairs into his own hands. Severity in the mode of collecting the appropriation for the invasion of Texas rendering Santa Anna unpopular, Herrera succeeded to power. Losing the esteem of the army, the chief gave place to Paredes, their new favorite. Subsequent distractions elevated and humbled Herrera and his successor, Farias; eventually bringing Santa Anna to the presidency (1853). A revolution headed by Alvarez brought that chief to power in the course of less than two years; but the fluctuation incident to popular feeling in this republic in a short space of time elevated Comonfort to the possession of power. Political power is constantly changing hands in Mexico. The sword is always at work. A hireling soldiery are ever ready to elevate a new favorite. Comonfort was not able long to retain their regard. The superior fortunes of Zulvago enabled him to win their smiles. A few days of terrible havoc at the capital caused him to rise upon the downfall of his rival (1858). But he fell as suddenly as he rose, and gave place to Miramon; whose power was soon overthrown by Juarez, during whose administration the invasion of the French, English, and Spanish occurred that brought Maximilian of Austria to the possession of imperial power, which, after his overthrow and execution, yielded to the forces of Juarez (1865).

Yucatan,* a portion of the republic of Mexico, took decided steps against the central system of Santa Anna. The contest was maintained for years under the command of Santiago Iman. Valladolid falling into the hands of the insurgents, their cause was triumphant. A congress was convoked, a constitution adopted, laws regulating trade enacted, and the state entered upon the enjoyment of an independence which Mexico has not been able to destroy.

The five central states have held a precarious power, which has been continually liable to the influences of their more powerful neighbors on the north and south. Political contests among its chieftains ran so high as eventually to cause one of them to offer inducements of a flattering description to the citizens of other lands to aid him in fastening his sway upon his countrymen. William Walker, a citizen of the United States, raised a small force composed of Europeans and Americans, with which he appeared in Nicaragua. Considerable success attended his movements for some time. In the end, however, the natives were roused to decided measures of opposition, and the invaders were expelled.

Brazil,† was placed in the possession of Portugal in the first year of the sixteenth century by a storm which diverted the fleet under the command of Cabral from its course. The troubles in Portugal forced its monarch to the shores of the colony (1807). So rapid was the progress of Brazil in improvement that in nine years from the arrival of John VI. it was elevated to the rank of a kingdom. European changes requiring the presence of the sovereign in Portugal, his son, Dom Pedro, took the regency. Convinced that further connection with the parent-power would impede its prosperity, Brazil became an inde-

---

* Norman's Yucatan. † Kidder's Sketches of Brazil.

pendent empire with Dom Pedro as its chief (1822). A constitution establishing monarchy, but lodging the legislative power in two representative bodies, was proclaimed. Montevideo was annexed, the rebellion in Pernambuco was overcome, and the independence of the new empire was acknowledged by the parent-power. A reverse, however, occurred in the affairs of Dom Pedro I. Montevideo withdrew from the confederation; the court measures became unpopular; and the emperor was compelled to abdicate in favor of his young son. Troublesome regencies followed. Order was eventually restored by the coronation of the emperor Dom Pedro II. A reformation of the criminal code, together with many salutary changes, rendered the emperor popular. Revolutionary movements have proved unsuccessful.

The people of the La Plata, indisposed to submit to the colonial restrictions of Spain, commenced revolutionary movements (A.D. 1810). A junta composed of Americans was created, into the hands of which the viceroy resigned his power. The first decrees of this body were published in the name of Ferdinand VII. This appearance of loyalty was retained until the concurrence of most of the departments was procured, when it was abandoned and the agents of the crown sent to Spain or the Canary Islands. Paraguay* was formed into a separate republic. The Argentine states † created a federal union. They were distracted at the commencement of their existence by the contentions between the federals and the unitarians; the former contending for a central government, the latter for a constitution similar to that of the United States. General Rosas, the champion of the federals, got possession of power in Buenos Ayres. Civil war raged through many of the

---

* Robinson's Paraguay. † King's Argentine Republic.

states. In the interior, the unitarian leader, Paz, defeated his enemies and maintained Cordova, his capital, against all their assaults. A congress at Cordova denounced Rosas, who appealed to arms and reduced the insurgent city. Seeking to attach Montevideo to the republic, of which he claimed to be of right the head, Rosas incurred the anger of France. Buenos Ayres was put under blockade. Taking advantage of this event, the unitarians of the interior threw off the yoke of the dictator, but were unable to maintain their stand. The Montevideans invoked the assistance of France and England, which frustrated the designs of the tyrant, who was eventually overthrown by the arms of Urquiza, whose sway was more brief than that of his predecessor.

The Peruvians* annihilated the power of Spain under the command of Simon Bolivar by the victory of Ayacucho (1824). The departments of Upper Peru constituted a republic, adopting a constitution which placed the law-making power in a legislature chosen by popular suffrage, the executive in a president selected in the same manner, aided by a ministry of his own adoption and by a council of state nominated by the legislature. In honor of the distinguished soldier by whom their independence was achieved, the confederacy adopted Bolivia as their national name. The departments of Peru properly so called established a government similar in its provisions to that of their neighbors. The political condition of both republics became unsettled in a short time. Discussions as to central and federal powers began to be agitated. The natural endowments, educational advantages, military experience, and political resources of Santa Cruz, president of Bolivia, enabled him to proceed step by step from the position of a

---

*For. Qu. Review, No. 39, 1837. Amer. and West Indies.

citizen to the possession of supreme power both in Peru and Bolivia. The inroad of the chieftain, however, on the constitution of his country was not permanent. Equally impotent have been the recent assaults of Spain both on this republic and on Chili, its southern neighbor.

New Granada* struck the blow for independence when Spain was invaded by France. In the first effort the Spanish forces were triumphant, the patriots scattered, and their congress dispersed. A fortunate event saved the republic. Simon Bolivar, at the head of a strong army, forced his way through appalling obstacles to Santa Fé, and entered it in triumph.

Venezuela† proclaimed its independence during the troubles in Spain. A congress convened at Caracas established a government. After repeated defeats Simon Bolivar was successful in maintaining the cause of freedom. The liberator was invested with the presidency of the republic. Contemplating a common league, Bolivar invited all the states of North and South America to meet in congress at Panama. Some assembled; others, questioning the purity of his motives, declined; while a general feeling of distrust was eventually engendered which brought the liberator to a disgrace in which he ended his days. Venezuela, New Granada, Ecuador, and Quito united together in a confederacy denominated Colombia (1819). The congress of the republic consisted of two houses: one a senate, composed of members from each state; the other a house of representatives, elected by popular vote. No sooner was the common foe vanquished than this state of things was disturbed. Quito first seceded from the union two years after its formation. Venezuela followed in seven years; the remaining states took a similar course in the

---

* Family History, in loc.   † Amer. and West In., in loc.

space of twelve years. Each state still retains its republican form of government, which is administered by an executive and a legislature chosen by popular suffrage.

In Chili* the revolutionary forces were scattered; but the leaders fled to Buenos Ayres, where they raised another army. The battles of Cacabuco and Maypu followed, in which the republicans were triumphant (1817). Domestic strifes disturbed the country for years. A form of government was eventually settled which provides for a supreme director, as well as a legislature consisting of two branches, which are elected by popular vote.

The improvement in the condition of the world has been very rapid since the Reformation. There has been more accomplished to promote science, to extend the arts, to advance civil and religious liberty, and to increase trade, commerce, and travel within the last three hundred and fifty years than was effected by both pagan and papal Rome during the two thousand years they swayed the destinies of mankind.

In the first days of Protestantism its advocates were, like the papists, proscriptive. However, as they became better acquainted with the Scriptures they imbibed and put in practice the mild teachings of the Divine Master. The Princes of Orange and Henry IV. of France led the way in the noble work of religious toleration. The Puritans of England, who fled from the tyranny of Mary to the Low Countries, adopted the liberal views of the Dutch, and on their return in the reign of Elizabeth openly maintained the duty of forbearance towards those who differed from them on religious points. But upon their establishment in New England they were guilty of enor-

---

* Fam. His., in loc.

mous atrocities on such as dissented from their sectarian dogmas. Nevertheless one of their number, who had suffered the full measure of their mistaken zeal, is entitled to the honor of first announcing the legitimate principles of religious liberty. This distinguished man, for forty years the revered pastor of the church of Providence, Rhode Island, openly maintained "that the exercise of private judgment was a natural and sacred right; that the civil magistrate has no compulsive jurisdiction in the concerns of religion; and that the punishment of any person on account of his opinions is an encroachment on conscience and an act of persecution."* These humane sentiments gradually pervaded all the colonies. After the revolution they were incorporated into the federal constitution and became the organic law of the republic. The United States of America, therefore, are fairly entitled to the credit of having inaugurated an era in the evolution of empire which must eventually affect for the better the religious and political interests of the whole human race. These facts properly considered throw much light upon the figurative language of Daniel and John.†

The events of the age are of a significant character. A crisis has arrived which indicates changes in the moral, religious, and intellectal condition of mankind that at no very distant period must produce a total revolution in human affairs. Serfdom is extinguished in Europe; slavery abolished, as well in the British dominions as in the United States; and the slave-trade is a crime.

Already nations have been born in a day. The savages of the Sandwich Islands have within half a century aban-

---

* Rol. His of Am., ch. x. Neal's His. of N. Eng., p. 141. Roger Williams.
† Dan. xii. 4. Rev. xiv.–xx.

doned the degradation of the past and become as civilized and Christianized as any nation on earth. Many large Indian tribes of America, whose sons and daughters were from time immemorial but little above the brute, have forsaken their migratory mode of life and become models of every social virtue. Events of an equally important character have occurred in Asia. India is in a condition which clearly indicates that the faith of the false prophet and the dominion of the native priest have passed their culminating points. Japan has received with delight the news of a better moral and religious system than she possessed. In China the middle wall of partition which separated her from the science and religion of Christendom has at last been broken down, and all her borders are now open to the approaches of truth.* Even downtrodden Africa has begun to shake herself from the slumber of ages, and her cheerless wastes have become the abodes of civilized men. If with the limited instrumentalities already employed such have been the triumphs of the Truth, it is fair to presume when the combined energies of Christendom shall be employed in the work of the world's emancipation that superstition, idolatry, and oppression will be dissipated and the daylight of millennial bliss break upon the kindreds of mankind.

In review of the events of history in all ages of the world, the language of that eminent scholar and distinguished author, Bishop Newton, is remarkably appropriate. "We have seen," observes he, "the descendants of Shem and Japheth ruling and enlarged in Asia and Europe, and the curse of servitude attending the descendants of Ham in Africa. We have seen the posterity of Ishmael multi-

---

* Huc's China. Orme's His. of India. Rev. xx. Is. liii. Numbers xiv. 21. Dan. ii. 44, 45.

plied exceedingly and become a great nation in the Arabians, yet living like wild men and shifting from place to place in the wilderness; their hand against every man, and every man's hand against them, and still dwelling an independent and free people in the presence of all their brethren and in the presence of all their enemies. We have seen the family of Esau totally extinct, and that of Jacob subsisting at this day; the sceptre departed from Judah, and the people living nowhere in authority, everywhere in subjection; punished severely for their infidelity and disobedience to their great prophet like unto Moses; plucked from off their own land and removed into all the kingdoms of the earth; oppressed and spoiled evermore, and made a proverb and a by-word among all nations, and their land lying desolate and themselves cut off from being the people of God, while the Gentiles are advanced in their room. We have seen Nineveh so completely destroyed that the place thereof is not and cannot be known; Babylon made a desolation forever, a possession for the bittern and pools of water; Tyre become like the top of a rock, a place for fishers to spread their nets upon; and Egypt a base kingdom, the basest of kingdoms and still tributary and subject to strangers. We have seen the four great empires of the world [evolved according to prophecy]; the fourth and last, which was greater and more powerful than any of the former, divided in the western part thereof into ten lesser kingdoms, and among them a power with a triple crown diverse from the first, with a mouth speaking very great things, and with a look more stout than his fellows, speaking great words against the Most High and changing times and laws. We have seen that power cast down the truth to the ground and prosper in practice and destroy the holy people, not regarding the God of his fathers nor the desire of wives, but honoring Mahuzzim—God's protectors or saints' protectors—and causing the priests of Mahuzzim to rule over many and to divide the land for gain. We have seen the Turks stretching forth their hand over the eastern portion of the Roman Empire in Asia, Europe, and Africa, the Arabians still escaping out of their hands."*

We now behold both pope and Turk, who were unknown two thousand years ago, fully manifested according to the foreshadowings of prophecy, with the doom of prophecy hanging over their heads! Who can doubt but that at the appointed time "God will dash them in pieces like a potter's vessel," just as he has done with all the enemies of the truth and the world's advancement who have flourished and fallen in former ages?

CHAPTER XXIV.

NATIONAL PROGRESS IN EUROPE AND AMERICA FROM THE FALL OF THE EMPIRE OF THE ROMANS IN THE WEST TO THE PRESENT TIMES.

At the fall of the Roman Empire in the West, Europe exchanged a military despotism for a military democracy. The Northern invaders were directed by chieftains whose claims to command arose from their superior characters as soldiers.† Conformably to a principle universally received among them, they seized their conquests as common property. Wherever they settled, the army was considered still in existence, being arranged under its proper officers, who in return for the land granted them by their general

---

* New. Dis., Conclusion, p. 625.
† Robertson's Charles V.: View of the State of Europe. Tacitus' Man. of Germans. Rus. Mod. Eu., Vol. I. p. 189. Kolrausch.

held themselves prepared to reassemble their forces on his call. A similar obligation to that upon which the general granted the land to the subordinate officers was imposed by the latter on their dependants. In the course of time personal attendance upon the chieftain becoming onerous, exemption was purchased by the payment of pecuniary assessments, denominated scutages, tallages, and subsidies.* Thus originated the feudal system, which, although excellent for the purposes of defence, was sadly defective in its bearings on the domestic condition of a state. The feudal lord exercising the right to coin money was incessantly engaged in private warfare. Conquest emboldening him to one assertion of privilege after another, eventually all subordination was subverted. Revenge became the motive, the sword the means, by which judicial proceedings were originated and executed.

Christianity was adopted by most of the Northern nations, but with such an admixture of pagan superstition that its essential features were obliterated. The disorders consequent on all these abuses attained their height before the conclusion of the tenth century. Causes began at this period to influence society which produced a revolution in the state of Europe. Chivalry, which by inculcating a sympathy for the forlorn, as well as a regard for female chastity, taught the haughty offender whom the sovereign could not restrain, to dread, in associated strength, a power superior to his own. The crusaders opened new sources of wealth, created a taste for foreign commodities, and laid the foundation for commercial intercourse. Large towns procured by arms or purchased their freedom. Sovereigns long trammelled by the power

---

* Tacitus, p. 545, note 6 (Mur.'s ed.). Rob. Am., Vol. I. Bk. I. p. 49. Rev. xiv.-xx. Dan. xii. 4. Mod. Eu., Vol. II. p. 176.

of their barons began to treat with respect the commons, in many instances constituting them a distinct estate. Possessed of the balance of power, the commons obtained the enfranchisement of that portion of society which cultivated the soil or performed menial services. The barbarous modes of judicial trial by ordeal and duel gave place to the present system. Private wars were interdicted by public authority. The discovery of the pandects at Amalfi, in Italy, was followed by important consequences. The world was charmed with the civil law; its study was commenced; professorships established. A new road opening to preferment, the ardor for military pursuits abated. A taste for science gradually pervaded Christendom; men of letters were encouraged; colleges founded; courses of education settled; academical honors invented; and though for a time a false taste and the too-common use of the Latin language counteracted the beneficial effects of these changes, yet they eventually accomplished the improvement of the manners of society. The discovery of paper in the fourteenth and printing in the fifteenth century introduced a new era in human progress.

Commerce, which had ministered to the necessities of men, produced luxuries between the beginning of the fourteenth and the middle of the sixteenth century. Italians commenced the culture of silk and the sugar-cane within their own borders. Flanders was not behind Italy. Its manufactories of woollen and linen caused foreign intercourse which resulted in extensive commercial relations. Architecture revived in Italy and was studied through the Low Counties; so that the inhabitants in these places lived in houses erected with elegance, while the residents of London and Paris were in possession of miserable cottages constructed without even chimneys. Still, literature was but in its infantile condition. The romances of the troubadours of Provence attest this fact. But having commenced existence, its course was onward. It broke with effulgence upon Europe in the productions of Dante, Petrarch, Boccaccio, and Chaucer. Italy claims the first three, England the last. Nor was France without her William of Lorris and John of Meun. Nevertheless Italy was destined to elevate the character of the moderns to the standard of the ancients in the productions of Arisoto and Tasso, the poets; Machiavel and Guicciardini, the historians. Navigation, and consequently commerce, received an unwonted stimulus from the discovery of the compass (A.D. 1302). The Portuguese navigators, under the reign of Don Henry, discovered the Azores and Cape Verd Islands; doubled Capes Blanco, Bazadore, Verd, and at last Sierra Leone. In the time of his successor, John II., many places in the interior of Africa were conquered and the Cape of Good Hope settled. Emanuel I., pursuing the policy of his predecessors, equipped a fleet under the command of Da Gama, who after numberless dangers succeeded in opening the line of navigation by sea to the East Indies, thus giving his countrymen possession of that trade by which Venice and the other Italian cities had been long enriched. The voyage of De Cabral, in addition to Brazil, placed Malabar in possession of Portugal. Albuquerque was commissioned; Goa, Malacca, and Ormus were subdued; and Lisbon made the mart of the world. Meantime a spirit of enterprise was awakened in Spain. The oft-repeated petitions of Christopher Columbus, a Genoese navigator, were granted (A.D. 1492). A small fleet was committed to his charge, in which he discovered that group of islands now known as the West Indies. A third voyage opened the way to the continent which ought to bear his name, but which is denominated America, from Americus Vespucius, a Florentine navigator employed by the merchants of Seville. Mexico was reduced by Cortes, Peru by Pizarro. A westerly passage to the East Indies was discovered by Magellan through the straits at the south of the American continent which bear his name. The trade from this source becoming a matter of the highest importance, it excited the jealousy of the Portuguese to such a degree that Charles V., not wishing to involve himself in further wars, secured it to them. Philip II. planted large colonies in the Manillas, which he named, after himself, the Philippine Islands. The tyranny of the king of Spain over the United Provinces turned the attention of the Dutch to the rich trade of the Indies. The successive voyages of Houtman, Van Neck, and Warwick wrested from the Portuguese not only the wealth of the East Indies, but their settlements in Brazil. These successful enterprises roused the ambition of the English. Bloody scenes of war ensued between the ships of the two nations, which eventuated in an arrangement that Moluccas, Amboyna, and Banda should belong in common to the parties, the English being entitled to one third, the Dutch to two thirds of the trade at a fixed price; that each should contribute in proportion to their interest for the defence of the islands; that the treaty should remain in force twenty years; that both should avoid clandestine contracts with the natives; and that all disputes which could not be settled by the Dutch and English trading companies should be determined by the crown of Great Britain and the states-general of the provinces. The rapacity of the Dutch broke the treaty by stripping the English of the Spice Islands. The feeble reign of James I. was insufficient to redress this outrage. Commotions in the times of Charles I. prevented any effectual interference. Cromwell rendered some assistance to the struggling interests of the company, but his needy successor, Charles II., almost reduced it to ruin.

England had not remained inactive in the West during the progress of her neighbors. John Cabot, a Venetian mariner in the service of Henry VII., not only landed on the island of Newfoundland, but prosecuted his voyage along the shore of the American continent from the Gulf of St. Lawrence to Cape Florida. No benefit was derived from these discoveries until the middle of Elizabeth's reign, when that queen, roused by the aspiring course of Philip II., induced adventurers to commit depredations on his American subjects. Sir Francis Drake was pre-eminent in this service. That brave commander, with four ships, passed through the Straits of Magellan into the South Sea and enriched himself by the capture of many valuable prizes. This success awakening in the kingdom a desire for foreign enterprise, suggested to Sir Walter Raleigh the scheme of a settlement within the regions visited by Cabot. A company was formed for this purpose; a patent procured from the queen; and two ships, commanded by Philip Amidas and Arthur Barlow, sent out. Landing in the Roanoke, the settlers planted a colony, to which they gave the name of Virginia. The settlement thrived for some time, but finally falling to decay, was abandoned. This unfortunate experiment threw a damper on the spirit of colonization during the remainder of Elizabeth's reign. It however revived in the reign of James I. in consequence of the voyages of Gosnard and other navigators. Two companies were formed under royal sanction; the one of adventurers, belonging to London, the other of residents in Plymouth, Bristol, and Exeter. The former equipped three vessels commanded by Christopher Newport. The colonists, being supplied as well with arms of defence as with implements of agriculture, landed in the Chesapeake. Obtaining leave from the natives to settle, they formed a colony (A.D. 1607) which was called Jamestown, in honor of the king. The settlement soon became of importance to the mother-country by reason of the trade in tobacco. On the same account the province of Maryland, settled in the reign of Charles II. by Cecil Lord Baltimore, a Roman Catholic nobleman (A.D. 1632), attained a high state of prosperity. The first successful settlement in New England was made at New Plymouth (A.D. 1620). It was composed of one hundred and twenty persons who, previous to their emigration, had resided at Leyden in consequence of religious persecution in England. The adventurers held a patent from the London Company, but on account of the jealousy of the Dutch in New York they were landed north of the territory of the corporation. In the course of ten years these colonists were followed by large bands of Puritans, who held their rights under the Plymouth Company,* the territory of which had been considerably enlarged by Charles I. Religious discussions from time to time gave rise to new establishments among the settlers, while the spirit of enterprise in the mother-country tended constantly to introduce adventurers in large numbers, so that in the space of fifty years New England became a populous and prosperous portion of the civilized world. The Carolinas were granted (A.D. 1663) by Charles II. to Lord Clarendon and others, who took immediate steps for permanent settlement. One year afterwards the Duke of York, having received a charter from his brother which covered the Dutch colonies in New York, reduced them to submission. A portion of the territory thus acquired, denominated New Jersey, was conveyed by the Duke to Lord Berkeley and Sir George Carteret. Eighteen years subsequent William Penn received his charter (A.D. 1682), and rapidly settled

---

* Marsall's Life of Washington, Introduction, pp. 12, 22, 78. Holmes' Annals. Rus. Mod. Eu., Vol. II. p. 188; Vol. III. p. 456.

Philadelphia. A corporation of twenty-one persons obtained a grant of Georgia, nearly half a century from the last settlement. In addition to the colonies in North America, the English founded an establishment at Surinam, on the borders of Guiana, in South America. Having seized many of the West India Islands, they acquired the sugar-trade early in the seventeenth century. This immense commerce was increased yearly by the industry of the colonists, fortified by the policy of the mother-country, through which its benefits were eventually secured by the Navigation Act.

About the commencement of the sixteenth century, the Russians, with whom a beneficial traffic had been opened by the English in consequence of the discovery of a passage round North Cape, commenced their manufactories, which in the course of a short period of time rivalled and finally excelled those of the Flemings. Though Spain and Portugal had received such quantities of gold from America, though the Dutch had derived such inexhaustible sources of wealth from the trade of India, though England enjoyed such flattering prospects from her western colonies, France, the most potent kingdom of Europe, possessed abroad at this time only the settlements in Louisiana and Canada, together with a few unimportant plantations in Martinique and Guadalupe; while at home her silk manufactories were in a state of but progressive improvement.

Society having attained the utmost point of refinement in Italy, began to decline. Other nations commenced improvement. France took the lead. In its first efforts it was involved in a course of manners disgustingly licentious. This result was produced by Francis I., who encouraged females to appear publicly at court.* The wise

---

* Sully's Mems. Rus. Mod. Eu., Vol. IV. p. 215; Vol. V. pp. 28, 403.

minister of Henry IV. could not totally destroy the vice of the times, but attempted its correction by blending with the evil from which it originated a spirit of heroism. Chivalric acts became the passport to a lady's affections. The favors of the softer sex being more hard to purchase, were less frequently enjoyed. The folly once corrected, though never so imperfectly, gradually disappeared. In the reign of Louis XIII., love, instead of being treated as a passion, was graduated by the most abstract if not refined principles. During the regency of the Austrian Princess Anne the tender passion received a more romantic turn than even that given to it by Sully's policy. Women became the leaders of factions, the advisers in matters of state. A change in the affections of a lady averted or produced revolutions. These evils found an effectual remedy in that elegant system which the refined mind of the polished Louis XIV. originated. The saucy freedom of sensuality, the rash feats of chivalry, the fickle rule of female factionists, were succeeded by the natural freedom, ease, and propriety of virtue. Woman was elevated to her true scale in society; becoming the patroness of every accomplishment, the pattern of chastity, the source of rational enjoyment. The court, completely regenerated in all its principles, was converted into a school of the strictest morality. The custom of settling matters of honor by duelling almost extinguished itself by rendering gentlemen more tender of personal feeling. Not only in France, but throughout the neighboring nations on this side the Alps, were sculpture, painting, and music brought to the highest degree of improvement. French literature was elevated during the reign of Francis I. by the productions of Rabelais, Montaigne, Marot, Voiture, Balzac, Corneille, and Pascal.

From the Reformation religious men and religious manners became more pure. The Protestants, pursuant to their professed attachment to the Scriptures, encouraged the study of the original languages in which they were written. In order to match their adversaries, the Catholics pursued the same policy. With an "open Bible and the right of private judgment on religious and moral subjects," the dogmas of Rome were regarded as "things of the past." Ignorance ceased to be the "mother of devotion," money the medium of access to God. Science began to be regarded as the food of the mind, the piety of the heart that homage most acceptable to the Deity. The pope, however, foresaw the danger threatening the stability of his empire. Hence originated the order of Jesuits, which was composed of a band of men free from monastic duties. His holiness quickly filled the world with a host of skilled, shrewd, and pliant tools who were employed as teachers of science; acted as confessors; were known as missionaries; bought up the produce of their converts, exposing it for sale in warehouses of their own founding in different parts of Europe. Wealth and power emboldened them to acts which at their commencement they would not have ventured to perform. Proverbially subtle, they introduced a supple casuistry which extenuated any crime or tolerated any vice that had for its object the interest of their ecclesiastical head. The world soon beheld again an effort to revive those doctrines which had enabled the pope in former times to triumph over popular liberty under pretence of superior sanctity and science. The attack was cunningly commenced upon the reformers. Every mode that ingenuity or learning could suggest was industriously applied to check the progress of the Reformation. But the light of truth was too resplendent to be eclipsed by such puny efforts, only showing what the Roman hierarchy would do if it had, as of old, the power. Knowledge attained a high state of perfection in England as early as the middle of Elizabeth's reign. Spenser and

Shakespeare gave a turn to national taste which placed British literature on that proud pre-eminence which it now occupies. Nor were the times of James I. destitute of great men, although the pedantry of the monarch unfortunately communicated to their writings a staidness not congenial to learning. The English language nevertheless was greatly improved by Hooker, Camden, Raleigh, Fairfax, Fletcher, Jonson, Drayton, and Daniel. Its force was fully tested by the disputes consequent on the high pretensions of Charles I. These awakened the brilliant genius of Milton. If no other work existed but "Paradise Lost" by which the strength of the English language could be established, that would be sufficient to confirm its claim to a close affinity, if not a strict equality, with the Greek. Still the English tongue was wanting in the refinement which a polished state of society is calculated to communicate. The productions of Dryden, Waller, Otway, Tillotson, Clarendon, Temple, Lee, supplied this deficiency in defiance of the corrupting influence of manners during the reign of Charles II. The sciences made greater progress than polite learning during the seventeenth century. Sir Francis Bacon, who lived in the reign of James I., not only broke the fetters of a false, but taught mankind how to acquire a true, philosophy, by reasoning experimentally upon both moral and intellectual subjects. Guided by this principle, Harvey commenced that series of investigations which resulted in the discovery of the circulation of the blood. Not long after the Restoration the Royal Society was founded. Under its auspices Wilkins, Wallace, Newton, and Boyle perfected their improvements in mathematics and natural philosophy. Metaphysical knowledge was mastered by the capacious intellect of Locke, who with a familiar freedom gave his discoveries to mankind, in which he traces the development of the human understanding.

Admirably indeed does the sententious language of the captive prophet portray this phase in the unfolding of the world's history, the age of liberty and activity, of art and science: "But thou, O Daniel, shut up the words, and seal the book, even to the time of the end: many shall run to and fro, and knowledge shall be increased." (Dan. xii. 4.)

From the commencement of this period of events, one improvement has rapidly succeeded another until the steamboat, the railroad, the telegraph, and the discoveries in science upon which they rest have effected radical alterations in the conditions of men and the relations of empires. It is a striking event of the times that the civil and religious tyranny prevalent for ages throughout Christendom has received a fatal blow from the advancement of popular education and the unrestrained right of private judgment upon all matters, whether of church or state.

The Navigation Act and the destruction consequent on the wars with England reduced the commerce of the Dutch almost entirely to the trade with the Indies. Thus contracted it gradually declined, while that of England constantly increased. Early in the reign of Louis XIV. Colbert established a French East India Company, which, in consequence of its want of prosperity as well as the failure of the Mississippi Scheme, was united with the West India Company. A disseverance eventually occurred which put both companies on an independent footing. France owes her wealth and commerce entirely to the genius and industry of her own citizens. The encouragement of Colbert perfected the manufacture of fancy articles, and enabled his countrymen to supply the world with these articles for half a century. This monopoly was destroyed by the revocation of the Edict of Nantes. The general condition of commerce, however, was not affected, inasmuch as the labor and wealth thereby subtracted from the nation were immediately thrown into trade in the countries where the Huguenots settled. England attributes much of her skill in the finer manufactures to this event. The same cause produced a sensible effect upon the fabrics of Germany and Holland. The increased supply of these articles consequent upon the instruction of so many nations in the fabrication of them would doubtless have been injurious to the market had not the demand for them been greatly increased by the flourishing condition of the Western colonies. They were exchanged in those regions for coffee, sugar, cotton, and other articles. An appalling evil, however, obstructed to a great extent the trade in this portion of the world. On the failure of the gold-mines in Hispaniola it was deserted by the inhabitants, who upon their departure left many of the necessaries, as well as some of the luxuries, which they had acquired. Lawless French and English outcasts were induced by this circumstance to make settlements on the islands. These desperadoes were called buccaneers, from the fact of their drying with smoke the flesh of animals in places called "buccans." The only mode of their subsistence, the wild animals, failing, the more daring spirits associated under the name of "the brothers of the coast." One degree of violence succeeded another, until these wretches became the scourge of the Western waters. In their ravages under Montbars, Basco, Lolonois, and Morgan they committed terrible enormities at Maracaibo, Porto Bello, and Panama. The defection of Morgan and the wars between France and England so divided these destroyers that in the course of time their existence was extinguished. Port Royal, in the island of Jamaica, had been the scene of their pleasures as well as the receptacle of their wealth. The curse of their vices rested on it after their names were known only by the recollection of their crimes. It continued to be a place of illicit traffic with the Spanish settlements, which was the more securely conducted under cover of that stipulation in the treaty of Utrecht which gave to the English the right of supplying the Spanish colonies with negroes. The Spanish government, to prevent these frauds, stationed the guarda costas at convenient points, whose outrages on British traders excited the retribution of their government.

The social system underwent great improvement during the eighteenth century. Russia, at its commencement in a state of barbarism, made rapid advancement in civilization. Sweden and Denmark did not deteriorate. Linnæus, the profoundest naturalist of modern times, was a native of the former country. Germany underwent little change in the general condition of its people, but science received a great impulse there by the patronage of Frederick, king of Prussia, and the genius of Gesner and Klopstock. The Swiss, instead of continuing the hurtful practice of hiring their surplus population as soldiers to the contending powers of Europe, found it to their interest to turn their attention to the establishment of factories and the cultivation of the soil. Italy acquired new lustre by the courts of Turin and Naples, the rapid improvement in music and poetry, and the classical turn given to its opera by the chaste airs of Metastasio. A taste for science and agriculture was communicated to Spain and Portugal after the expulsion of the Jesuits.

A bitter controversy between the Jansenists and Jesuits about points of theology produced distraction in France during the days of Louis XIV. The former having the advantage in argument, the latter submitted one hundred and three propositions to the pope for his decision. A bull, denominated Unigenitus, pronounced all the points but two heretical. The parliament, the archbishop of Paris, fifteen prelates, many of the most respectable clergymen, and the mass of the people opposed the bull, alleging that it was an infringement on the rights of the Gallican church and a violation of the laws of the kingdom. Two parties consequently arose, the acceptants and the recusants. The death of Louis XIV. gave a temporary cessation to the dispute, inasmuch as the Duke of Orleans, who succeeded as regent, directed the recusant bishops to receive the bull with certain explications, which they deemed satisfactory. Confessional notes signed by a priest who adhered to the bull being demanded in order to receive extreme unction, the flames of discord were again lighted. The new archbishop of Paris took part with the acceptants. The parliament of that city adhered to the recusants. Louis XV. forbid the parliament to interfere in the matter. Disregarding the command, that body were proceeding against the bishop of Orleans when they received a lettre-de-cachet directing them to suspend all further prosecutions relative to the sacraments. Resorting to remonstrance, the parliament was anew directed to transact its legitimate business. Upon their reply that duty and oath required them to complete what they had commenced, the members were banished to different parts of the kingdom. A royal chamber was created to supply the place of the dissolved parliament. Popular indignation fell so heavily on the new court that it was impossible for it to conduct public business. Louis was compelled to recall the exiles, who entered Paris amid extravagant expressions of joy. Former scenes of commotion raged with redoubled acrimony. Hoping to rid himself of further responsibility, the king submitted the case to the pope. Benedict decided that the bull must be acknowledged as a universal law. Indignant at the invasion of its rights, the Parisian parliament suppressed the papal brief by an arrêt. This manly boldness enraged the king to such an extent that he suppressed the fourth and fifth chambers of inquests. Resolved neither to be oppressed nor insulted, fifteen counsellors of the great chamber and one hundred and twenty-four members of the other courts of parliament deposited their resignations. This prompt yet decorous movement secured the popular voice in favor of the parliament. A general expression of disgust at the royal measures succeeded throughout the kingdom. Louis eventually banished the archbishop of Paris and accommodated differences with the parliament. Popular feeling, thus far completely triumphant, now turned against the Jesuits, who from the commencement of the struggle had been the supporters of the bull Unigenitus. On their refusal to discharge the debts of one of their members who had become bankrupt, they were cited before the parliaments and ordered to do justice to their creditors. Although they did not demur against the correctness of the decisions, yet they avoided a compliance by a variety of pretexts. More energetic measures were considered necessary to carry into effect the popular will. Accordingly new suits were commenced against them on account of the pernicious tendency of their writings. In the progress of these proceedings the Jesuits were compelled to produce their institutes, which were found on examination to contain principles totally subversive of government and morals. This discovery accomplished their ruin; their colleges were wrested from them, their effects forfeited to the crown, and finally the sovereign banished them from the realm. A victory so complete over ecclesiastical tyranny, backed by royal authority, induced the parliament to curb the power of the king. Registration of unpopular acts was accordingly refused, the right of remonstrance exercised with unusual freedom, and prosecutions instituted against provincial governors. Amidst these distracting theological disputes the French did not lose sight of literature and the arts. Indeed it was their good fortune to produce some of the brightest intellects that have ever appeared in the world. Political economy was profoundly developed by the Baron de Montesquieu. Moral science was treated with precision by Helvetius, whose efforts to strip it of Jesuitical subtleties were eminently successful. Buffon did equal benefit to the race by his inimitable survey of the natural world. Duhamel, by ingeniously expounding the principles of husbandry, rendered it a popular study. The former measure of glory which had been accredited to France by reason of the writings of Racine and Corneille was greatly increased by the brilliant genius of Voltaire, Rousseau, the Crébillons, Marmontel, Diderot and D'Alembert, the latter of whom produced that incomparable compend of science, the Encyclopædia. It is, however, a source of regret that the French writers of this period should have been so strongly tinctured with infidel principles.

Nor was England behind France in the progress of the arts and sciences. The revolution which ushered into power the Protestant succession was conducive to this end. Although the reign of William III., by driving the Tories from court, relaxed the energies of some learned men, yet the accession of Anne opened to the world the brightest period of British literature. Poetry was carried to its highest perfection by Prior, Armstrong, Akenside, Thomson, Gray, Collins, Shenstone, and Pope. Unrivalled prose composition was produced by Addison, Steele, Rowe, Swift, Bolingbroke, Chesterfield, and Johnson. Fielding, Smollett, and Richardson introduced a new species of romance, both comic and tragic in its character, entirely stripped of that military heroism which been had considered its necessary accomplishment. Sated with this sort of literature, public attention was powerfully attracted by the appearance of a description of composition much more profound and no less elegant in the historical writings of Robertson and Hume. The subsequent times of the two Georges were not congenial to the progress of genius. Nevertheless the arts and sciences were not neglected. Painting, statuary, architecture, and engraving were promoted by the efforts of Reynolds, Wren, Bacon, and Strange. Modern gardening was greatly improved by the classic suggestions of Kent. Mathematics and natural philosophy found patrons in Halley, Gregory, Maclaurin, and Tull. Metaphysics and moral science were treated by Hume and Hardey: of Hume, however, candor compels the admission that notwithstanding the manner of his writings is elegant and his reasoning luminous, still some of his principles if carried out would subvert both natural and revealed religion.

Two Spanish mathematicians, Juan and Ulloa, were employed by Philip V. in a survey of Peru; whose observations confirmed the opinion of Sir Isaac Newton that the earth is an oblate spheroid flattened at the poles and projecting near the equator. The Russians turned their attention towards exploring. Behring and other navigators visited the seas which lay between the northern parts of Asia and America. The result of these voyages was the discovery of the northern archipelago. After the peace of Paris the English monarch equipped Byron on a voyage of this description. Taking a southwest direction, the navigator passed through the Straits of Magellan; traversed the Pacific, where he discovered what he called King George's Islands, together with two others which he named after the Princes of Wales and York; steered for Tinian, which he reached; thence proceeded to Java, and returned home by the way of the Cape of Good Hope. In the following year Wallis and Carteret made their voyages. The former was the first who discovered Otaheite and other islands of less importance in the Pacific, while the latter rendered some service to his country by exploring the coasts of New Britain and New Ireland. Determined not to be outdone, the French made preparations for a grand nautical enterprise. The command of their force was committed to Bougainville. Little more can be said of this exploit than that it was the first voyage made by a Frenchman round the world. Cook, under the direction of the English government, made his first voyage, which resulted in the discovery of the Society Islands, the settlement of the latitude and longitude of various places, as well as the exploration of the eastern coast of New Holland, to which he gave the name of New South Wales. A desire to determine the dispute as to the existence of a great southern continent induced the king of England to put another force under the command of Cook. After an absence of two years the captain returned home, having settled in the negative the question which gave rise to his voyage. The Spaniards continued their explorations from their landing in St. Domingo.* In the forepart of the sixteenth century Hernando Cortes penetrated as far as the coast of California. Eight years afterwards an expedition was conducted by Cabrillo. Its object was to proceed as far north on the Pacific front as possible, with a view to discover positions susceptible of permanent colonization. Before the completion of the voyage the commander died and Ferrelo succeeded to his authority. The result of the enterprise was a critical examination of the coast from the thirty-fourth to the forty-third parallel of latitude. Intent upon something more than mere geographical knowledge, the enterprising Castilians followed

---

* Greenhough's Mem. Dix's Speech.

up their discoveries on the western coast of America by settlements of quite an extensive character. Towards the latter end of the sixteenth century the Spaniards equipped an expedition under command of the Greek pilot Juan de Fuca, with a view to discover the straits by which the north Pacific was supposed to communicate with the north Atlantic Ocean. In pursuit of this object, Fuca entered what he considered an extensive inlet from the sea between the forty-eighth and forty-ninth parallels of latitude, where he sailed for more than twenty days. This strait bears the name of its discoverer to this period of time. Eleven years subsequent to the voyage of Fuca, Vizcaino, under the direction of the crown of Spain, added two new items of information in a survey of the coast of California as far north as the thirty-seventh, and in the exploration of the whole front of the continent to the forty-third, parallel of latitude. The voyages of Berkeley in the same quarter produced misunderstandings between England and Spain which were arranged by the treaty of the Escurial. England procured by this instrument a right to trade in the north seas. Grey, an enterprising navigator from Boston, commanding the ships Columbia and Washington, having entered the Pacific in the latter part of the eighteenth century, eventually penetrated a large river of fresh water, to which he gave the name of Columbia. The government of the United States pursued this discovery by the land explorations of Lewis and Clark and the Missouri and Pacific Fur Companies. Much speculation existing among the English in regard to a northern passage by water through America, Cook was sent out five years subsequent to the treaty of Paris. After protracted labors, during which he discovered the islands denominated the Sandwich, he determined that Asia and North America were separated by a channel thirteen leagues in width. The suggestions of Cook upon the fur-trade which might be conducted with the savages that occupied the regions he had visited were adopted by the English; an association styled King George's Sound Company was formed, and an expedition projected under the command of Portlock and Dixon. Near about the same time Louis XVI. equipped two vessels under Perouse for a purpose similar to that, which gave rise to the last voyage of the unfortunate Cook. No tidings were ever received of the commander or his force. Vancouver's voyage was a confirmation of Cook's determination as to a northern passage. Although the expedition of Ross, in the early part of the nineteenth century, cast little new light on this subject, the suggestion of his second officer, Parry, has by means of the efforts of Simpson and Dease gone far towards settling the existence of a naval passage in the North. The fate of Franklin, Kane, and Hall still leaves the subject in uncertainty.

The protracted wars of the eighteenth century deeply affected the commerce of Europe, by impairing the power of its kingdoms to furnish their wonted products. After the treaty of Paris this evil speedily wrought its own remedy. Woollen fabrics, iron, steel, tin, lead, copper, brass, leather, were afforded by the British; fine stuffs, brandies, wines, by the French. Oil, madder, salt, cork, barilla, liquors, fruits, were produced in the southern peninsula; velvet, lace, brocade, corn, paper, mirrors, coral, flax, wool, hemp, silk, in the Italian cities. Carpets and dyes abounded in Turkey; copper, timber, hemp, flax, potash, peltry, in Russia. The Swedish trade consisted of iron, copper, timber, fish, oil, pitch, tar; the Prussian, of porcelain, corn, timber, glass, potash, madder, antimony, hemp, flax, tin, copper, spices, wine, brandy. Silver, iron, lead, copper, cobalt, hemp, flax, saffron, hops, abounded in the Palatinate; linen, coarse woollen, paper, glass, gold and silver lace, in the Hanoverian possessions; while Austria was able to supply valuable mineral productions, and the Swiss were not deficient in provisions, linen, cotton goods, silks, laces, and watches. The Genevans for a long time possessed the monopoly of the last article; eventually it was destroyed by the superior workmanship of the English.

The genius of the French was much deteriorated by the revolution; still in the midst of their wars national ingenuity was displayed in improving the construction and management of field-pieces, in affording unwonted facilities in the communication of intelligence by means of telegraphs, and in introducing a new mode of discovering the position or tracing the course of an army by the use of air-balloons. The arts and sciences were not totally abandoned. Natural philosophy flourished under the care of Macquer, Lavoisier, Arago; statuary and painting were produced by numerous masters. Napoleon's accession to power was attended by the restoration of learning in all its branches, as well as the amelioration of society throughout every department. However questionable it may be with some authors whether many of the compeers of the emperor might not have risen to the same height of power he attained had they been as reckless of human life as he was, yet it may be safely asserted that no man could have made a better use of power than Bonaparte, at all events so far as the internal condition of France was concerned.*

The advancement of science was never greater in England than from the latter part of the eighteenth to the middle of the nineteenth century. Black, Cavendish, Priestley, Kirwan, Hutton, Herschel, Miller, have advanced natural philosophy. A Royal Institute was founded; ethical science canvassed by Warburton, Hurd, Watson, Paley,

---

* Al. Eu., in loc.

Louth, Porteus, Blair; medicine improved by Jenner's discovery of vaccination as a preservative against the smallpox, as well as by the dissertations of Cullen, Brown, Darwin. Literature owes much to the genius of Burke, Gibbon, Gillies, Ferguson, Kames, Tooke, Beattie, Cowper, Southey, Sheridan, Cowley, Byron, Moore, Montgomery, Scott, Dickens. Nor have any of these luminaries outshone their contemporaries in the United States: Franklin, Fulton, Godfrey, Ramsay, Marshall, Kent, Story, Cooper, Irving, Prescott, Bancroft, Longfellow. During the same period the Dutch have advanced general science; the Swiss have produced Haller, Bonnet, Senebier, Mallet: mineralogy and chemistry have flourished in Germany under the patronage of Werner and Humboldt; belles-lettres have attained a high degree of perfection by the productions of Schiller, Goethe, Lessing. Sweden has produced chemists and statuaries; Russia, mathematicians and historians; Italy has retained her fame as the nursery of the arts. Charles III. of Spain gave an impetus to science within the borders of his realm which has enabled it to accomplish great things in that kingdom. Austria has not kept pace with the improvements of the age, although it may be reasonably hoped that within its limits learning has got the better of ignorance and reason commenced its triumph over superstition. Commerce has received a new element and impulse from the cotton and tobacco, the sugar and rice, the drugs and precious metals of America, where the industry of over a hundred million of people are engaged in supplying the demands of trade. Those wonders of former ages, the canals of China,* as well as those constructed by Peter the Great of Russia, lose much of their importance in comparison with the canals and railroads of the Swedes

---

* Phillips' Inland Navigation.

and Dutch, the French and English, the people of Canada and the citizens of the United States.

The discovery of electricity in the clouds during the year 1752 by Franklin,* and of the quadrant in 1724 by Godfrey at Philadelphia;† the application of steam to navigation in 1807 by Fulton, of New York,‡ and of electricity in 1837 by Morse, of the same place,§ to the transmission of thought, form the principal agencies in completing the measure of human advancement to the present period. For some time after its invention the telegraph seemed destined to act only as an auxiliary to the railroad and steamboat, but it soon outstripped its rivals, crossed trackless worlds, passed boisterous seas, twice circled the Atlantic, and bids fair at no distant period to embrace all nations in its grasp.

---

* Nicholson's Nat. Phil., p. 427.
† Franklin's Memoirs. Walsh's Appeal, pp. 274-284.
‡ Colden's Life of Fulton. Walsh's Appeal, pp. 257-269.
§ Turnbull's Telegraph.

NOTES OF THE PLACES IN THIS WORK WHERE PROPHECY IS FULFILLED.

Introduction.—General coincidence between history and prophecy.

Chapter I.—Downfall of Assyrian Empire predicted by Nahum.

Chapter II.—Conquest of Babylon predicted by Isaiah and Jeremiah.

Chapter IV.—The whole subject of prophecy as to Medo-Persian, Greek, and Roman empires reviewed.

Chapter V.—The prophecies of the Incarnation stated. The Apocalypse analyzed, which gives a brief review of the leading imperial events during the Christian era, religious and civil.

Chapter VI.—The pale horse of St. John indicates the gloomy twenty-five years of the Roman Empire in which one fourth of the human family was destroyed by violence.

Chapter X.—The "ten toes" of the image of Daniel, the ten nations of Europe that are presented to view after the fall of the Western branch of the Roman Empire.

Chapter XI.—How the king of France formed the Western Empire and elevated the hierarchy of Rome to supreme power, as was predicted by John.

Chapter XII.—Rome makes war on its opposers, and thus verifies Rev. xiii. 7.

Chapter XV.—Pope claims supremacy and puts to death those who opposed—John Huss and others—as predicted (Rev. xiii.).

Chapter XVI.—The predicted overthrow of the Roman hierarchy.

Chapter XVII.—Papal Rome overthrown (Rev. xiv. 6-8).

Chapter XVIII.—William panders to the pope. "None to buy," etc. (Rev. xiii. 17).

Chapter XIX.—Protestants put to death in the time of Henry V. and Mary (Rev. xiii.).

Chapter XXIII.—The age of advancement (Dan. xii. 4). Newton's conclusion.

www.ingramcontent.com/pod-product-compliance
Lightning Source LLC
Chambersburg PA
CBHW020334240426
43673CB00039B/938